PRAISE FOR STRIKING DOWN THE HOME

"*Striking Down the Home* in no-nonsense and common sense form, takes the reader through America's everyday judicial and governmental operations. The book, in satirical fashion, exposes the divorce, child support, and child protection industries.

"Sadly, author Toby Strebe's story in this work is all too commonplace. Strebe couldn't be more accurate when he writes, 'your innocence is elusive.' The author articulates invaluable tidbits of information, intertwining American history and religion, in arguing that American Family Courts trigger parentectomies.

"In this system that operates in Loco Parentis and in kafkaesque fashion, nobody is safe (including your children), and you could be next. From no-fault divorce to false abuse allegations, *Striking Down the Home* is a cathartic resource for all parents who find themselves struggling in child custody court. Read it and tell your friends."

—**Dean Tong, MSc.,** CFC is a nationally-known Forensic Trial Expert who has worked court cases from all 50 states, and a multi-published author whose web site www.abuse-excuse.com has been on the Internet since 1997.

STRIKING DOWN THE HOME

The Propaganda of Family Court and Child Support Mechanisms

Toby Strebe

Published by:
Toby Strebe
Trenton, OH 45067
www.strikingdownthehome.com
strikingdownthehome@protonmail.com

Book Layout © 2018 by BookDesignTemplates.com
Cover Design by BuzBooks

Library of Congress Control Number: 2021909139
Striking Down the Home / Toby Strebe
ISBN: 978-1-7372025-0-9
Printed in the United States of America

Dedicated to my children:

Addison, Kyndall, Tobie, Paige, and Lincoln

"For we wrestle not against flesh and blood, but against principalities, against powers, against the rulers of the darkness of this world, against spiritual wickedness in high places."

—EPHESIANS 6:12

TABLE OF CONTENTS

PROLOGUE..1

PART I: THE ATTACK

1) FOUNDATIONS...11
2) INFLUENCES..27
3) BATTLE FOR CONTROL..35
4) CHILLING EFFECTS...45

PART II: THE WARFARE

5) A SUBTLE ABDUCTION..59
6) MASTERS OF DECEIT...73
7) THE PSYCHOLOGICAL SEDUCTION OF CHILDREN....................97
8) TAKEN INTO CUSTODY..107
9) THE INVISIBLE ROBBERY..117
10) THE PRICE OF BEARING FALSE WITNESS.............................137
11) THE SUBVERSION OF INDIVIDUALITY AND PROPERTY........147

PART III: PREPARING FOR COMBAT

12) RECOGNIZE THE BATTLE LINES.......................................161
13) BATTLE LINE 1: THE POSITION OF AUTHORITY......................165
14) BATTLE LINE 2: THE POSSESSION OF AUTHORITY.................183
15) THE COURAGE TO RESIST...203
16) THE FREEMAN'S RESOURCE..219

PART IV: PLANNING YOUR STRATEGY

17) PROTECT YOURSELF...233
18) MINIMIZE THE DAMAGE...247

19) ENDURE ADVERSITY..253

20) LAUNCH ATTACKS..265

21) PLANT OBSTACLES...279

22) BYPASS LANDMINES...293

PART V: RESTORING FREEDOM

23) VICTORY: THE LORD'S TIMING.....................................311

APPENDIXES

A) REFERENCE GUIDE...323

B) FICTITIOUS OR FACTUAL...327

C) THE SCIENCE OF MARRIAGE...331

D) THE CONFLICT OF MARRIAGE: BIBLICAL V. SECULAR..........339

E) ADDITIONAL RESOURCES..345

PROLOGUE

Pulling away from the curb, mom headed home. It was September 3, 2016, and she had just picked me up at the Cincinnati-Northern Kentucky International Airport. I must have stared out the window for the entire trip. I was glad to see her, but not under these circumstances.

The past three months were almost more than I could bear. The streets had turned into a living nightmare. Fear and paranoia often gripped my thoughts. I was constantly on guard and panic-stricken each time I caught a glimpse of a police car. For the first time in my life, the police had become my enemy—right here in America.

Propaganda spread throughout the city like wildfire and burned down my means of survival. There was no place I could seek refuge —no place to be left alone. What I endured was only a small taste of tyranny—never to be forgotten. And my flight to freedom was only the beginning of my fight *for* freedom.

Only three months earlier, on May 24, 2016, my 9-year-old daughter had written me a note bragging about how I was the best dad in the whole world. But that evening when I dropped her off with her mother, I would never see her or my other four children again.

For the first time in my life, I have a firsthand account of the spiritual warfare. In Ephesians, Paul warns:

> *"For we wrestle not against flesh and blood, but against principalities, against powers, against the rulers of the darkness of this world, against spiritual wickedness in high places."* (Ephesians 6:12)

Deception and propaganda always trickle downward. Only governments can annihilate freedom, and in America, the rise of the bureaucratic State serves to launch a war against freedom. This is a war on multiple fronts, but one of the means to their end is by initiating an attack against men, children, and the family. That's right! Our government has secretly waged war against your children. The enemies of freedom don't care how many casualties they create. The end of freedom justifies the State's means to achieve it.

Understanding the principles of freedom is necessary to defend life, liberty, or property. Propaganda is the method to enlist soldiers in the fight against freedom, while ignorance produces casualties. There is no neutrality. Each citizen has the responsibility to protect their own life, liberty, and property. However, believing that our government protects those things results in the dereliction of duty. Contrary to popular opinion, our service members are unable to protect our freedoms precisely because the enemy is within.

How often are our actions misguided? We act when we shouldn't, and we don't act when we should. But after witnessing the horrors of tyranny, I have a much greater appreciation for the work accomplished by the founding generation. Patrick Henry's speech delivered to the Virginia House of Burgesses on March 23, 1775 bring on a whole new level of understanding:

> *"Gentlemen may cry, 'Peace! Peace!' — but there is no peace. The war is actually begun! The next gale that sweeps from the north will bring to our ears the clash of resounding arms! Our brethren are already in the field! Why stand we here idle? What is it that gentlemen wish? What would they have? Is life so dear, or peace so sweet, as to be purchased at the price of chains and slavery? Forbid it, Almighty God! I know not what course others may take; but as for me, give me liberty or give me death!" (Wirt, 1817)[1]*

---

[1] William Wirt, *Sketches of the Life and Character of Patrick Henry* (Philadelphia: Published by James Webster, 1817).

The past several years have been very trying for me, but I'm grateful to have the opportunity to share my experiences while exposing the devil's devices. My trials and tribulations have opened the door for the publication of this book, and I pray that I can help another person in the process. I don't want Satan to take advantage of one more soul.

Striking Down the Home: The Propaganda of Family Court and Child Support Mechanisms is the real-life account of an American family and the 6 innocent lives that were shattered on the altar of tyranny. As the State continues to prey on its citizens, will your family become the next casualty in our war-torn land?

The composition of this book accomplishes several tasks.

Chapter 1: Foundations builds the structural integrity of this book. It's the presupposition. Before I present my case, I must begin by laying down a Biblical and historical foundation. This chapter addresses the rights of mankind, the rule of law, and the proper role of government.

Chapter 2: Influences conveys a brief history of my wife, Amy, and the manipulation techniques that guided her decisions. This true story illustrates how dangerous it is to be "under the influence" – the influence of alcohol, drugs, television, propaganda, etc. These techniques altered her mind and shifted her thinking patterns, which ultimately, controlled her actions.

Chapter 3: Battle for Control logs the events of Amy's war against me. Whenever there's divorce, conflict is inevitable. But since I didn't fight back, she was strategically setting the stage prior to the divorce. She sought a quick and easy checkmate.

Chapter 4: Chilling Effects records the State's hostility against me. Since the criminal court's checkmate failed, family court stepped in to steal my livelihood. They were, in essence, attempting to finish me off by nailing the coffin shut.

Chapter 5: A Subtle Abduction provides some history on the origins of family court and the doctrine of Parens Patriae. With the rise of an invisible government, children, like mine, are being abducted at will, but packaged under the pretext of "protecting the children."

Chapter 6: Masters of Deceit exposes the operations of this invisible government. It amounts to the largest child abduction scheme within the United States. But there are inherent dangers of kidnapping children for their own good. Be aware that Satan is actively bidding for the soul of your child today.

Chapter 7: The Psychological Seduction of Children opens the road map to the psychological and oftentimes, irreversible damages created by the government's method of protecting children. By shifting a child's thinking patterns away from God's design and social order, later in life, they'll develop more conflicts within their relationships.

Chapter 8: Taken into Custody parallels Germany's physical genocide with America's psychological genocide. America has traditionally taken criminals into State custody, but we've entered a new age – an age where children are collectively targeted, taken into State custody, and their ability to think and reason for themselves is, in fact, exterminated.

Chapter 9: The Invisible Robbery unmasks the largest fraud ring operating within the United States. By examining the raw numbers in my case, you'll discover that child support was never intended to support children. But regardless of what it's called, stealing, by any other name, is still stealing.

Chapter 10: The Price of Bearing False Witness addresses the selfishness and greed of the recipient of child support. The covetous condition of their heart distorts the values of the exchange, resulting in an unequal trade-off. You need to understand that there is a high reward on your child's head.

Chapter 11: The Subversion of Individuality and Property sheds light on the dehumanizing effects of the divorce and child custody apparatus. Those who are sucked into the system must choose between obeying God or "supporting their children." No person can do both.

You'll either lose your respect for the law or you'll lose your moral sense.

Chapter 12: Recognize the Battle Lines identifies where the battle is being fought and how the enemy is dressed in a robe of authority. This chapter and the next two are knowledge-based. You'll learn how to correctly identify enemy forces from friendly forces. In this warfare, you are helpless if you lack knowledge and understanding.

Chapter 13: Battle Line 1: The Position of Authority examines the legitimate offices of authority, which God has established. All others are false and destructive to a free society. But there are distinguishing marks that separate genuine from artificial positions, so you must remain sober and vigilant.

Chapter 14: Battle Line 2: The Possession of Authority analyzes the occupants who hold the office of authority. Since all authority is delegated, beware of those who occupy the position (or office) without delegation.

Chapter 15: The Courage to Resist provides a standard of comparison by covering misconceptions about Biblical resistance, choosing your battles wisely, and how God pours His blessings out on His children for resisting.

Chapter 16: The Freeman's Resource educates the reader on methods of proper resistance and differentiates between your moral responsibilities and your legal obligations. This chapter is action-based. Once you know where the battle lines are drawn and can identify the enemy, it's time to put your knowledge into action. In this warfare, a true patriot and advocate of freedom goes into action. Only slaves surrender.

Chapter 17: Protect Yourself examines the necessary steps to protect yourself prior to entering a marriage contract. It offers some pointers in finding a future spouse who will help you keep the State out of your home. This way, you won't find yourself in a bad situation.

Chapter 18: Minimize the Damage addresses how to identify hostile behavior and offers practical advice in hopes to neutralize the aggression before a full-blown attack is initiated. This isn't fail-proof, nor does it mean you'll come out on top. But you may have a higher probability of surviving the fallout.

Chapter 19: Endure Adversity was written specifically for those who didn't get a copy of this book until after the State's assault against your family. I suggest ways to help you remain positive during a dark period of your life. You need to keep busy in healthy and productive ways because idleness always precedes mindless behavior. Who can help you better than the one who has gone through it himself?

Chapter 20: Launch Attacks lists several ways for you to turn the table on your spouse. You can't win by playing defense. Offensive maneuvers are necessary if you intend to triumph. Maintaining a defensive mindset is suicide.

Chapter 21: Plant Obstacles offers practical ways for you to derail your State's attack and hinder their movement. But be on guard, these aren't permanent solutions, just temporary roadblocks.

Chapter 22: Bypass Landmines alerts you to various traps that the government plants in your pathway. You cannot avoid the minefield, but you can move slowly, deliberately, and cautiously to prevent stepping on a mine.

Chapter 23: Victory: The Lord's Timing acknowledges the hand of God during uncertain times of tribulation. Your entire life and the lives of your children will shatter overnight. This chapter explains how God desperately wants to bestow His blessings upon you – but you must make the first move by placing your faith in Him. Reading this book will give you good direction, but once you've finished it, then it's time to put these truths into action.

Appendix A: Reference Guide is an outline, which can be copied, shared, or posted. This outline covers chapters 17-22.

Appendix B: Fictitious or Factual differentiates between the signs and symptoms of bona fide sexual abuse and fabricated sexual abuse. Most child advocates have never been trained to identify these differences, nor are they required to report objectively. With proper understanding, you can distinguish between the attacker and the victim. This is crucial in situations where the attacker yells, "HELP!"

Appendix C: The Science of Marriage proposes practical ways to increase the health of your marriage. Happy and healthy marriages can only be achieved when both spouses recognize their roles and understand the importance and contribution it brings to the marriage.

Appendix D: The Conflict of Marriage: Biblical v. Secular scrutinizes Biblical verses secular marriage. This section includes the origins of marriage licenses, the function they perform in marriage, the weaponizing of their statutory requirement, and Biblical alternatives to the marriage seeker.

Appendix E: Additional Resources supplies you with several website addresses and book titles to increase your knowledge and understanding. These websites and materials will provide you the necessary strength to live and fight another day. These invaluable and timeless resources are like nutrition for your mind. When you stop feeding yourself, it's at that moment you begin to deteriorate. Your mind requires the proper mental nutrition to remain strong.

Striking Down the Home: The Propaganda of Family Court and Child Support Mechanisms is a case against the rulers of darkness. It's a presentation of truth. It's an exposure of deception. It's an educational resource. It's an encouragement. Brace yourself, as you won't read this material anywhere else.

Truth must be sought, recognized, and put into action.

PART ONE

THE ATTACK

CHAPTER ONE

FOUNDATIONS

I t's not surprising how many people claim that truth is relative but never question the existence of government or the purpose of law. Let's face it, if truth is relative, why do we have government? Why do we have laws? Why do we have courts? Truth must be absolute if there is a law prohibiting a type of behavior or compelling some type of action. Our criminal justice system prosecutes lawbreakers, and the physical evidence presented in court is an illustration of truth being absolute.

The reality that truth is absolute has never been disputable. The actual problem is who gets to determine truth? Those who believe that truth is relative are dodging the real issue. They usually just confuse truth with opinion.

Absolute truth is self-evident, which explains why it's constantly attacked and suppressed. Truth is simply defined as reality. And reality must be sought and recognized. Fantasy, however, is invented from the imagination of men. Portraying fantasy as reality is called deceit. If the deception spreads (or propagates) throughout an entire area, region, nation, or world, this is known as propaganda.

The existence of a higher law helps us identify reality. The higher law exists independent of our internal faculties. It transcends our physical bodies and our circumstances.

Denial of this higher law suppresses truth. It reduces man to a cog who cannot see beyond his physical body. He is restricted to the use of his imagination and fantasizes over his inventions.

The higher law is a self-evident truth and is the foundation that we must build upon. Without a solid foundation, our structure collapses. Matthew Trewhella explains:

> *"God's moral law as the 'higher law' provides an objective standard whereby one is able to discern right from wrong or good from evil. The 'higher law' exists independent of the authority of any government, and all governments of men are accountable to it. The tyrant State abhors an objective standard to which it is accountable, rather it flourishes in a subjective environment. It wants to be accountable to no one."* (Trewhella, 2013)[2]

Before we can dive into the material presented in this book, it's imperative to lay our foundation upon the Rock. Just as a wise man builds his house upon a foundation, I will build my argument upon God's Word. This helps us correctly determine right from wrong and justice from injustice precisely because our objective standard is the Bible. Jesus' parable illustrates the necessity of a foundation.

> *"...a wise man, which built his house upon a rock: And the rain descended, and the floods came, and the winds blew, and beat upon that house; and it fell not: for it was founded upon a rock."* (Matthew 7:24-25)

* * * * *

In a business or organization, an industrious person with ability and ambition may, by hard work and ingenuity, rightfully gain a position of authority over others who voluntarily submit. But throughout

---

[2] Matthew Trewhella, *The Doctrine of the Lesser Magistrates: A Proper Resistance to Tyranny and a Repudiation of Unlimited Obedience to Civil Government* (North Charleston: CreateSpace Independent Publishing Platform, 2013).

history, there are those who have had an insatiable desire to control and maintain power over others without their permission. However, in America, the Constitution stands in the way.

Laws that protect people from hurting one another will, by their very nature, grant the government a monopoly on power. As a result of the incredible sinfulness of mankind, their monopolistic control naturally subjects our rulers to the overwhelming temptation to practice the art of deception and spread propaganda which always increases their own power.

- The power of constitutional interpretation...
- The power to change or erase history...
- The power to shift cultural trends...
- The power to pursue one's enemies...
- And the power to elevate oneself.

The ruling class in America continually disseminates deception and propaganda. In this manner, people can be persuaded that oppressive behavior is genuine freedom while man's freewill is perceived to be oppressive. The American Constitution cannot safeguard against such backwards or progressive thinking. Each one of us must seek the truth, recognize the truth, and then put the truth into action.

The apostle Paul makes it clear that the soldiers of darkness labor within the political arena. It's manifested from the usage of his words, *"principalities, powers, rulers, high places."* Yet, I've often wondered why preachers and teachers in the church don't filter politics through the Scriptures. In today's age, it's difficult to get the church leadership and the disciples of Christ engaged in this spiritual and political warfare.

On January 30, 1750, Jonathan Mayhew preached "A Discourse Concerning Unlimited Submission and Non-Resistance to the High Powers." His sermon was based on the text of Romans 13; yet, he was criticized for "preaching politics and not Christ." This dichotomy is a logical fallacy considering Christ (God incarnate) instituted government in the beginning. But Mr. Mayhew was strong in the Lord and continued preaching the whole counsel of God.

The Bible has much to say about government, but political sermons or Bible studies on the administration of government and its policies are treated as if they're spiritually forbidden. However, the truth in God's Word can only be revealed if we filter our ideology through the Scriptures.

The greatest asset to the mind is the *Knowledge of Truth*. You can deposit into the mind, but you can't deplete it. You can share knowledge, but you can't steal it. This asset produces independency of thought, private judgment, and psychological strength. Additionally, it's the number one cure for most mental illnesses.

Possession of the knowledge of truth is far superior to silver or gold. The Bible tells us that our strength comes from the Lord (Psalm 46:1); but strength does not come apart from knowledge (Proverbs 24:5; Hosea 4:6). Knowledge is truth, and without truth, there can be no knowledge.

Contrast this to the spiritual forces that push deceit. The continual flow of propaganda is designed to control the input of thoughts, which ultimately determines the output of actions. In other words, the people are programmed to behave in a manner contrary to their best interest. Once an individual's ability to choose is suppressed through deception, their freewill ceases to exist, and he or she lives in a state of oppression.

German writer and statesman Johann Wolfgang von Goethe, member of a secret society known as Illuminati, nailed the art of propaganda with deadly accuracy. In his 1809 classic, *"Elective Affinities,"* he writes:

> *"None are more hopelessly enslaved than those who falsely believe they are free. The truth has been kept from the depths of their minds by masters who rule them with lies. They feed them*

on falsehoods till wrong looks right in their eyes." (Goethe, 1809)[3]

Propaganda is like ingesting small doses of poison. A relatively small amount can be filtered out, but the long-term effect poisons the mind and shifts your thinking patterns. Separating politics from Scripture—government from God—is the result of a poisoned mind.

Let's examine what the Bible has to say about rights, law, and government. This will help us answer questions, such as:

- Is child support a right?
- Is it just for family court to impose child support obligations?
- Should fathers obey a child support order?
- Should government enforce child support laws?

The Rights of Man

God has given all of us the inherent power to choose for ourselves: *"Of every tree of the garden thou mayest freely eat."* (Genesis 2:16). Therefore, you and I, as well as every individual on Earth, possesses the right to exercise his or her God-given power. This is the freedom to choose. Freedom (or liberty) can simply be defined as, "the power to act for oneself." Mankind is the only one created with this right (Genesis 1:27-28), and this is the only right a person possesses. There are no other rights.

Animals live by instincts. They don't have the power to choose for themselves. They can't reason. They can't understand. They're in subjection to mankind. When a person allows others to control their choices through deception and propaganda, they are living like an animal. They don't choose for themselves. They don't reason. They don't understand. They're in subjection to the propagandists.

---

[3] Johann Wolfgang von Goethe, *Elective Affinities*, trans. David Constantine (New York: Oxford University Press 2008).

America is not the same country as it was during its Founding Era. The colonists recognized that our rights come from God through the very wording of the Declaration of Independence:

> *We hold these truths to be self-evident, that all men are created equal, that they are endowed by their Creator with certain un-alienable rights, that among these are Life, Liberty, and the Pursuit of Happiness...* (US, 1776)

Self-evident truths stand on their own—no evidence required. As our founders declared, it's a self-evident truth that all men are created by God and equally possessing the same rights. The "three" rights listed in the Declaration are not distinct and independent of the others. They are all summed up into just one: *the right to choose*. It's natural for you to choose life over death, liberty over slavery, and happiness over misery. Thus, do not be confused, every person is born with only one right: *the right to choose*.

This historical acknowledgment of God and their proclamation of self-evident truths wasn't exclusively understood by Thomas Jefferson and his committee, but it was the atmosphere of the colonies in those days. The Second Continental Congress unanimously approved of the wording and adopted the declaration.

Historical examples abound during the Founding Era. During the Constitutional Convention of 1787, Benjamin Franklin reminded the delegates of their daily prayer during the war. *"In the beginning of the contest with G. Britain, when we were sensible of danger, we had daily prayer in this room for the Divine Protection. Our prayers, Sir, were heard, and they were graciously answered."*[4]

Franklin (PA) then suggested that the convention should open each daily session with prayer. Sherman (CT) seconded. Hamilton (NY) and others expressed their apprehensions that opening with prayer is

---

[4] James Madison, "Thursday June 28th. In Convention," In *The Records of the Federal Convention of 1787*, ed. Max Farrand (New Haven: Yale University Press, 1911), Vol 1.

proper had it been initiated earlier. At this point during the debates, prayer might arouse fear in the community. Williamson (NC) also pointed out that the convention had no funds to pay a clergy. In lieu, Randolph (VA) proposed a fourth of July sermon instead; Franklin seconded. The convention adjourned without voting on the motion.[5]

But on Wednesday, July 4, 1787, the convention adjourned to attend an oration[6] at Philadelphia's Reformed Calvinist Church. Rev. William Rogers delivered an introductory prayer for the Constitutional Convention, which appeared in The Massachusetts Centinel on August 15, 1787.[7] This began the tradition with the Senate and House of Representatives to open each daily session with prayer to God requesting his aid in governing the new nation.

In addition to the convention delegates and representatives of the several states, the Constitutions of all fifty states mention God in some form, usually in the Preamble. It's quite evident that the colonial governments and the citizens acknowledged God and understood where their rights came from. Since God is the origin of our freedoms, as this truth is self-evident, then the Holy Bible becomes our source document.

Unfortunately, in present-day parlance, the word "rights" has been misconstrued and redefined. Today, the word "rights" has been detached from the choice and affixed to the object of the choice. For example, let's say you walk into a store and see your dream television costing $500.00. You have the right to choose between alternatives: (1) take the TV and pay the price or (2) leave the TV and keep your money. Your choice to take or leave the television is determined by the cost of the object. You may choose what you will, but it's a packaged deal.

---

[5] Ibid.

[6] George Washington, *The Diaries of George Washington*, ed. Donald Jackson and Dorothy Twohig (Charlottesville: University Press of Virginia, 1979), Vol. 5: July 1786 to December 1789.

[7] The Massachusetts Centinel 7, no. 43 (August 15, 1787), Accessed April 29, 2021, https://www.loc. gov/item/sn83021269.

Without the cost, there can be no choice. If the cost is eliminated by government decree, then taking the TV without paying for it prevails. However, the value of the object has been distorted by theft. In other words, the television holds no value because you received it for free.

Using this example, let's create an analogy. What would happen if the government created a right to own a television? You would lose the freedom to choose the type of television you want. If government is responsible to ensure everyone has access to a free television, then government will choose what television you're allowed to have.

A short time later, the government might pass an edict requiring television manufactures to incorporate spy technology into their products to secure your home from intruders. How convenient! If the government isn't catching bad guys, they can spy on you instead. But of course, you have nothing to hide, right?

Afterwards, the government is positioned to criminalize speech, prayer, or the Bible. How dangerous to surrender your right to choose by replacing it with the right to an appealing object.

This same principle is applied to healthcare, medical, education, school tuition, housing, food, employment, social security, child support, alimony, and virtually every government program available. Calling these objects "rights" doesn't change the action. The Bible refers to this as "coveting." This subtle shift away from the choice easily persuades many to stake claims to objects they're not entitled to. But hardly anyone is attentive to recognize that this is removing their freedom of choice by replacing it with an appealing object. These false and deceptive "rights" do not come from God. They're invented from the imagination of those controlling governmental power.

Nearly everyone is duped because these "rights" are crafted to prevent opposition. Here's how it works. These advocates will say that you have a right to eat. But notice what's been left out. They omitted the words "to choose." The word "rights" carry two distinct meanings. If you have the right [to choose] to eat, then you also bear the responsibility to choose how best to obtain food, how much, and what kind to get. On the other hand, if you only have the right to eat without individual choice, then government has assumed power over those choices. (The Women, Infants, and Children program is a model for rationing and dieting set by the government.) But statements that affix the word "rights" to the object are invalid and incomplete. Let's face it, who's going to say that you don't have a right to eat?

Free choice and responsibility is, and always has been, individual. This individualism is self-evident. But when your free choice is removed, the power to choose shifts to a collective group. This is known as collectivism (or collective rights). These rights are not self-evident, so government must decree and enforce them.

To initiate the process, government first creates a new "right," which didn't previously exist. That "right" is attached to an appealing object. Government also specifies the party or group responsible to provide this new right. Once the law passes, it's time to publicize it and let everyone know. When the people learn about a new right that benefits them, they rush to cash in.

In some circumstances, the government assumes the responsibility to dispense these benefits, like food stamps or free education. In other cases, the responsibility might fall on employers to provide things such as minimum wage or overtime pay. Still, other situations place the responsibility on fathers, like child support or alimony. But in every example, free individual choice has been abandoned and replaced with government control. This is what happens when "rights" are attached to an object and disconnected from the individual choice.

There's a plethora of examples which are too numerous to count, but the operations are the same. Here's an exercise for you to chew on. One day while you're at work this week, look at your company's bulletin board. This is the place where the law requires certain posters to be displayed. One of those posters will read, *"If you have the right to work, don't let anybody take it away."*

Notice how the "right" is detached from the free choice and connected with the object. The right to work is not self-evident, so government had to create it and proclaim it. On the contrary, it's self-evident that we were all created equally with the right to choose. We have the right to choose where to apply for work, how to present ourselves during an interview, and how we will conduct ourselves on our employer's property, but no one has the right to compel others to facilitate a work environment for us.

This government-created right is categorized under a collective group termed "Employee Rights." But the responsibility to provide these "rights" is the employer, while the choices are being made by the government – not the individual. This subtle lie, however, is intended to pit workers against entrepreneurs by holding the employer responsible for the actions of his employee.

Collectivism is defined as *"...the idea that the individual's life belongs to the group or society of which he is merely a part, that he has no rights other than those the group or society gives him, and that he must sacrifice his values and goals for the group's 'greater good.' The individual is of value only insofar as he serves the group."*[8] Collective rights are counterfeit because God never created groups or classes of people. He created two individuals in His image—male and female (Genesis 1:27). Then He gave both individuals freewill (Genesis 2:16).

Collectivism opens the door for the government to decide which groups or classes are permitted to have rights and which are not. (Where are the government signs informing me about my employers' rights? How come I don't ever hear about men's rights?) This is a prime example of a subjective standard. The law does not apply to everyone equally, because it was crafted to target a select group of people. Hence, the law's enforcement is dependent on their subject.

---

[8] Gai Ferdon, *A Republic If You Can Keep It: America's Authentic Liberty Confronts Contemporary Counterfeits* (Chesapeake: The Foundation for American Christian Education, 2008).

Overlooked is the fact that these fictitious rights come into existence by depriving another individual of their God-given right to choose. Here's several examples:

- Women's Rights—at the expense of the men.
- Victim's Rights—at the expense of the accused.
- Children's Rights—at the expense of the parents.

These *"rights"* are not listed in the Declaration of Independence, the Bill of Rights, or God's moral law, and the reason is simple: they do not exist. Rights, when attached to the object, is only a fantasy. It's been invented from man's imagination.

Since it's a self-evident truth that our rights come from God, we must be mindful about government's subtle tactic to define those rights. Allowing the government to define our rights is tantamount to allowing children to define the rules of the home. Parents don't set the rules, but allow their kids to decide what they mean, how to interpret it, and whether they're exempt from obeying it or not? That's just ludicrous. It's time to obey God's Word and discontinue our government program. They're from the devil.

The Rule of Law

Law comes from God (Isaiah 33:22) for the purpose of protecting our right to choose. God gave us the right to choose (Genesis 2:16) so we may choose what we will, but we may not choose to take away someone else's freedom of choice. Furthermore, we may not choose to give up our own right. God doesn't give us the freedom to give away the right He gave us.

The first law God gave mankind was a prohibition: *"But of the tree of knowledge of good and evil, thou shalt not eat of it: for in the day that thou eatest thereof thou shalt surely die"* (Genesis 2:17). The law did not impose God's will on man; rather, it was to protect man's right to choose life. This is simply known as the rule of law. Frédéric Bastiat sums up the purpose of law and outlines the consequences when law doesn't fulfill its purpose:

> *"When the law keeps a person within the bounds of justice, they impose nothing but a mere negation. They oblige him only to abstain from harming others. They violate neither his personality, his liberty, nor his property. They safeguard all of these. They are defensive; they defend equally the rights of all.*

> *"But when the law...imposes upon men a regulation of labor, a method or a subject of education, a religious faith or creed – then the law is no longer negative; it acts positively upon people. It substitutes the will of the legislator for their own wills; the initiative of the legislator for their own initiatives. When this happens, the people no longer need to discuss, to compare, to plan ahead; the law does all this for them. Intelligence becomes a useless prop for the people; they cease to be men; they lose their personality, their liberty, their property."* (Bastiat, 2007)[9]

Earlier, I addressed the redefinition of "rights." This paradigm shift packages these "rights" as some form of compassion. Yet, this perversion cannot be confronted and corrected. Any opposition targets the object, not the removal of free choice.

For instance, to argue that somebody doesn't have a right to eat, people envision an attack against food to advocate mass starvation and death. They are completely oblivious to the reality that they are surrendering their freedom to choose in exchange for the government to impose, by force, the will of the lawgiver. The majority unknowingly elevate their government to a position that controls their choices. However, any right created by the government can also be revoked by government. But if the right to choose remains with the individual, not the right to eat, then their freedom [to choose] to eat cannot be restrained or revoked.

---

[9] Claude Frédéric Bastiat, "The Law," In *The Bastiat Collection* (Auburn: Ludwig von Mises Institute, 2007).

This applies to every government program. The right to an education, the right to healthcare, the right to housing, the right to work...
It can go on and on and on. In each scenario, the freedom to choose is
missing. Without the freewill of the individual, government makes
the choices. But any opposition attacks the object of choice, not the
loss of free choice.

Every time the law creates a new "right," government must either
provide or they must force the party responsible to provide. This is
called legal plunder. To identify legal plunder, see if the law takes
from some persons what belongs to them, and gives it to other persons
to whom it does not belong. See if the law benefits one citizen at the
expense of another by doing what the citizen himself cannot do without committing a crime.

Child support and food stamps are examples of legal plunder. The
consequence of legal plunder is how it erases from everyone's conscience the distinction between justice and injustice. Frédéric Bastiat
addresses this problem:

*"No society can exist unless the laws are respected to a certain
degree. The safest way to make laws respected is to make them
respectable. When law and morality contradict one another,
the citizen has the cruel alternative of either losing his moral
sense or losing his respect for the law."* (Bastiat, 2007)[10]

Laws prohibiting certain behavior are intended to protect free
choice. But as the word "rights" was shifted from free choice to the
object of choice, public laws and statutes naturally shifted as well.
The laws compelling certain behavior are designed to enforce objects
for free. Law was no longer reserved for a prohibitive act but was
necessary to coerce and compel to satisfy the greed of the people.

Compulsive laws, and the enforcement thereof, repeatedly violate
an individual's God-given right to choose. The Patient Protection and
Affordable Care Act (aka Obamacare) is an example of a compulsive

---

[10] Ibid.

law. When the law's opponents were fighting for a repeal, you could hear the screams of people claiming that their rights were being violated and healthcare was being taken away. Undoubtedly, the law's proponents attributed this "right" to the object. But the right to receive free healthcare sacrifices the individual right to choose.

The laws and justice of every nation should mirror the laws and justice of God because *"The law of the Lord is perfect...The statutes of the Lord are right..."* (Psalm 19:7-8). Positive and compulsive law is counterproductive and destroys liberty. For example:

- No-fault Divorce Law—to defraud the faithful spouse by removing accountability when a legally-binding contract is violated.
- Protection Orders—to force parents away from their children and children away from their parents.
- Child Support Orders and Laws—to defraud by deceptive means and to rob by confiscating private property.

The Role of Government

God has given each person the inherent right to defend his person and those under his charge, his freedom of choice, and his property (Nehemiah 4:13). From this individualistic right stems the freedom to form and organize a governmental force to protect these civil liberties.

After the fall, God instituted government. *"Unto the women He [God] said, '...and he [husband] shall rule over thee'"* (Genesis 3:16). This is the first instance where God delegated authority for one person to rule over (or govern) another. The functions of government encompass three parts: to give the law, to execute the law, and to judge according to the law (Isaiah 33:22). These three components are essential for order and stability.

In America, the people retained the authority to govern themselves. A governmental force was organized to protect the people's freewill.

This concept is known as political sovereignty. You are supreme and your government is subservient. You extend your authority to the government for the sole purpose of preserving your individual rights —the right to choose. Since you, acting on your own, don't have the authority to deprive another person of their freedom of choice, this power cannot be delegated to the government. In simple terms, you cannot give what you do not have. Our Founders even clarified: *"...that to secure these rights, governments are instituted among men deriving their just powers from the consent of the governed."* (US, 1776)

To safeguard against the misuse of power, God directed America's founding generation towards representative government (Exodus 18:13-27) and the decentralization of governmental power. This was to maximize freedom by protecting your right to choose.

The purpose of decentralization is nullification. Due to our sinful nature, power would be abused. By creating a government with de-centralized power, God enabled one level of government to nullify the power of another. The Bible lists four vertical levels of government: Self (Genesis 2:16), Family (Genesis 3:16), Church (Matthew 16:18), and Civil (Romans 13:1-4). Each realm of government has its own distinct jurisdiction and limitations. If one level of government invades the jurisdiction of another, chaos ensues.

From the four levels of government, only civil government is an institution of force. *Executing wrath on him that doeth evil* is an example of negative force. This Biblical principle is often overlooked and easily ignored when applying for and receiving government assistance. Civil government was not created to pamper its citizens with handouts. Unfortunately, our government has transformed itself into a positive force—to do things for people. When government helps one person, it must first take from others to provide it.

The more programs and services provided by the government, the more manpower it requires to administer them, and the more resources it consumes from the productive individual. These programs and services exist solely through creating new "rights" that are affixed to objects, and then enforcing the new compulsive law.

By redefining the word, "rights" to remove the individual's freedom of choice, government must shift into a positive force. If the individual won't make their own choices, government will. And legal plunder (or theft) is what happens when government enforces their own choices.

Government's negative force is a Biblical principle (Romans 13:4), but their positive force violates a Biblical commandment. *"Thou shalt not steal"* (Exodus 20:15). Don't be fooled, but this expansion of governmental power is naturally an obstruction to liberty due to its transformation of the law from prohibition to compulsion.

In today's age, the people sense that something is wrong in America, but they do not know what. They're unable to differentiate between needs and wants, between individual rights and collective rights, between the rule of law and the perversion of the law, between a negative force and positive force, between production and consumption. The person devoid of understanding doesn't possess the power to protect their own life, liberty, or property. They do not know what happens to a people when their government is allowed to exceed its boundaries.

I've witnessed firsthand in my divorce case that the horror of government intervention far exceeds that administered by an average criminal.

CHAPTER TWO

INFLUENCES

" *Most of us have had the experience, either as parents or youngsters, of trying to discover the 'hidden picture' within another picture of a children's magazine. Usually, you are shown a landscape with trees, bushes, flowers, and other bits of nature. The caption reads something like this: 'Concealed somewhere in this picture is a donkey pulling a cart with a boy in it. Can you find them?' Try as you might, usually you could not find the hidden picture until you turned to the answer page farther back in the magazine, which revealed how cleverly the artist had hidden it from you. If you study the landscape, you realize that the whole picture was painted in such a way as to conceal the real picture within, and once you see the 'real picture,' it stands out like the proverbial painful digit.*" (Allen, 1972)[11]

My ex-wife, Amy, was very artful in her portrait of my family. She painted one picture, which masterfully disguised the real scene. In the process, false authorities added their own personal touch. If you can see through the camouflage, you'll notice the donkey, the cart, and the boy that were there all along.

---

[11] Gary Allen, *None Dare Call It Conspiracy* (Seal Beach: Concord Press, 1972).

The stage for this sad story and its camouflaged setting is Las Cruces, New Mexico. Amy's modus operandi was to control family decisions without making them. In this way, she could rule without responsibility. She could impose her will but escape the blame when things went wrong. When confronted with differing opinions or perspectives, Amy handled the situation by asserting her power. She accomplished this by threatening, intimidating, ignoring, or dramatizing her role as the victim. She never attempted to disprove me or refute the evidence. It couldn't be refuted. When her threats, intimidation, and ignorance failed to coerce me into making destructive decisions, she attacked me with false allegations to divert attention from the facts. This forced me to abandon my effort of exposing her abuse and caused me to exhaust my time and resources defending myself.

Although Amy has caused catastrophic damage and irreparable harm to our five children, to my relationship with my children, and to our family as a whole, in the long run, she has failed to bury me. This is a case where the truth sounds stranger than fiction. This chapter provides some background information, which will help you connect the future dots. The chronological breakdown allows you to follow the timeline of events, observe its progressive nature, and gradually detect the subtle transfer of roles. In other words, the superhero in the beginning is painted as the villain by the end and vice versa. I must begin in the year 2014 for you to understand what facts Amy wanted to suppress.

2014: The Condition of Oppression

Amy was involuntarily hospitalized at the El Paso University of Behavioral Health because of suicidal ideation. On June 25, 2014, she was diagnosed with severe Borderline Personality Disorder (BPD). The hospital had also been treating Amy for insomnia, depression, and anxiety. Following several weeks of inpatient care, she was stabilized, on the appropriate medication, a safety plan was created, and outpatient therapy was scheduled.

However, upon her discharge, she discontinued all treatment and canceled all appointments. She didn't want to be under a doctor's care. For me, the burden of working full time, keeping up with house-work, nurturing my children without help, and caring for a wife who refused treatment was extremely stressful.

She never slept at night, but she mentioned to me on numerous oc-casions that she would get some sleep during the day (while I was at work). That meant she required our 8-year-old to babysit her two younger sisters, one of which is autistic. During this time, Amy lived in a state of idleness; she never did anything. She frequently followed me around the house but wouldn't lift a finger to help. Her untreated insomnia and depression certainly played a major part in her life.

Little did I know, these were the least of my problems. At the time, I was unaware of the dangers of BPD. A summary is essential to help you understand Amy's motivation for attacking me and what she needed to conceal. The American Psychological Association charac-terizes Borderline Personality Disorder in this way:

- *Frantic Efforts to Avoid Real or Imagined Abandonment—* Amy felt isolated, anxious, and terrified at the thought of being alone. She was constantly looking for cues that might reveal I was about to abandon her. Going to work or making a phone call might be interpreted as a signal that I was plotting to leave her. She would panic and erupt into a rage, make accusations, seek revenge, puff up her chest to assert her power over me, or do other destructive things.
- *A Pattern of Unstable Relationships Characterized by Alternat-ing Between Extremes of Idealization and Devaluation—*Amy had a difficult time integrating my good and bad traits; her cur-rent opinion of me was always based on her last interaction with me. She would perceive me as either the fairy godmother or the wicked witch—a saint or a demon. When I seemed to be

meeting her needs, she would cast me in the light of a super-hero. But if she perceived that I failed her, I became the villain. This is the all-or-nothing approach.

- *Poor Self-image and Chronic Feelings of Emptiness*—Amy expected me to provide things that she found difficult to supply for herself, such as self-esteem. Most of all, she looked to me as a nurturing caregiver whose never-ending love and compassion would fill the black hole of emptiness and despair inside.

- *Impulsiveness and Reckless Behavior*—Amy tried to fill the emptiness and create an identity for herself through impulsive behaviors, such as reckless spending habits and binge eating. These negligent actions carried over to her parenting, that is: my children suffered from a lack of nutrition in vitamins and minerals, inconsistency with rules and discipline, an unstable bedtime, and little (but poor) supervision.

- *Recurrent Suicidal Behavior, Gestures, or Threats*—Suicide and other impulsive, dysfunctional behaviors are adapted for solutions to overwhelming, uncontrollable emotional pain. Amy had previously revealed her thoughts about the world being better off without her. Her involuntary hospitalization resulted from her desire to walk into traffic to make her death look like an accident.

- *Severe Mood Swings*—Amy's mood would swing from intense anger to depression, depression to irritability, and irritability to anxiety within a few hours. Her unstable mood cycle repeated several times within a week.

- Difficulty Controlling Anger—Amy's rage was usually intense, unpredictable, unprovoked, and unaffected by logical argument. She was like a person with third-degree burns over 90% of her body. Lacking emotional skin, she felt agony at the slightest touch or movement.

- *Severe Dissociative Symptoms*—Amy was severely dissociative, that is, she felt unreal, strange, numb, and detached. I watched her on numerous occasions. She acted as if she wasn't part of the family and didn't belong. I personally believe that her idleness and severe depression were contributing factors.

- *Undefined Boundaries and Control Issues*—Amy attempted to control me by putting me in no-win situations, creating chaos that no one could figure out, and accusing me of trying to control her. Her accusations were always constructed to prohibit a defense.

- *A Game of Projection*—Amy denied her own unpleasant traits, behaviors, and feelings by projecting them onto me. Sometimes, her exaggerations had a basis in reality. Other times, she twisted my words and actions out of context. To Amy, this served a higher purpose: If I found out she wasn't perfect, I might abandon her. Therefore, she transferred her negative behaviors, feelings, and traits onto me.[12]

The characteristics described above apply to low and high functioning borderlines. There are other BPD characteristics that I have omitted since they don't apply to Amy. Although the hospital never labeled Amy as high or low functioning, Amy displayed the characteristics of a high-functioning, invisible Borderline. This type of Borderline are as follows:

- Amy acted perfectly normal most of the time to people outside the family. Being on the inside, I was the only one who witnessed her destructive behavior.

- Amy coped with her pain by acting out and inflicting it onto me. This included threats, verbal abuse, intimidation, and even physical provocations.

- Marriage counseling and therapy proved to be non-productive because Amy used it as a platform for her agenda—to accuse me before a counselor and set herself up as the victim.

---

[12] Paul Mason and Randi Kreger, *Stop Walking on Eggshells: Taking Your Life Back When Someone You Care About has Borderline Personality Disorder* (Oakland: New Harbinger Publications, 2010).

- Amy kept her distance from our friends and family so they could never really get to know her. Therefore, no one ever believed my stories of her rage, intimidation, and verbal abuse. Others either ignored my plea for help or accused me of lying.
- Amy's denial was so persuasive that she convinced herself that what she said was true and what she did was really my fault.[13]

Then one particular day, Amy handed me a worksheet. I was saddened by what she wrote. *"I'm good for nothing / People would be better off without me / I always mess things up."*

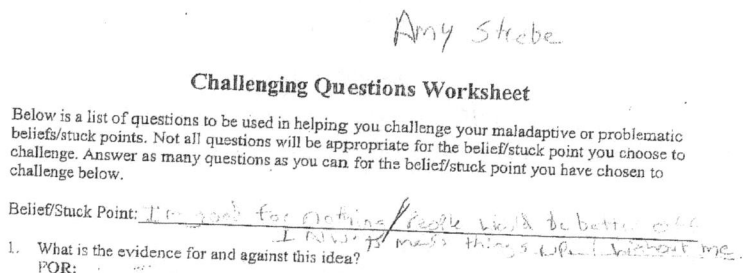

Amy Strobe

Challenging Questions Worksheet

Below is a list of questions to be used in helping you challenge your maladaptive or problematic beliefs/stuck points. Not all questions will be appropriate for the belief/stuck point you choose to challenge. Answer as many questions as you can for the belief/stuck point you have chosen to challenge below.

Belief/Stuck Point: I'm good for nothing / People would be better off
                    I always mess things up without me.

1. What is the evidence for and against this idea?
   FOR:

Figure 1: Amy's Worksheet

I wasn't the only person who witnessed Amy's behavior. When our daughter, Kyndall, was receiving services with Pacific Child and Family Associates, their report observed, *"Kyndall's mother...has difficulty participating and remembering strategies that were recommended in session. She will often report Kyndall's poor behavior to the staff via text and state that she doesn't know what to do."*

Parent Participation

Kyndall's father has been consistently present two times a week for session. He will ask questions and participate in the session for 20 minutes. Kyndall's mother is the parent that is present in the majority of the sessions has difficulty participating or remembering strategies that were recommended in session. She will often report Kyndall's poor behavior to the staff via text and state that doesn't know what to do. The team is currently working on a "cheat sheet" for the family for follow when staff is not in the home. Parent's participation is imperative to Kyndall's progress and the team will continue to work with the family to find all barriers that preventing them from implementing strategies during and outside of session.

Figure 2: Pacific Child Report

---

[13] Ibid.

2015: Under Satanic Power

The following year, Amy's father, John, moved into our home to ostensibly care for her and assist her with childcare while I was at work. But his move into our home was quite ironic, since my wife had previously verbalized to me accusations of her father molesting her sisters. This led to her opening about how she was raped when she was a young child by her dad's best friend.

With these several accusations, however, I can only vouch for number two. In the case of the State of Ohio v. Timothy Smithers, the defendant was convicted for sexual penetration of Amy Topmiller (her maiden name). But whether any of those other statements are true or not is irrelevant. She believed them at the time she spoke them, but then turned around to move her father into our home.

Unfortunately, John's presence was also merely idle. He operated as an extension of Amy's arm and reported to her everything he saw and heard. Initially, I thought nothing of it because I had nothing to hide, not realizing that I still had everything to protect.

Amy stayed awake all night and slept during the day, while John stayed awake all day and slept at night. Thus, I was never alone, except at work. Amy or John attempted to engage me in casual conversation, but their body language spoke much louder than our simulated communication. I was always under surveillance, so our family and its relationship deteriorated.

This 24-hour observation required Amy to demand control over my communication with others. I no longer had any privacy. Amy insisted on listening in on all my phone conversations. She sought proof that I was hiding information from her and plotting against her. In addition to eavesdropping on my phone calls, she imposed a strict time limit for my commute to and from work. Leaving work late, catching an extra light red, or getting stuck behind a slow driver would cause me to walk in the house just minutes after Amy expected me home, but in her mind, I was late. And her response was no different than any other situation. She promptly started an argument, throwing false accusations in my face.

Naturally, this behavior turned me off. Since this demonic personality destroyed her beauty, I was no longer attracted to my wife. But regardless, Amy always demanded sex. On several occasions, I just gave up, even though I hated every minute. My fourth and fifth child were conceived under these circumstances. However, if the roles had been reversed, this would have been classified as rape.

This progressive change in Amy's behavior became far more evident once her father moved into the house. And since her focus now revolved strictly around her Borderline-induced fears about me, she couldn't be bothered with the children. While my 8-year-old daughter, Addison, readily picked up her mother's parenting responsibilities, I found that within my own home, my freedoms were eroding away. And worst of all, I never even saw it coming. Unaware at the time, this oppressive state was just beginning.

March 10, 2016: Divine Intervention

Through Divine intervention, the Lord removed me from under satanic control. I moved into a 2-bedroom apartment about a mile down the road from Amy and the kids. By the end of March, Amy moved into government housing with her father and my kids. In that environment, the children were not safe, but Amy's constant surveillance and iron grip smothered their relationship with me. Force would be necessary to loosen her hold, and the only lawful and appropriate use of force was due process under law.

On this day, Amy lost direct control over my life. But thanks to the government, they paved her another avenue to regain power over me. My circumstances are about to turn from bad to worse.

BATTLE FOR CONTROL

On April 11, 2016, Amy gave birth to our fifth child, Lincoln. (My fourth child was born in 2015.) I didn't know she had gone into labor, so I wasn't there. Naturally, my absence left others with the impression that I wasn't present because I didn't care about my wife or family. Numerous people assumed that I had been notified but refused to show.

The morning following Lincoln's birth (thirty-three days after our separation), Amy filed for divorce. How could she file for divorce while lying in the hospital still recovering from childbirth? Did someone else file for the divorce on her behalf? Were insiders working behind the scenes to undermine our family?

For the next six weeks, the fellowship I enjoyed with my children started to deteriorate. And Amy was always in the center. When she filed for divorce, the terms of visitation and child support obligations were attached. This is where things turned ugly.

While the terms granted me the "right" to see my children on certain days and times, it specifically denied me access to them at the same time. I could visit my children two days per week, three hours per day. (I could choose any two weekdays, but the three-hour block was set to after-school hours.) Then, with harsh language, the document specified that my children were never allowed weekend or overnight visitation.

The visitation terms imposed on me was not standard practice. Amy persuaded the State-appointed attorney to word the document in that manner. Visitation orders commonly specify the days and times that visitation is authorized—an approval for access, not the denial of it. Outside of that agreement, Amy has the power to deny me access to the kids. Why then should the order deny me access?

This is an example of Amy's modus operandi. She rules without exercising any visible power. She imposes her will but shifts the decision to the courts. In other words, the State is denying me access, she's not. The tactic of ruling in darkness. I refused to sign this agreement, so Amy threatened to turn me over to the government.

A few days later, I phoned her to speak with my children. She promptly asked if I signed the child support agreement. I said that I'd sign and agree to her child support terms only if visitation were modified. She argued that the terms of visitation contained exactly what I wanted and gave me no more than I needed. "You'll be sorry!" After threatening me, she hung up the phone. I didn't even get to speak with my children—the initial reason for the call.

In the meantime, Amy's attorney, Elena Hansen from the La Morena Law Firm, sent me a letter where she ensured I was denied access to my children unless I followed certain procedures; yet the rules were crafted in such a way as to prohibit me from complying. For example: I was *only* allowed to visit my children if I texted Amy first. Amy knew full well that I didn't own a cell phone because she previously asked why I didn't have one. Therefore, calling with my home phone denied me physical access to my kids. But she might give me permission to speak with them.

However, that same letter portrayed an element of disappointment. Amy and her attorney were allegedly concerned about my lack of participation in the lives of my children. They were encouraging me to be a father and to get involved with my children.

To cleverly deny me access to my children while encouraging me to participate in their lives revealed my wife's motive. The self-contradiction is intended to impose her will but hold me accountable. I responded to Miss Hansen correcting the falsehoods, but my letter fell on deaf ears.

Amy falsified visitation appointments on more than one occasion. She deceived my children into believing I had arranged to pick them up, but when the fabricated appointment slipped by without my appearance, the children's spirits were crushed. This cruelty led to more deception, and Amy conveniently blamed me. But when I showed up at her house, she refused to open the door. On one occasion, Amy wasn't there and so her father opened the door. Later that day, I received a phone call from Miss Hansen threatening me with police action. I was to never go over to her house again, or she would file a police report against me for stalking, harassing, and threatening my wife.

By painting me as an unloving and uncaring dad, my children reacted with animosity and hatred towards me. They no longer wanted to see me, and since Amy had effectively silenced my voice in the lives of my children, they were forced to believe their most verbal source. Thus, they easily believed and repeated their mother's bombardment of lies.

Amy was setting the stage. She anticipated her need to declare war against me and prepared my children to rebel against my authority. In addition, government force lurked right around the corner.

Amy eventually severed all phone contact. In May, I called and left several messages wishing my daughter a "Happy Birthday" and requesting a call back. But the call never came.

This psychological assault against my children was devastating. I attempted to petition the court to have my children removed from their mother to protect them from the lethal effects of Parental Alienation—

the most dangerous form of child abuse. The court denied my petition, citing an unlawful attempt to bypass judicial protocol. It turns out that in my effort to bring charges against Amy, I must serve her with a set of interrogatories (written questions). This is, I am told, to prevent an ambush in court. She would then have 30 days to respond to the interrogatories and mount her defense. On May 19, I served Amy with a set of interrogatories. On May 28, I received her response.

May 28, 2016: Waging War

Someone advised Amy[14] to contact the Las Cruces Police Department and file a police report against me for allegedly molesting, kidnapping, and threatening my eldest daughter, Addison, who was now 9 years old. On May 28, 2016, the police responded to Amy's residence, took down her statements, and opened a criminal case.

Within two weeks, there was a court hearing that I was denied access to. Judge Douglas Driggers presided over that secret hearing. And Amy perjured her testimony by pretending to be victimized. There was no evidence! There were no witnesses! The other side of the story was not presented! I, the defendant, could not hear the charges brought against me! All that existed was a one-sided story and a dark conspiracy. In the shadows of the courtroom, Judge Driggers found me guilty and issued a protection order (also known as a restraining order) against me.

If you remember, I had been under 24-hour house surveillance for more than a year. I worked a full-time job while Amy stayed home. Following our separation, I was denied access to Addison and my other four children. So when did I even have an opportunity to commit this horrific act, and where was Amy's 24-hour surveillance team

---

[14] This advisory was recorded in the police report, but no name or entity was mentioned.

when it happened? What we see is a conspiracy building a case upon a false foundation, all based on Amy's emotional accusations, not on fact.

The first week of June, the police interviewed Amy and recorded her official statements at the police station. She informed the questioning officer that I had called several times and threatened her. (The last few phone calls, I left messages wishing my daughter a "Happy Birthday.") Unfortunately, the Las Cruces police weren't interested in the truth. They accepted her statement without asking one question. "Ma'am, what did he say? Did anyone else happen to hear it? Did he leave any messages? What time did he call? Who answered the phone? May we see your phone's call log?" Why didn't they question her? The more information they have, the better the case against the person who's harassing her with threatening phone calls. Wouldn't you think?

Then later, they transported Addison to the Children's Advocacy Center (CAC) where she echoed her mother's false accusations of molestation. Because Amy's accusations always contradicted the facts, sometimes Addison couldn't remember what to say or how to answer certain questions. In addition, Amy's continual dose of deception grayed Addison's distinction between truth and error. As a result, her recorded interview showed inconsistencies with the police report. Regardless, the police used this interview to obtain a search warrant and arrest warrant. I was criminally charged, jailed, and subsequently indicted by the Grand Jury. Two days later, the court released me on bond.

Around the first half of July, Addison returned to the CAC to make further accusations against me. This time, she claimed to have engaged in illicit sexual behavior with three neighbor boys (ages 6, 8, and 9 at the time of the alleged crime). That incident supposedly took place a year earlier. All three boys denied any sexual impropriety. Regardless, the police filed new felony charges. They rearrested me, and once again I was indicted—based exclusively on Addison's slanderous testimony. In addition, to make it appear as if those three young boys corroborated her testimony, Las Cruces Police Detective Guerra offered perjured testimony before the Grand Jury. In a nutshell, he lied—plain and simple. This is a clear case of malicious prosecution.

When the Las Cruces Sun News obtained a copy of the police report, they doctored up their findings (exaggeration), flavored their content (fabrication), removed their nutrients (omission), and polished their publication to paint me as a child predator, who was stalking children in Las Cruces. That fictional news story caused me to get fired from my job and evicted from my apartment.

My incarceration, coupled with the eviction, resulted in a loss of many of my material possessions. Although my parents drove down from Ohio, they were unable to haul everything home. I sat in jail for 5 weeks until the judge lowered bail and approved my request to live with my parents. They released me in September, but I no longer had a job, a place to live, or any money. My parents paid for my airfare to Ohio, so within a day, I was thankfully boarding a plane and leaving New Mexico.

November rolled around and Amy transported Addison back to the CAC. Amy was so determined to have me convicted that she constructed more accusations against me. It was imperative that her voice was heard through Addison, so this time she accused me of rape. At the conclusion of her two previous interviews, Addison said, *"That's all he did. There's nothing else."* The inconsistencies of the second and third interviews demonstrate that the State, collectively was working hard to prove me guilty of a crime that never happened by manufacturing evidence where none existed.

Thankfully, the prosecutor, Rebecca Duffin refused to charge me with rape. Why? Was it because of the progressive nature of the accusations and a strong indication of brainwashing and coercion? This indicates that Miss Duffin knew I was being falsely accused and wrongly charged, so why was she still pursuing the two other cases?

The prosecution was certain they could obtain a conviction, especially when Amy started turning over evidence she had gathered from her government-issued house. Interestingly, a house I never lived in was somehow full of evidence of sexual abuse. One piece of evidence (a post-it note with the date, time, and name of the boy Addison allegedly had sex with) didn't even corroborate with my work schedule. I was on the clock at work during the alleged behavior. This crime, if true, would have been committed under Amy's care. However, no medical examination was ever brought to light.

When my attorney interviewed Addison on May 5, 2017, their cases began to crumble. This evaluation brought to light more inconsistencies in her testimonies, and then Addison admitted fabricating evidence for the police. Also, my attorney exposed the Las Cruces Police Department for committing perjury before the Grand Jury. I passed two polygraph examinations. All three boys continued to deny any sexual impropriety. In addition, searching my apartment and seizing my property left the police without one scrap of evidence. The prosecution failed to produce a shred of paperwork on a medical examination for my daughter. They couldn't find a single witness nor the slightest bit of evidence to lend credence to the accusations and charges filed against me.

There was nothing left to investigate.

Yet, the kindling of their hatred darkened my days for another 9 months.

Ironically, only four days after Addison's interview with my attorney, Amy petitioned family court to finalize her divorce and receive financial support. This hearing was scheduled for July 24. (I requested the hearing be continued after the criminal case was resolved, but my request was denied.) During the July hearing, I was prohibited from mounting a defense or proving my innocence because I was still pending criminal charges. I was only permitted to answer questions, but Amy had no restrictions. Judge Manuel Arrieta finalized the divorce at Amy's request, awarded her permanent custody of my children, and ordered me to pay her spousal support of $200 per month for two years.

February 27, 2018: A Murder Threat

My criminal trial was scheduled for mid-February. However, just three days before I was to appear in court, the prosecution dismissed the criminal charges against me for lack of evidence.

At that time, another court hearing to address the temporary restraining order was on the calendar for February 27. I showed up for court but couldn't foresee what was about to unfold. During my testimony before the court, Amy ambushed me with a bombardment of more false allegations. These included building a tent for Addison and the neighbor boys' sexual activity, choking my wife, looking at child porn, lusting after my children in my sleep, suffering from Post-Traumatic Stress Disorder, the military conditioning my mind to outwit and beat the justice system, etc. (Wait a minute, wasn't Amy unlawfully bypassing judicial protocol? Where were my interrogatories? Why wasn't I allowed 30 days to respond to these questions and mount a defense?)

How can anyone defend themselves against an onslaught of accusations? It was simply my word against hers. How can you prove that you're not lusting after your children in your sleep? Everything she accused me of, she couldn't prove; nor could I disprove. Yet, those things have a way of leaving trace evidence around the perpetrator. No one lusts after children without a visual stimulation (child pornography). And if a person looks at porn, it's either physically or digitally stored somewhere. Where's the evidence?

You can't prove a negative. That's why the burden of proof rests with the prosecution (or accuser). Amy even had the assistance of the prosecutor and the entire Las Cruces Police Department, who dismantled every piece of my electronics looking for proof—any proof—that I'd been into illegal activity, especially child pornography. And after all that, the prosecutor dismissed the charges for lack of evidence.

Anyway, he still required Amy and Addison to take the stand to testify. My attorney caught Amy lying under oath when he questioned her about her mental illnesses. He also pointed out inconsistencies during Addison's testimony where she admitted that she couldn't remember.

Then the judge allowed Amy to question Addison. Amy asked Addison several questions and then concluded with, *"What will happen if your dad gets custody of you?"*

Addison's startling response was, *"I will be killed."*

Prior to this point, there wasn't a single recorded interview with a murder threat. But her response didn't include who made the threat; just that the threat was made. Yet, due to the restraining order, I hadn't seen or talked to her in nearly two years. With some critical thinking, it's not too hard to figure out that Amy (or someone under Amy's influence) threatened to murder my daughter.

My attorney discredited both, Amy and Addison. My daughter received a murder threat under her mother's care. And my ex-wife didn't prove a single accusation. Nevertheless, Judge Jerabek Isabel favored Amy by extending the restraining order against me for another two years. This is what prejudice looks like.

CHAPTER FOUR

CHILLING EFFECTS

About three months later, in the shadows of the Child Support Division (CSD) office, they prepared a stipulated order against me. In that order, they demanded $972.00 per month in child support, $5.00 per month in medical support, $200.00 per month in spousal support, and $40.00 per month in past-due spousal support. Total monthly support would be $1,217.00.

06/05/2018 JUDGMENT AND ORDER   RS   1

Stipulated Judgment and Order Ordered that Rsp. Toby Strebe pay $972.00/month for child support, $5.00/month for cash medical support, $200.00/month for spousal support and $40.00/month for spousal support judgment Total monthly $1,217.00

Figure 3: Stipulated Judgment and Order

The CSD did send my attorney a copy of the stipulated order requesting our consent. But without waiting, they moved forward and rushed their stipulated order into court on June 5, 2018, where the judge's stamp of approval finalized it. When we notified the CSD of the impossibility of complying with such oppressive demands, it was too late. A judgment and order had already been issued against me. Pay the monthly amount or go to jail for contempt.

Therefore, on July 5, I filed a motion with the court to relieve me of their previous judgment. I eventually managed to appear in court telephonically on November 27, 2018 to make that request. Judge

Jeanne Quintero allowed my attorney to speak, but we were limited to making our request and the reason for our request. Amy spoke without restraint, and her accusations flew all around the courtroom. Since Amy appeared unrepresented by legal counsel, Judge Quintero assumed the role of Amy's defense attorney and the prosecutor. Hearsay in support of Amy's accusations was admissible, but physical evidence to aid my defense was irrelevant. Judge Quintero criticized me for refusing to support my children and equated that to a form of child abuse.

Amy denied me access to my children, withholding from them their father's love, my financial support, and my parental guidance. She filed several false police reports against me, which led to my false arrest and unlawful incarceration, a termination of my employment, an eviction from my home, and the loss of many personal possessions. She committed perjury on numerous occasions and cost me tens of thousands of dollars in my criminal defense.

Yet, Judge Quintero thinks I'm a deadbeat for not voluntarily showering her with hundreds of dollars per month to ostensibly provide for my children. Since Amy took the children by force (with government assistance), I can't help but wonder why she's now refusing to support them. For Judge Quintero to deny my children financial support by favoring Amy—that, in and of itself, is child abuse.

Amy presented the judge a report printed by the Children Youth and Families Department (CYFD). This report only substantiated Amy's allegations, which had never been disclosed before now.

I'm unable to appear in court, even against government agencies, without being ambushed. The CYFD wasn't present for me to cross examine. I wasn't served interrogatories or allowed 30 days to mount a defense. Evidence used in court was not even turned over to me. Do you see a trend here? Apparently, this conspiracy can't compete with the truth, so the only way for them to prevail is to suppress it.

Standard judicial protocol protects the right of the accused to hear the arguments against them, cross examine their accuser and witnesses, and see the physical evidence. Every time I appeared in court, judicial protocol was shredded. This unlawful practice infringed upon my God-given, constitutionally-protected rights to hear the arguments against me, cross examine my accusers, and see the evidence used against me. This method of interference is to ensure that it's only my word against Amy's, so I can't prove my innocence.

I was, allegedly, digging my own grave. Judge Quintero approved my relief on a mere technicality but expedited my case to the CSD. I was now required to stand trial before the same CSD that previously conspired against me.

December 18, 2018: The Enactment of Child Support

I appeared telephonically before hearing Officer John Trujillo solely to determine the level of support they expected from me; not to debate the issue of support itself. His position required a child support judgment to be issued. But he was also very vocal in repeating the line that fathers are responsible to support their children.

The CSD was demanding retroactive support from March 10, 2016 (the date of my separation from Amy) until December 18, 2018 (the date child support was officially ordered).

Mr. Trujillo, however, suspended the retroactive support until a custody evaluation could be conducted. (I elaborate on the custody evaluation a little later.)

But to satisfy current support obligations, he ordered me to pay $400 per month in child support with an additional $5.00 per month for medical coverage. Judge Arrieta's order in the amount of $200 per month for spousal support remained in effect. Monthly support totaled $605.00.

But there were still so many unanswered questions—questions I'm forbidden to ask.

- If family court is really pursuing what's in the best interest of my children, why am I prohibited from seeing them, loving them, and caring for them?
- If Amy wanted the children, why won't she at least help to support them?
- If the courts are concerned about protecting children, why did they give their mentally ill and emotionally unstable mother total control over them?

I get the impression they wanted to label me a deadbeat dad. The courts must hate fathers who are involved with their children. Have they added my name to the list of the hundreds of caring fathers they've driven from their own homes in the name of child protection?

How can you hold one person accountable for the decisions of someone else? I am only responsible to support my children if I am free [to choose] how to support them. If I'm not free to choose, then I can't possibly be responsible to support them. This was Amy's dream come true—she rules while I bear the responsibility of her decisions.

Since John Trujillo is only a hearing officer, he doesn't possess power to eliminate child support, remove children from an abusive spouse, or return children back to their caregiver. In other words, he has no power to rollback injustice; only to further it.

April 11, 2019: The Garnishment of Wages

Two days ago, but unknown at the time, my employer, Publix, received a court order to withhold my earnings. Surprisingly, Publix started withholding $139.62 of my weekly pay for what they falsely assumed to be "child support." They also withheld an additional $20.00 to process the government's request, and then $3.00 per payday thereafter.

After all I'd been through, why would Publix favor government oppression? *Because of propaganda.* Publix thought they were doing what was right by helping the government provide support for these poor neglected children and their over-worked mom who was left holding the bag when their dad ditched them. But like so many Americans these days, they're ignorant about the government actions.

I filed a written complaint with Publix's corporate payroll department. Relaying a message from corporate, my store manager stated, *"We're not allowed to say 'no.'"* This response was more than just informal. It was downright unprofessional. The payroll department never sent me a formal letter addressing my objection or explaining their legal position in the matter. They just ignored me.

Why was Amy's voice allowed to be heard—through Addison and the government—but my voice was still being suppressed?

Regardless, my store manager's statement was far from the truth. Court orders are only binding on the parties in court, so this court order placed Publix in the cross hairs. It's a civil responsibility to interpose on behalf of another by refusing to enforce an unlawful order— an opportunity they clearly missed.

But to take it a step further, does any judge possess the authority to compel an individual or business to take private property without the voluntary consent of the owner? Is this not the very definition of stealing? The law prohibits this action, irrespective of the reason for the action.

Forfeiture of pay (or wage garnishment) is only lawful with a conviction. The court order Publix received was only a judgment against me. A judgment without a conviction invalidates the order. Thus, if an order is null and void, then the law which prohibits the action is still in force. Yet, there was no conviction precisely because there was no crime or wrong-doing.

If you or I take property from Publix without their consent (or anyone else for that matter), we'd be arrested. It is crystal clear that the laws in our land do not apply, nor are enforced equally with all people. Enforcement of the law is selective, depending on the subject (or the violator). How can your life, liberty, or property be secure in a subjective environment?

June 13, 2019: Summoned for Unknown Reasons

The court proceeding in Dona Ana County began at 8:30 a.m. (10:30 EST). My name was on the roster, but I wasn't present. Wait, let me back up and set the stage!

On April 20, I received my first statement from the Child Support Division. CSD demanded a monthly payment in the amount of $786.19. This was $181.19 higher than the amount ordered by the court. My continued refusal to pay these bandits infuriated them, so about 12 days later, I received a demand for payment. Since I had ignored the CSD for the past four months (January–April), they now demanded payment of $3,165.15. If I didn't pay half within two weeks, they threatened to report it to the three credit bureaus. If payment wasn't made in full within 30 days, they threatened to suspend my driver's license.

Where do you find this type of law and order? In a bank robbery? *"Give me your money or else I will hurt you!"* This isn't justice; it's criminal. They've already destroyed my livelihood and finances once. Now they're coming after me for more money before I've even recovered from their last attack.

By mid-May, a court hearing was scheduled. There was no motion filed or reason specified for the hearing. Don't you find this a bit strange? A motion lets the judge and the other party know what the dispute is over. A request for hearing is usually ignored if a motion doesn't precede the request. Yet, in the shadows of the courthouse, I was discreetly summoned to court again. And with no reason given for the hearing, I had no way to prepare for their next attack. This was an ambush waiting to happen.

I don't even know who summoned me. But regardless, weren't they (whomever "they" may be) unlawfully bypassing judicial protocol and preventing me from mounting a defense? Not if you're a slave and *have no right to a defense*!

Slaves aren't entitled to due process under law. Slaves aren't privileged to the equal protections of the law. Slaves don't have the right to make their own free choices. Slaves are only classified as property, not human beings. Slaves are bound to unconditional obedience to their owners. And this is a classic case of a disobedient slave being drug before his master to receive punishment. All freedom-loving Patriots must abhor the evil institution of slavery within the doors of family court and the Child Support Division.

To complicate matters, a telephonic appearance in court is very expensive. My family law attorney had covered the cost out of my retainer. But towards the end of March, I was forced to discontinue her representation due to the high cost of attorney fees. I didn't have any money to appear in court. But at the same time, I didn't want to appear in court. I was tired of standing in the middle of the courtroom (in person or via the telephone) just to be mocked, lied about, falsely accused, and degraded by every member of the judicial mafia.

Yet, to this day, they have never heard a true account of both sides of this story. They have only heard (and believed) distorted views of this embellished fairy-tale, both of which were told from the perspective of the one with Borderline Personality Disorder—the one who has no true grasp on reality.

July 18, 2019: Driven from Employment

Without any notification, warning, or reminder, Publix increased their payment by $181.19 (from $605 to $786.19). Why couldn't Publix send out a notification or reminder beforehand?

If Publix just wanted to obey the government (and not say "no," as my manager claimed), what's wrong with notifying their employee? If their notification prompted me to resign prior to withholding my earnings, that's not Publix's problem; it's the government's. Publix's element of surprise indicates that they were a voluntary accomplice with the government. They love what the government is doing and want to help anyway they can.

Apparently, what was ordered in court increased by the time it was officially documented. During the December 18, 2018 court hearing, John Trujillo informed me that I would be paying $405 per month in child support, and the $200 for spousal support would remain in effect. Period!

The written order that followed the court hearing specified that I would pay $405 per month for the first six months (January–June) in child support. Then starting in July, child support would increase to $586.19 per month with no change in spousal support. This increase in support was never ordered in court but inserted later into the written order that Publix received on April 9, 2019. (This was prior to the June 13 court hearing that I refused to attend.)

Also, last December, my attorney (prior to discontinuing her representation) successfully argued that my children should remain with government medical insurance. Since I resided in a different state with different laws, it just made since. I was ordered to pay $5.00 per month for my children's government medical insurance. However, the courts changed their mind without notifying me, but were quick to contact Publix.

Employers usually mail information to their employees with open enrollment dates for employer-provided health insurance. Employees usually have the option to decline the coverage if they choose to, but in my case, this option was not available. Open enrollment was quickly approaching, and the decision to enroll myself and family had already been made—a decision contrary to my will.

I have reason to believe that this was ordered by family court, but neither New Mexico, nor Publix, ever sent me a copy of this order. Publix just sent me a letter telling me what the court ordered. Once again, this was contrary to the agreement made in court.

The day I received that letter (July 18), I resigned from Publix.

There are two sides to this ongoing battle: oppression (the devil's side) or freedom (God's side). Publix has, unknowingly, chosen to favor the oppressor—the enemies of freedom. But I continued to resist government tyranny for the sake of freedom.

August 12, 2019: A Quick Pursuit Emerges

It was disheartening to leave Publix because I really liked my job, but I thought it was for the best. Since I didn't have a new position lined up, I was on the search. When I applied to work for Hobby Lobby, they offered me a seasonal position, which I gladly accepted. I started on August 12. Ten days later (August 22), I received correspondence from the New Mexico Child Support Division acknowledging my new employment with Hobby Lobby.

I certainly didn't expect the CSD to move this fast. The letter was mailed only two days after I started work. First, I didn't live or work within the state of New Mexico, and second, all legal-based paperwork such as my I9 or W4 was processed through the federal government. Therefore, it would've been impossible for the CSD to retrieve my employment information within days unless there were insiders within our federal government. In other words, the CSD needs federal assistance to automatically retrieve private information about an individual.

Three years ago, the police obtained a search warrant on me. However, the CSD easily bypasses the requirements of the law. This conspiracy that goes far beyond our local and state government agencies.

Appallingly, laws have been enacted to prevent businesses from disclosing, distributing, or selling private or confidential information to protect their customers. Yet, the federal government isn't bound by law to protect its citizens. It's evident that these laws do not apply equally to all. They are subjective.

The very first paycheck I received, Hobby Lobby followed in the footsteps of Publix when they seized my wages and handed it over to the family court-run mafia. What would possess Hobby Lobby to do such a thing? *Propaganda!* The government's use of propaganda is so effective that many businesses and individuals have been convinced that, *"War is peace. Freedom is slavery. Ignorance is strength."* (Orwell, 1961)[15]

It worked in Germany, and it's been very effective in the United States. American's are inundated with the ideology of protecting the young and the weak—even against their own parents. The stronger, ostensibly, possesses no self-restraint—instinctively attacking the weaker. And government is our savior. This ideology, however, is propaganda, which caused Hobby Lobby to also miss an opportunity to interpose on my behalf.

Yet, one benefit of my employment with Hobby Lobby was the hours I received. I worked an average of 47 hours per week. Although child support increased to $586.19 per month, spousal support dropped off (the two-year expiration date had elapsed). While working at Hobby Lobby, I noticed that only 25.63% of my salary for "child support" was taken. In addition, since I was only a seasonal employee, I was thankful that I didn't qualify for medical insurance.

October 17, 2019: Suppression of an Evaluation

I received a notification that a court hearing was scheduled for October 17 to establish retroactive support. If you'll remember, John

---

[15] George Orwell, *Nineteen Eighty-Four* (New York, Signet Classics, 1961).

Trujillo had suspended the support last December. Here's a brief background on its suspension, which will help you understand why it's being lifted now.

Throughout this whole ordeal, I had argued for a custody evaluation. My arguments were largely ignored. That was, until last November. (The same court hearing to relieve me of the CSD's previous judgment.) My attorney presented the need for an evaluation by turning my ex-wife's arguments upside down to reveal her psychological problems. I was unaware how Judge Quintero deceptively granted the evaluation. I say "deceptively" because she also granted Amy the power to veto the evaluation through a back door.

Since I chose a private evaluator, I would have to pay upfront for the cost of his services—regardless of the outcome. His impeccable reputation often generated referrals from the Dona Ana County family courts to their litigants for his services, so he was in high demand. Unknown to me at the time, but later revealed in court, I happened to choose a private evaluator the courts revered.

Unfortunately, Amy had too much to hide to allow a thorough evaluation by an unbiased source who would undoubtedly reveal the truth, so she requested another evaluator. And the judge, who obviously wanted her to retain custody of the children, regardless of her mental or emotional state, had no qualms in granting Amy's request.

Judge Quintero ordered the evaluation but set a trap in the process. She allowed Amy to choose the evaluator, while ordering me to pay for the evaluation. Sounds like a reasonable compromise. But was it? By using this method, Amy screened evaluators and selected one that she had the opportunity to prejudice against me. I would foot the bill for a biased evaluation that would cement Amy's triumph over me— even at the expense of my children.

This was equivalent to paying for my own assassination. Judge Quintero also provided Amy a second weapon. Her order was crafted to prevent Amy from interfering with the evaluation, but it did not order (or compel) the evaluator to perform the evaluation.

Upon contacting Amy's hand-picked evaluator, my attorney and I learned that he had already refused to perform the evaluation. He felt uncomfortable performing an evaluation involving such a delicate nature of sexual allegations. Now how did he know about that?

With that information—be it truth or error—he could no longer perform an unbiased evaluation, so he declined. It mattered not if he refused to evaluate or favored her. Either way, she won.

Since I wasn't allowed to choose an evaluator, and the evaluator Amy chose declined to evaluate, the order for the custody evaluation was meaningless—it didn't order anything.

Retroactive support had been suspended until after the completion of a custody evaluation. In the eyes of the courts, Amy fulfilled her role by choosing the evaluator. But since he declined and the judge had stripped me of the right to choose an evaluator, the subject was now closed. Therefore, it was time for this suspension to be lifted.

PART TWO

THE WARFARE

CHAPTER FIVE

A SUBTLE ABDUCTION

These tactics deployed against me (and the strategic involvement with all divorce cases) have their roots grounded in juvenile court—the precursor to family court. In 1899, the Illinois legislature passed the Juvenile Court Act which established the nation's first juvenile court in Chicago. By 1903, seven other states had followed suit. The old English Common Law, *Parens Patriae*, served as the rationale for the creation of the juvenile court system in America.

The Origins of Parens Patriae

The early origin of *Parens Patriae* dates back from feudal times but has endured a varied history of usage and interpretation. Historically, it has referred to the king as "father and protector of his people." The royal prerogative formed one of the central tenants for the common law. Blackstone describes the notion of a royal prerogative as such:

> *"By the word prerogative we usually understand that special pre-eminence, which the king hath over and above all other persons, and out of the ordinary course of the common law, in*

right of his regal dignity. It signifies, in its etymology, some-thing that is required or demanded before, or in preference to, all others. And hence it follows, that it must be in its nature singular and eccentrical; that it can only be applied to those rights and capacities which the king enjoys alone, in contradistinction to others, and not to those which he enjoys in common with any of his subjects: for if once any one prerogative of the crown could be held in common with the subject, it would cease to be prerogative any longer." (Blackstone, 1765-69)[16]

By virtue of the Prerogative Regis (a declaration defining certain feudal and political rights of the Crown), the king was understood to be personally sovereign and to have pre-eminence over all within his realm. He was the representative of the State in its dealings with for-eign nations. He was part of the legislature, the commander of the army, the fountain of justice, the arbiter of commerce, and the head of the church.

Parens Patriae was an expression of the king's prerogative. As Chitty explains:

"The king is in legal contemplation the guardian of his people, and in that amiable capacity is entitled (or rather it is his Majesty's duty, in return for the allegiance paid him) to take care of his subjects as are legally unable, on account of mental incapacity, whether it proceed from first nonage (children); second, idiocy; or third, lunacy: to take proper care of them-selves and their property." (Chitty, 1820)[17]

The king exercised his functions through the keeper of his con-science, the chancellor, and subsequently to the Court of Chancery, which operated under his supervision.

---

[16] William Blackstone, *Commentaries on the Laws of England* (Oxford: Clarendon Press, 1765-69), Vol 1.

[17] Joseph Chitty, *A Treatise on the Law of the Prerogative of the Crown and the Relative Duties and Rights of the Subject* (London: Printed for Joseph Butterworth and Son, 1820).

The court's parental jurisdiction extended to cases where a parent or guardian dies intestate, leaving behind property and minor children or a mentally incapacitated adult, who are unable to care for themselves. In short, under the *Parens Patriae* prerogative, the State's authority could only extend over certain individuals where no other person was already entrusted with it. *Parens Patriae* established the king as a protector or supreme guardian over those people.

The English Common Law forbade the king or his chancery court to claim jurisdiction over criminal matters. Although other areas of the king's prerogative might justify such intrusions, *Parens Patriae* was limited to a parental guardianship for the dependent.

Undermining American Jurisprudence

Today's modern usage of *Parens Patriae* is a doctrine claiming that State power over the lives of children is inherent. However, all inherent power comes from God. (I elaborate on this principle in chapter 13.) Inherency must precede its own doctrine—it cannot have a beginning.

Regardless, in their impulsiveness and haste to embrace the theory of *Parens Patriae* as its justification for the juvenile and family court movement, the reformers and child advocates of both nineteenth and twentieth centuries ignored three fundamental aspects in relation to the king's prerogative, the chancery court's jurisdiction, and American law.

First, they failed to recognize that *Parens Patriae*, was an extension of the State's authority over individuals, but strictly on the condition where no other person was already entrusted with it. Yet, this condition doesn't exist in divorce and child custody cases. Since both natural parents are still alive, *Parens Patriae* becomes an invalid argument. Stripping power away from the parents and claiming it for itself isn't inherent; it's a usurpation.

Second, they ignored the jurisdiction of the court of chancery, which was extended to the dependent child, not the delinquent child. English children who received royal protection and care had not violated the norms of society. These children summoned the care of the crown because of their dependent and propertied status. The motivating reason to apply the *Parens Patriae* was the need to support and care for children, not to reform or rehabilitate them.

Lastly, but more significantly, the reformers and child advocates utterly disregarded the American Constitution, which forms the basis of law and freedom in our nation. The American government receives its authority from the Constitution—not from the legislature, the courts, rebellious wives, or English Common Law. The *Parens Patriae* prerogative was never integrated into our Federal or State Constitutions. Therefore, it holds no legality.

These early juvenile reformers saw the application of *Parens Patriae* to the delinquent as "merely a logical extension of the principle of chancery and of guardianship applied to the court of chancery."[18] They were delighted to foster a theory to treat the delinquent child as a dependent child. The juvenile delinquent stood in sharp contrast to the notable innocence of childhood. Therefore, reformers proposed plans to save the delinquent from himself and to place him on the straight and narrow path. By focusing on the hopes of rehabilitation, it was possible to conceal any element of social fear of the child.

The straight and narrow path, however, was often barricaded by the reformers themselves. Since they were convinced that juvenile delinquents were social deviants threatening public safety and order, part of their rehabilitation process was to restrain the child from activities that were contrary to the social norms of the reformers. It was common practice for juvenile asylums to place an emphasis on atonement and punishment, not redemption. This is how the managers of the New York House of Refuge viewed their task in the early 1800's:

---

[18] Herbert Lou, *Juvenile Courts in the United States* (Chapel Hill: North Carolina University Press, 1927).

"These little vagrants, whose degradations provoke and call down upon them our indignation, are yet but children, who have gone astray for want of that very care and vigilance we exercise towards our own. They deserve our censure, and a regard for our property, and the good of society, requires that they should be stopped, reproved, and punished." (Hart, 1832)[19]

The children must be persuaded of the error of their ways and made to suffer for them. This was an appropriate method of rehabilitation for the reformers. These contrasting themes: "fear of the child" and "hope of rehabilitation" found an easy reconciliation in the concept of *Parens Patriae*, which had been completely detached from its historical purpose and original intent.

The Supreme Court of Pennsylvania was one of the earliest judicial endorsements of this concept's role in the rehabilitation of the delinquent child. It was articulated in Ex parte Crouse in which the father of Mary Ann Crouse brought a habeas corpus suit against the Philadelphia House of Refuge. Mary Ann was being held at the house of refuge against the wishes of her father, but at the bequest of her mother, who felt Mary Ann had become unruly and unmanageable. Mary Ann had not broken any laws or committed any crimes, but regardless, the court denied the father's petition and endorsed the actions of the State and institution:

"The object of the charity is reformation, by training its inmates to industry; by imbuing their minds with principles of morality and religion; by furnishing them with means to earn a living; and, above all, by separating them from the corrupting influence of improper associates. To this end, may not the natural parents, when unequal to the task of education, or unworthy of it, be superseded by the Parens Patriae, or common

---

[19] Nathaniel Hart, *Documents Relative to the House of Refuge, Instituted by the Society for the Reformation of Juvenile Delinquents in the City of New York, in 1824* (New York: Mahion, 1832).

guardian of the community? It is to be remembered that the public has a paramount interest in the virtue and knowledge of its members, and that, of strict right, the business of education belongs to it. " (Ex parte Crouse, 1839)[20]

The court's invention of *Parens Patriae*, under the force of such judicial reasoning essentially resulted in the evolution of *Parens Patriae* from a theory to a doctrine. The State could invade the home, replace the parents, and take custody of the child. The conflict between due process and *Parens Patriae* is clearly present. However, the purpose of such governmental action was never intended to protect or provide for the child's well-being. Rather, it was to protect the security and best interests of the State.

Juvenile reformers and courts were (and still are today) totally convinced that a child is the product of his environment. Therefore, if you remove the child from the corrupt influence of his natural parents, he ceases to be bad. A child's mind was a blank slate, which could be written on. The popularity of juvenile reform stemmed largely from its parental nexus, which the State is viewed as capable of achieving only good.

This environmentalist psychology was the conceptual framework of the *Parens Patriae* theory, which formed the basic justification to establish the first juvenile court system in 1899.

The Divorce Revolution

Shortly thereafter, the New Jersey legislature contemplated expanding the breadth of their experiment—from a court with jurisdiction over the legal matters of children to one over the law as it pertains to entire families. Thus, in 1912, the New Jersey legislature vested

---

[20] Ex parte Crouse, 4 Whart 9; 1839 Pa Lexis 171 (Supreme Court of Pennsylvania, 1839).

county juvenile courts with jurisdiction to hear and determine all domestic relations disputes.[21]

Two years later, Ohio followed suit with a court consolidation by creating the Division of Domestic Relations in Cincinnati. Although it wasn't labeled "Family Court," the Domestic Relations Division is credited with achieving the nation's first family court consolidation.[22]

With roots planted in New Jersey and Ohio, the idea spread throughout the first half of the century. A model family court legislation was drafted by three national organizations:

- The National Probation and Parole Association
- The National Council of Juvenile Judges
- The U.S. Children's Bureau

In April 1959, the Standard Family Court Act was presented to the states for consideration.[23] Rhode Island was the first state to adopt the act in 1961, which established the first system of family courts. By 1980, thirteen states had engaged in operating the family court system. Sixteen short years later, the number of states had risen to 35.

The family court system, however, wasn't intended to operate under fault-based divorce. Therefore, no-fault grounds emerged to complement the rise of the newly devised court system. It's evident that the conspiracy was implementing a Communist system, which is intended to bring America to her knees. So in 1953, Oklahoma became the first state to incorporate no-fault provisions to their traditional grounds for divorce.[24] But the divorce revolution started in 1969 with

[21] New Jersey Legislature, *Acts of the One Hundred and Thirty-Sixth Legislature of the State of New Jersey and the Sixty-Eighth Under the New Constitution* (Trenton: Secretary of State, 1912).

[22] Hunter Hurst, *Ohio Family Court Feasibility Study* (May 1997), Accessed April 13, 2021, https://ohiofamilyrights.com/Reports/Reports/Special-Reports-Page-3/Ohio-Family-Court-Feasibility-Study-.pdf.

[23] The Committee on the Standard Family Court Act. *Standard Family Court Act* (New York: The Association, 1959).

[24] Denese Vlosky and Pamela Monroe, "The Effective Dates of No-Fault Divorce Laws in the 50 States," In *Family Relations* 51, no. 4, Families and the Law (October 2002): 317-324, Accessed April 13, 2021, http://www.jtor.org/stable/3700329.

the California Family Law Act (Cal. Civ. Code §§ 4000-5138).[25] For the first time in American history, no-fault was the sole ground for divorce. But the law made no provisions for child custody or support.

No-fault grounds, after all, isn't exclusively reserved to cases where divorce is a mutual agreement. Rather, it extends to cases where wrong-doing is alleged. Nevertheless, the misleading term, "no-fault," is imposed upon all divorce cases. My ex-wife filed for divorce under no-fault grounds, even though she was accusing me of fault.

If the law prohibits finding fault as grounds for divorce, then the guilty party has an incentive to weaponize the law in their favor. By filing under no-fault grounds, the petitioner isn't held responsible to prove harm or injury. This sets the stage for a scapegoat. In theory (on paper), neither party accuses nor can they defend without an accusation. But in practice (off the record), the petitioner attacks, and the respondent takes the fall.

When accusations of wrong-doing surface after the filing (as with my case), the original grounds for divorce aren't invalidated. The petitioner isn't required to re-file under the fault-based system. If the accusations occur prior to the filing, similarly, the petitioner is encouraged, prompted, or even required to file under no-fault conditions. This convenience saves time, money, effort, and resources since the petitioner doesn't have to prove fault. However, it comes at a great expense to the respondent (who may be innocent) and any children shared between the couple.

Yet, when allegations of wrong-doing are presented in court, how can a judge side favorably with both sides? Fault must be placed!

A divorce is a civil dispute (or conflict) between family members —plain and simple. And similar to a criminal dispute (a conflict be-

---

[25] Richard Osborn, "Dissolution and Voidable Marriage Under the California Family Law Act," In *Loyola University Law Review* 4, no. 2 (April 1971): 331-361, Accessed April 13, 2021 https://digitalcommons.lmu.edu/llr/vol4/iss2/5.

tween the prosecution and defense), an investigation must be conducted to find truth and dispense justice. Without an investigation, truth is suppressed, and justice cannot be administered.

Suppose I'm a judge presiding over a civil divorce case. The parents disagree over the custody and care of their children. Without regard to the merits that each parent might bring, I enter my courtroom with a preconceived idea. My orders will follow 3 principles.

- I accept *only* the arguments or evidence that support my theory.
- I *reject* any and all clues that disagree with my theory.
- I *fabricate* my own argument or evidence, when necessary, to prove my predetermined conclusion.

Without investigating or looking into both sides of an argument, my rulings and court orders will slant towards my predetermined conclusion, ignoring the facts in the process. When this happens, I cease to be a judge and become a propagandist. Instead of judging according to the law or the merits of a case, I am spreading misinformation about an individual through my court orders. This is called, "libel."

American judges have traditionally been restrained by law. And a jury has always served as the last line of defense for the innocent. By removing these, court proceedings can effectively be manipulated to favor the judge's prejudiced opinion, which can never be challenged. No-fault legislation removed the law's restraints, and the Standard Family Court Act destroyed the last line of defense.

Communism Grips America

This shift in government policy resulted from the infiltration of communist ideals, which advocates social justice in replace of due process (lawful justice). Through a gradual, but strategic process, a metaphorical nation emerged and integrated itself within America's boundaries, which has subverted the American Republic by stealth. This symbolic nation is invisible. but nevertheless, it fulfills the requirements of nationhood. There are no physical borders, but two neighbors could live, theoretically, under two separate and distinct forms of government. One family might live under American jurisdiction, but their next-door neighbor could live under family court's jurisdiction (a communist dictatorship). This dictatorship is fully operational and has its own:

- **Form of Government**—Oligarchy! A judge is the figurehead, while the ruling class remains in the shadows.
- **Police Force**—Social agencies such as, the CAC, CPS, CYFD, and others perform police functions. They receive criminal reports of child abuse or neglect and perform investigations.
- **Court System**—Family court is consolidated to decide criminal cases (restraining orders), civil cases (divorce), and domestic disputes (child custody and visitation).
- **Laws**—Court orders are written rules by some governing authority for the purpose of regulating or restraining some sort of action in private life.
- **Community**—Enslaved families within the divorce machinery. The judicial order dissolving the marriage usurps the constitutional jurisdiction over each member of the family.
- **Source of Revenue**—Child support is a form of taxation since government revenue is attached to those payments. This tax is levied by the State with attached penalties for failing to pay.
- **Treasury Department**—The Child Support Division collects, enforces the collection of, transfers, and distributes funds.

The infiltration of this independent nation undermines the virtues on which America was built. But when any nation is governed by social justice, the most coveted status is victimhood, which people will go to absurd lengths to attain.

We are witnessing a controlled conflict. The stated objectives of the government have always been pro-child, pro-family, and pro-fatherhood. However, in the shadows of family court and their bureaucratic accomplices, they deceive and distribute propaganda.

Like double agents, they:

- Divide the family, which *weakens America's backbone.*
- Undermine parental authority, which *encourages crime in later years.*
- Terminate the relationship between father and child, which *transfers the child's loyalty to a new god and promotes perpetual adolescence and irresponsibility.*
- Remove the child's hedge of protection, which *increases child abuse.*
- Sever the child's life support, which *creates poverty and the entitlement mentality.*

The public rhetoric is intended to mask their actions, and in the process, the father becomes the scapegoat. America goes the way of the families. When the family collapses, so does America.

The Bible warns us not to be ignorant of Satan's devices, or he will get an advantage on us (2 Corinthians 2:11). Clearly, the price of ignorance is catastrophic. This strategy has effectively bound, gagged, and drug many into this system by deceit or by force. But very few comprehend what's going on.

Let's end this chapter with a simple exercise. Speak to one or two men who you know to be paying child support. Ask him to share his story with you.

- What was the root cause of his divorce?
- Who filed and why?
- What are the custody and visitation arrangements and who proposed them?
- Does he prefer those arrangements, or did he just accept the proposal?
- Does he pay child support and support his children when they're with him?
- Would he prefer paying the Child Support Division or taking his children shopping (if this was a choice)?

- Is he free to take his children anywhere he chooses, or does he have to ask permission from the court or his wife?

You'll discover that, in many cases, women are walking out on (or abandoning) their husbands. Other couples just decided to part ways together. But it's rare to hear a father say that he walked out on his family. It's always the government, the media, and feminists who spread disinformation about men abandoning or abusing their wives and children.

Thomas Jefferson, the author of the Declaration of Independence, had a much deeper understanding about freedom. In a letter to Charles Yancey, he wrote:

> *"If a nation expects to be ignorant and free in a state of civilization, it expects what never was and never will be. The functionaries of every government have propensities to command at will the liberty & property of their constituents. There is no safe deposit for these but with the people themselves; nor can they be safe with them without information. Where the press is free and every man able to read, all is safe."* (Jefferson, 1816)[26]

I've often asked myself why freedom was such a hard sell. After much thought and consideration, I realized that you can't offer something to someone who already believes they have it.

The true weight of freedom can only be measured by your free choices. Without governmental intervention, the individual must bear the responsibility for their own choices. Each time government intervenes in the private affairs of individuals or businesses, responsibility is transferred and freewill is dissolved.

This governmental system, its false authorities, and their positions must be dismantled (addressed in chapter 16). The great news is that dismantling this system doesn't require a majority—a small minority

---

[26] Thomas Jefferson, "Letter to Charles Yancey, 6 January 1816," In *The Papers of Thomas Jefferson: Retirement Series*, ed. Jefferson Looney (Princeton: Princeton University Press, 2013), Vol 9: September 1815 to April 1816.

can be just as effective.   The possession of knowledge, strength, courage, and God's direction during adversity enabled me to endure.

CHAPTER SIX

MASTERS OF DECEIT

Imagine that you're sitting in an auditorium waiting to watch a presentation. Have you ever given it much thought on its preparation? There are three parts necessary for a successful performance. You must have a director, a cast, and a script. The director oversees the program from start to finish. Every aspect of the play—from the script and the cast, to the costumes and the props—has the director's fingerprints. To lessen his workload, he will delegate assigned tasks to the assistant directors. Someone is responsible for the actors' costumes and make-up, whereas another may oversee the design of scenes and props. The lead director helps the cast rehearse their lines and directs the emotional tone of the scene they're rehearsing.

Other skilled experts are brought in for specialized areas of interest. One talented make-up artist applies the makeup on the cast. A designer makes the costumes. A handy-man might build the set. During this preparation, nothing takes place without the director's initiation, knowledge, and approval. Once complete and the auditorium opens, the cast takes their places, and the audience takes their seats. The play can now commence.

During the performance, there's usually music, dancing, and various scenes. The cast moves and speaks so naturally. Even their emotions change depending on the scene their enacting. Suddenly, the curtains close, the cast changes clothes, and the run crew sets up the stage for the new scene. Within minutes, the curtains open and the play resumes, but everything looks different.

The directors have complete control over the outcome, and the audience only sees what the directors want them to see. In the end, it's only an act; not reality.

This is an illustration of the subtlety of the deception within our political environment. But more precisely, it illustrates the assassination of the family behind the curtain. The government is only putting on a presentation—pretending to protect the family while depicting the father as a destroyer of his own family.

But we must ask ourselves, "Why would a man destroy his own wife and children, while government officials rush in to save somebody else's family. How many people do you know vandalize their own property? Yet, this is what the government wants you to believe that every man in America does. That's absurd!

The enemies of freedom have waged war on America's families. And the political performance (illustrated above) is their success formula to conquer and disassemble the traditional family.

Under the inspiration of God, Paul warns us about this warfare when he tells us *"For we wrestle not against flesh and blood, but against principalities, against powers, against the rulers of the darkness of this world, against spiritual wickedness in high places."* (Ephesians 6:12).

This warfare isn't waged by the audience deceived by the act, the performance of the politicians and judges, or the bureaucratic artists and designers. Paul's usage of words: *"principalities, powers, rulers, high places"* is evident that he is referring to the directors. These directors prepare the script, control the cast, hire the artists and designers, set the stage, determine the appearance, and influence the audience.

Divorce Mechanisms: A Satanic Design

Carefully examining my historical record (chapters 2–4), identifying the Principle of Reversal was quite evident. Throughout the whole ordeal, the State's actions against me, from the first accusation until the final establishment of child support, were firmly entrenched in Communist deceit and slogans. In a speech delivered by Robert Welch on April 11, 1961, he explained:

> *"The trick in the slogan...is the Communists' habit of taking their greatest weakness and, by daring and bluff, converting it into their greatest item of strength in a particular situation, large or small. This is the Principle of Reversal applied with a vengeance."* (Welch, 1966) [27]

The Principle of Reversal transforms criminality into righteousness while demonizing virtue. But tragically, these tactics are deployed universally across all 50 states. This is the consequence for trashing our fault-based system. Without fault, custody cannot be determined by action or merit; but rather, by discrimination based on sex.

My circumstances might be extreme compared to most cases, but the government's hidden objective remains the same. By giving women the upper hand with priority of custody, they aren't held accountable for their actions—their husbands are. (In all fairness, switching these roles in society would not solve the problem, only a fault-based system would.)

Generally speaking, the severity of the psychological attack against the children is the yard stick to gauge how much force the government will use against the father. In other words, the mother who attacks her children's mental faculties can be sure that the government will attack her husband. He's being held accountable for the actions of his ex-wife. The more brutal she is, the higher price he pays.

---

[27] Robert Welch, *The New Americanism and Other Speeches and Essays* (Belmont: Western Islands, 1966).

Don't be fooled, but the government is lurking in the shadows waiting for you to become vulnerable, so they can also devour you and your children. And if you refuse to plead guilty to crimes you never committed, the government will be compelled to bring out their makeup artists and designers to dress you as an offender while they apply the victimized makeup to your spouse and children. This successful performance is humanly impossible without a central direction (namely: a spiritual director—the devil).

The people entangled in this conspiracy encompass the directors (disguised), the cast (Amy, Addison, the police, judges), and the artists and designers (the social agencies). The actions of each member within this conspiracy complemented the others. They were all united in view of the same object.

The bureaucratic Child Protective Services (CPS), however, wasn't directly involved with my case, but they were notified of my situation. The CPS flagged me as a child abuser and recorded Amy and Addison as the victims. This devious tactic automatically "discredited" me if I reported child abuse. Furthermore, Amy's victimhood status gave her immunity from being reported.

Unfathomable! My ex-wife can't be investigated for child abuse or neglect through the CPS. Any evidence discovered by neighbors or teachers were attributed to me. The very agencies charged with protecting children provided Amy an open invitation to perpetrate child abuse while shielding her from prosecution.

State agents are merely arms of the conspiracy. Each bureaucracy must focus and strengthen themselves with one specific task.

Agency 1 — Children's Advocacy Center (CAC)

- Task: "Trained professionals" advocate for the child against parental authority using false abuse claims as a pretext to conduct forensic interviews.

- Weapon: "Trained professionals" possess enormous, unchecked power over language during their forensic interviews. Thus, usurping police investigative powers.
- Ammunition: "Trained professionals" have expertise in setting traps during questioning by choosing the questions, the choice of words, the arrangement of words, the words to avoid, and the questions to omit.
- Crimes: "Trained professionals" are guilty of language manipulation, the redefinition of words, social engineering, manufacturing false evidence, and ignore cues that negate.

Agency 2 — Children Youth and Families Department (CYFD)

- Task: "Community-based" representatives utilize a consensus to uphold abuse claims, even falsified claims.
- Weapon: "Community-based" consensus usurps police investigative powers, and the "community-based" verdict usurps jury powers.
- Ammunition: "Community-based" programs operate through the ideology of social justice. Creating victims, real or imagined, empowers their programs.
- Crimes: "Community-based" justice produces false witnesses, perjures statements, manufactures false evidence, and spreads deception.

Agency 3 — Child Support Division (CSD)

- Task: To "serve families" by transferring wealth from the parent producing to the parent and agencies who will not produce.
- Weapon: To "serve families" by taking away the father's responsibility to support his children. Thus, usurping the police's seizure power.

- Ammunition: To "serve families" by confiscating all their wealth and removing their means of survival.
- Crimes: To "serve families" makes them guilty of stealing private property, defrauding, establishing excessive taxation, and denying due process.

Notice how the existence of these bureaucracies currently operates upon collective principles, which is opposed to the individual. Remember our foundational structure presented in chapter one?

If a burglar broke into your child's bedroom, you wouldn't expect the CYFD or the CPS to respond, even though they claim to protect children. However, your local police would. The difference is based on the principles within the agency or organization. The police have a job to protect the individual; whereas, social agencies have a job to protect children. But this creates a problem. How can social agencies protect children if they reject your child as an individual?

Within itself, each bureaucracy lacks the power of physical force. Their only power is the power of deceit. A court with unlimited and centralized power was the perfect scene to impose the will of these agencies. From its inception, family court was kept apart and distinct of the judiciary, which allowed it to utilize dictatorial-type powers. This court is the all-powerful motor driving these three dangerous bureaucracies; four if we include CPS.

Non-Judicial Family Court

- Task: To overthrow God's social order by using the State's police powers against responsible and law-abiding parents.
- Weapon: To rule against (and usurp) your paternal role and authority over your family.
- Ammunition: To shift fault to the masculine-born spouse while transferring responsibility to the wealth-creator.
- Crimes: Black-robed tyrants are guilty of kidnapping, robbery, slavery, creating poverty, increasing crime, and murdering your

family institution. They're guilty for denying you the equal protections of the law, depriving you of due process, violating standard judicial practices, wrongfully jailing you, and issuing unlawful orders.

Family court, however, issues orders and condemns individuals based primarily on the false foundation laid by these bureaucracies. But since the government rejects the individual rights of your child (contrasted to the collective rights of all children), they are, in essence, building a house upon the sand (Matthew 7:24-27). As a result, your children will not, nor can be, protected by them. But if your children are ever caught up in this diabolical performance, they will inevitably be harmed by them. The operations of family court and their bureaucratic accomplices "seemeth right" unto the judges and agents, *"but the end thereof are the ways of death."* (Proverbs 14:12)

The Systematic Suppression of Truth

Several states and county jurisdictions have hidden powers that continually reassign judges. After a judge presides over one hearing, they are removed from your case and a new judge is assigned. These judges are not retiring, dying, or being impeached. Rather, the powers that be are strategically reassigning them to other divorce cases to prevent them from sitting on your case for more than one hearing.

On July 24, 2017, Judge Manuel Arrieta presided over my first hearing in the divorce and child custody case. He dissolved my marriage against my wishes. He refused to postpone the hearing until after the criminal case was settled. He awarded my spouse full and permanent custody of my children. He ordered me to pay her $200.00 per month. Then two months later, on September 29, 2017, he was removed from my case and a new judge was assigned.

On November 27, 2018, Judge Jeanne Quintero presided over my second hearing in the divorce and child custody case. She approved my motion to relieve me from a previous CSD judgment but only on a technicality, not on merit. She expedited my case to the Child Support Division. She deceitfully ordered a custody evaluation but allowed my ex-wife to nullify her order to prevent an evaluation from being conducted. Then exactly four weeks later, on December 27, 2018, she was pulled from my case and a new judge was assigned.

HEARINGS FOR THIS CASE				
HEARING DATE	HEARING TIME	HEARING TYPE	HEARING JUDGE	COURT
11/27/2018	1:30 PM	MOTION HEARING	Quintero, Jeanne H.	LAS CRUCES DISTRICT COURT
07/24/2017	10:00 AM	MOTION HEARING	Arrieta, Manuel I.	LAS CRUCES DISTRICT COURT

Figure 4: Court Hearing w/ Presiding Judge

JUDGE ASSIGNMENT HISTORY			
ASSIGNMENT DATE	JUDGE NAME	SEQUENCE #	ASSIGNMENT EVENT DESCRIPTION
12/27/2018	Duran, Grace B.	4	Administrative Assignment
02/27/2018	Quintero, Jeanne H.	3	Assignment By Supreme Court Designation
09/29/2017	Perea, Conrad F.	2	Administrative Assignment
04/12/2016	Arrieta, Manuel I.	1	INITIAL ASSIGNMENT

Figure 5: Judge Assignment History

This tactic prevents the judge from getting to know the individual parties in the case and observe any oddities that surface. These judges are forced to believe the very first thing they are told that appeals to their emotions. Any records or other forms of evidence subpoenaed by the court become meaningless, since a new judge will be seated. The judge who orders, for instance, a custody evaluation doesn't have an opportunity to rule based on its results. You would have to plead your entire case to a new judge and persuade them to silence your spouse. If the other side of the argument is presented, the judge doesn't have the means to seek the truth. Following that hearing, he or she is pulled off the case. Thus, it forces the judge to rule based on whichever side is emotionally appealing.

Tragically, these judges don't realize that they're puppets on a string—cogs in a machine. Goethe's words ring in my ears, *"The truth has been kept from the depths of their minds..."* The powers that be hide the truth from these judges—the suppression of truth. Any judge who seeks the truth never gets to rule based on his discovery and findings. He's been reassigned.

Not all states and county jurisdictions operate in this manner. So consider yourself fortunate if your county doesn't operate this way. However, this operation is spreading if the people and fathers of our nation don't bring down the system. I'll address how to take down this machinery in another chapter.

Additionally, family court and these agencies have no oversight. The laws and policies that govern these bureaucracies are vague and very liberal. This allows them a great deal of latitude to interpret, modify, and manipulate the language of the law and policy to produce the exact same outcome in each case. In the hands of these agencies, they can turn over a 100% conviction rate. No "child abuser" can slip past them. Interestingly, this is because no child abuser is ever turned over to them.

Child abusers commit their crimes in the dark. And the abuse is so traumatizing that children don't tell others about it and are hesitant to answer questions in a truthful manner. When an instance of actual child abuse is brought to light, the perpetrator never makes it past criminal court. He's convicted and receives his due sentence.

These agencies don't need evidence of child abuse, like criminal court. They'll convict an innocent person for being born a male. But what I find most disturbing is the inconsistency of their actions. To protect children, they'll convict fathers of child abuse but won't re-move them from society. How does that make any sense?

The CYFD claimed that my deeds were substantiated, however, their verdict was withheld until after my criminal case was closed.

The CYFD didn't sentence me or remove me from the community to protect other children. Is that how the CYFD protects children?

These bureaucratic agencies don't have the authority to sentence or remove anyone from society. Without the means to execute judgment, rendering an in-house verdict—a false conviction—does more harm than good.

By convicting an innocent person, the CYFD is conspiring with the child abuser. But if they happen to convict a guilty person, without the ability to sentence and pronounce judgment, the agency is failing to protect children.

Family court and these bureaucracies are accomplishing the opposite of their stated objective. They are convicting the innocent nearly 100% of the time. And in the process, nearly 100% of child abusers are protected by these very agencies.

Let's take a look to see how this happens. Only criminals attack the innocent. Thus, child abusers tend to shift blame to their innocent spouse. Then comes along the social agencies and family court to convict the accused—the innocent spouse.

On the flip side, a law-abiding citizen doesn't attack other people (future criminal). So naturally, if there aren't any signs of abuse or the abuse hasn't started yet, the innocent spouse never accuses their mate (future child abuser). Then comes along the social agencies and family court to protect the child abuser since they weren't accused.

Challenging these bureaucracies is discouraging because their crimes never violate any law or policy. To complicate matters, family court cannot be penetrated. Its creator (the legislature) has the power to abolish it, and the citizenry retains the power to defy it.

The Avenue to Control the Future

Regardless of how many cases the states cycle through each year, why is it that children only need protection from the breadwinner?

The bureaucracies in this drama embody three complementary roles in chronological order: language (CAC), protection (CPS, CYFD), and provisions (CSD).

The CAC forensic interview is usually the first step of the process to initiate prosecution. This is because words are powerful (Psalm 12:6) and are used to build up or tear down (James 3:6-12). If the conspiracy intends to remake society, they must first tear down the traditional family. With a few lies, half-truths, and misrepresentations of facts, the interviewer easily furnishes a deceptive appearance that children are in danger.

The words of the interview are recorded on a physical device. That physical device, whether it's a tape, disc, digital file, or paper manuscript, is classified as physical evidence. But if the same interview is spoken on the witness stand in court, it's considered a testimony (or testimonial evidence), not physical evidence. But notice how the defense can cross examine a witness in court, but not in the office of the CAC. What should this type of trickery tell us? False evidence is being manufactured behind the closed doors of the Children's Advocacy Center.

The State has now justified the need to protect children from their father. For the conspiracy to reshape the thinking pattern of the next generation, they must first have access to your child's mind. So along comes the Children Youth and Families Department or the Child Protective Services. They render a faulty verdict, attempting to persuade judges, therapists, and others involved to remove (or demand the removal) of children from their homes. This is to ostensibly protect children from further harm. But the State is the beneficiary, not your children.

Sadly, this "protection" deprives children of much more than just physical provisions—they are robbed of everything they hold dear. But this is of no concern to the State. If a child's life support is removed, the State gains access to their minds. What should this delusion tell us? Family court and these social agencies are forcing children into a state of financial, physical, spiritual, and emotional poverty. For the State to possess god-like powers, they must be the giver of life. But they can only give life to those who are destitute.

The State intervenes again to "provide" children what they first deprived them of. This is tantamount to a mother giving her children some food, but a group of men intervene. They snatch the food from her hungry youngsters and beat up their mother for not feeding her children. Then, as the others look on with complete satisfaction, while the woman lays bruised and bleeding on the floor, one of the men gathers the food and gives it to the children as if he were their protector, provider, and defender.

However, for this conspiracy to control the thoughts, beliefs, and actions of the next generation, government must maintain their role as the only source of life for American children—your children. It's now time for the Child Support Division to step up and transfer wealth into the private pockets of non-productive individuals for the next 18 or more years.

But what do they gain by doing such a thing? They'll possess the entire world and all within. The government doesn't want you. You think for yourself. The government lusts after those who are vulnerable, impressionable, and dependent on others, because those are the ones that will depend strictly on government subsistence. Therefore, they mostly target children. And your children gain nothing but lose everything. They're only used as leverage. And this deceptive domino effect begins with one little lie.

It makes perfect sense that family court and these bureaucracies always target the breadwinner. To succeed, fathers must be deprived of due process, and it's essential that mothers are exempt from rules and laws, which are enforced upon fathers—a subjective environment.

Doesn't this sound remarkably similar to the actions of a hostage-taker? The government takes your children captive by force. They hold them as security and demands money from you for the next 18 or more years. Their hostages will be released from captivity once the legal adult age is reached. The State would keep them in bondage longer since it generates revenue, but justification for such action is squashed. But after years of brainwashing, propaganda poisoning, and governmental indoctrination on how Uncle Sam rescued them, cared for them, loved them, provided for them, and protected them, the government has them for life.

Family court is the force necessary to execute this 3-step process. These bureaucracies, with the force of family court, work in tandem day and night to deprive children of their God-given and loving father. And in the process, the State creates crime and poverty.

This is the standard script for governmental intervention. The government first creates a problem. Then they present themselves as the solution to the problem they just created. The government is busy concocting the antidote and the poison in the same laboratory.[28]

The success in abolishing the family rests with subtle deception that cannot be detected. If this deceit were ever exposed, the truth embraced, and then the citizenry and lesser magistrates responded accordingly, the system would collapse. The various bureaucracies are intended to serve four functions:

- The various bureaucratic agencies are unobservant to their surroundings. Each agent tends to focus on their specific job functions, oblivious to the actions of another agent within another agency.
- The separate arms fulfill a unified purpose; their actions complement one another. Therefore, tunnel vision deceives agents with good intentions.
- The independent bureaucracies cannot revert or undo the actions of another. Even family court lacks the power to reverse the effects of a manipulated interview.
- This interdependent system produces the delusion that fathers collectively have destroyed their own families. Thus, the pub-

---

[28] George Charles Roche III, *Frédéric Bastiat: A Man Alone* (New Rochelle: Arlington House, 1971).

lic tends to believe that *you* must have brought all this suffering upon *yourself.*

Sadly, well-meaning citizens and government employees with good intentions support or push forward the destruction of America's families and children without realizing it. Even God acknowledges the people working behind the scenes. *"But evil men and seducers shall wax worse and worse, deceiving, and being deceived"* (2 Timothy 3:13). The directors of this diabolical drama always produce the intended outcome, never the stated objective.

The stated objective is only a mask:
- It's the picture painted to conceal the hidden image...
- It's the act performed on stage that the public sees.

The true objective, which I just revealed, remains out of sight.
- It's the hidden picture of the boy, the cart, and the donkey that's been there all along...
- It's what occurs behind the curtains and back-stage, where the public doesn't see it.

Are you beginning to see through the camouflage?

It doesn't take a political genius to realize that this is mob rule. The Las Cruces Sun News was a complete misrepresentation of the facts. Amy, the Las Cruces police, the State's prosecution, the CAC, CYFD, CSD, and family court are the real child predators, and all children—my children and yours, are the prey. Unfortunately, these child predators remain at large—preying on other children and seeking whom they may devour (1 Peter 5:8).

The conspirators' end goal is to bring about a one-world government. The systematic and wholesale annihilation of the family is the means to achieve their goal. To recruit followers that will execute the means to their end, the conspirators must deceive government employees into believing they are protecting the family while you (the parent) are destroying it. To maintain one's enlistment in this conspiracy, government officials, employees, and bureaucrats become dependent on the rewards and incentives offered by the conspirators.

Cast	Objective	Performance	Hidden Agenda	Invisible Actions
Local Police	To serve, defend, and protect by enforcing the law (crime deterrence).	IN MY CASE: Police notified, abuse claims investigated, father arrested.	IN MY CASE: To favor women at the expense of men and impose the will of the judge.	IN MY CASE: Distorted and misrepresented words and actions; perjured testimonies.
Prosecution	To prosecute criminals and lawbreakers.	IN MY CASE: Evidence of guilt is presented, and the father is criminally charged.	IN MY CASE: To railroad the father, thus, awarding the State permanent custody and control over his child.	IN MY CASE: Lacked proper investigation; suppressed exonerating evidence.
Local News	To report the facts and keep the people informed.	IN MY CASE: Child predator caught and indicted according to police.	IN MY CASE: To misrepresent the facts and spread propaganda to sway public opinion.	IN MY CASE: Libels the innocent father to create drama and spark conflict.

Table 1: On the State Actors in Public

Artists	Scripted Lines	Performance	Hidden Agenda	Invisible Actions
CAC	Upholding the rights of the child through forensic interviews carried out by trained professionals.	The child is interviewed, and abuse is exposed.	To advocate for the child by usurping parental authority.	Socially engineers the interview; constructs logical fallacies to force the desired answer; manufactures evidence.
CYFD	Protecting children by early detection of abuse with community-based programs.	Society and their social representatives detected and identified child abuse.	To establish and substantiate child abuse allegations by a consensus.	Renders a false verdict; prints deceptive report; fails to substantiate and support claims; spreads propaganda.
CSD	The father is responsible to support his children.	To collect funds and enforce court orders to support children.	To transfer wealth from the breadwinner. Thus, rewarding the non-productive spouse and State.	Stalks, threatens, and attacks the father; manufactures fake debt; demands excessive payments.

Table 2: Behind the Scenes Bureaucracies

Cast	Scripted Lines	Performance	Hidden Agenda	Invisible Actions
Ex-wife (spouse)	To protect their children and report domestic violence.	Child confided with their loving mother; displays fear and trauma from abusive father.	IN MY CASE: To usurp power, so his children could be used as leverage in stealing his property and livelihood.	IN MY CASE: Betrayed her husband; accused falsely; committed perjury.
Family Court Judges	To serve the best interest of the child —to protect children and ensure their needs are being met.	DIVORCE: Family in conflict, so the court intervenes to resolve problems.	To divide the family and overthrow the authority of the father.	Usurps parental authority; creates chaos; rules by force; dispenses injustice.
		PROTECTION ORDER: Protecting the child from abuse is their first priority	To remove the child from life support and exile the father.	Abducts children; protects child abusers; creates poverty.
		CHILD SUPPORT: Supporting the child is the responsibility of the father.	To use the force of government to ensure the monetary transaction takes place.	Pursues innocence; enslaves family; robs children; transfers the loyalty of the child.

Table 3: On the Stage Actors in Court

The Trail of Money

The money seized (or a portion of it depending on your state) is turned over to your ex-spouse, but let me address how this benefits each state of the union that operates their own Child Support Division. These government employees wouldn't actively bid for and lust after your children if it didn't benefit the State (and ultimately, themselves).

As in my case, New Mexico doesn't, nor have they ever, cared about Amy or my children. New Mexico was just helping themselves. These bureaucratic agencies and the family court in all 50 states have been bribed into action by our federal government.

> *"The child support program is a federal matching grant program under which state and local governments must spend money in order to receive federal funding. For every dollar a state or local government spends on the child support program, it receives 66 cents from the federal government. The federal government also provides incentive payments, which are designed to encourage states to operate strong performance-based child support programs."* (Sorensen and Morales, 2017)[29]

When divorce is filed and minor children are shared between the parties, the entire family is automatically enrolled into the child support program, even if a mediator is not necessary. Divorce implies conflict—and conflict requires government intervention.

Spending money on the child support program is the money paid out to the recipients. Suppose the CSD collects $1,000 but pays out $800 to the recipients. The federal treasury sends them $528 ($800 × $0.66).

---

[29] Elaine Sorensen and Melody Morales, "Child Support Funding: 2008-2016," *Office of Child Support Enforcement* (May 2017), Accessed April 14, 2021 https://www.acf.hhs.gov/css/ocsedatablog/2017/05/child-support-program-funding-2008-2016.

Now consider, in 2018, the Office of Child Support reported a collection of $32.3 billion. However, they distributed $27.39 billion to the child support recipients.[30] The balance of $4.91 billion was paid into child support but didn't support the children. In addition, the federal matching grant program awarded the state and local governments with $18.08 billion ($27.39 × $0.66).

As we can see, child support is not intended to support the children, it's a profit-driven business. The State cannot allow fathers to support their children, lest they run into bankruptcy. But what's more, an intact family threatens their livelihood.

Receiving 66 cents for every dollar and extra incentive payments was a well-thought-out bribe. The more money flowing through their office, the wealthier these agencies get. This greed, however, is the motivation of numerous problems:

- It encourages and even promotes, the division of families—dragging more fathers into the system.
- It attacks the father's responsibility to provide for his children—favoring an abusive and neglectful mother over a loving and caring father.
- It results in excessive and onerous levels of child support—strangling the father's motivation to increase his wealth.
- It cripples the parent financially—interfering with his ability to actively participate in the lives of his children.

If the federal government is going to pay the states through their federal matching grant program, we should ask where the feds are getting the money. The money must first go from the states to Washington before it can get paid back to the states. And all of this is made possible from our income tax. *"As columnist James J. Kilpatrick remarked: '...power to control follows the Federal dollar as surely as that famous lamb accompanied little Mary.' As soon as the states and*

---

[30] Office of Child Support Enforcement, *FY 2018 Annual Report to Congress* (March 2021), Accessed April 14, 2021 https://www.acf.hhs.gov/css/report/fy-2018-annual-report-congress.

local governments get hooked on the federal funds, the controls will be put on... "[31]

The power of family court and these bureaucracies are united in view of the same objective. When Benjamin Franklin delivered his speech to the Constitutional Convention of 1787, he warned:

> *"There are two passions which have a powerful influence in the affairs of men. These are ambition and avarice – the love of power and the love of money. Separately, each of these has great force in prompting men to action; but when united in view of the same object, they have, in many minds, the most violent effects. Place before the eyes of such men, a post of honour that shall be at the same time a place of profit, and they will move Heaven and Earth to obtain it."* (Madison, 1787)[32]

This deep conspiracy has produced the most violent effects, which has rippled throughout our culture. By targeting fathers, they intend to bring America to her knees, so a New World Order can be ushered in.

A Silent Revolution

This diabolical drama is set against the backdrop of the psychological warfare that communists have been engaged in for decades. The book *"The Naked Communist"* by Cleon Skousen lists 45 current communist goals. Originally published in 1958 (prior to family court's existence), the pertinent communist goals for *Striking Down the Home* are 27, 32, and 38 – 41. The following goals are:

---

[31] Gary Allen, *None Dare Call It Conspiracy* (Seal Beach: Concord Press, 1972).

[32] James Madison, "Saturday June 2d. In Committee of Whole," In *The Records of the Federal Convention of 1787*, ed. Max Farrand (New Haven: Yale University Press, 1911), Vol 1.

27 Infiltrate the churches and replace revealed religion with social religion. Discredit the Bible and emphasize the need for intellectual maturity, which does not need a religious crutch.

32 Support any socialist movement to give centralized control over any part of culture—education, social agencies, welfare programs, mental health clinics, etc.

38 Transfer some of the powers of arrest from the police to social agencies. Treat all behavioral problems as psychiatric disorders, which no one but psychiatrists can understand or treat.

39 Dominate the psychiatric profession and use mental health laws as a means of gaining coercive control over those who oppose communist goals.

40 Discredit the family as an institution. Encourage promiscuity and easy divorce.

41 Emphasize the need to raise children away from the negative influence of parents.

Skousen goes on to state that:

"If the student will read the reports of congressional hearings together with available books by ex-communists, he will find all of these communist objectives described in detail. Furthermore, he will come to understand how many well-meaning citizens have become involved in pushing forward the communist program without realizing it. They become converted to communist objectives because they accepted superficial communist slogans. Soon they were thinking precisely the ways the communists wanted them to think." (Skousen, 1961)[33]

But even these communist goals are not actually the end in itself; they are only a means to an end. All six of the communist goals listed above are fulfilled through the divorce and child support mechanisms.

---

[33] Cleon Skousen, *The Naked Communist* (Salt Lake City: The Ensign Publishing Company, 1961).

The divorce architecture is similar to a vehicle. First, the car must be designed. Secondly, the car must be built according to its design. Thirdly, the car is ready to operate in the manner it was designed.

Now, consider what the government has been doing. First, the systematic design of divorce and family law was initiated in 1839 to operate in this manner. Then, throughout the twentieth century, the government was building this new "justice system."

- The Parens Patriae Prerogative, resurrected in 1839.
- Juvenile Court, established in 1899.
- Juvenile Court jurisdiction extended to all domestic disputes in 1912.
- The U.S. Children's Bureau, established in 1912.
- Domestic Relations Division, founded in 1914.
- No-Fault Divorce Provisions, incorporated in 1953.
- The Standard Family Court Act, adopted by Rhode Island in 1961.
- The California Family Law Act, enacted in 1969.
- The Divorce Revolution, started in 1969.
- Child Protective Services (CPS), instituted in 1974.
- Child Support Division (CSD), formed in 1975.
- Children's Advocacy Center (CAC), established in 1985.
- Children Youth and Families Department (CYFD), began in 1989.

The U.S. Children's Bureau was paramount to family court's existence, but the bureau was initially created to wrestle away private charity. *The Tragedy of American Compassion* by Marvin Olasky points out how the government used children as leverage to replace private charitable organizations and the work requirements with welfare entitlements and free handouts. Following the successful implementation of the welfare state, the U.S. Children's Bureau didn't just dissolve into oblivion. They turned their attention to helping devise another plan to wrestle children away from their biological parents. After all, the establishment of the federal income tax and the creation of the Federal Reserve, both occurrences in 1913, made this completely possible.

We see a trend, and its progressive nature, as this system was being built throughout the years. This shocking revelation is nearly identical to the trend and progressive nature of my New Mexico case. This system didn't exist within the first 180 years of our Republic. Divorce was rare and the family was strong. So what changed? The government!

Sadly, you are surrounded by many who undermine the truth. Movies, such as "Courageous," produced by Sherwood Baptist Church out of Albany, Georgia shifts the blame to fathers. The father was ruler over his family during the early days of our Republic, and he's still ruler over his family today. The father's authority hasn't changed, but the government's power has.

Finally, this "justice system" is ready to operate according to its design. Do you remember the first time you drove a car? You were probably nervous and started driving slowly, but gradually picked up speed as your comfort level increased. As people became familiar with this operation, the vehicle used to destroy the family naturally picked up speed. We currently live in a state where the speed is at full throttle. The design was successful, the social agencies were built, and its operation runs accordingly. Sadly, it continually attracts more drivers each day, like Amy.

We are witnessing a satanic design. Author William Norman Grigg explains this design:

> *"The adjective 'satanic' is properly used when describing the hideous bloodshed which has resulted from the centuries-old campaign to bring about the terrestrial perfection of mankind...*

> *"Although misery and tragedy can come in individualized allotments, it is only through the State that wholesale annihilation or misery can be achieved...Only governments fight wars, and it takes the power of a totalitarian State to commit genocide...*

"The satanic design inspires the tactics used in pursuit of the total State. One of the titles by which Satan is known is 'The Accuser.' The Holy Bible's book of Job describes Satan's attempt to ruin Job by provoking him to sin—and then accusing him before God. In a similar fashion, tyrannical governments create or exacerbate 'problems' or 'crises' which serve as rationales for enriching their own power." (Grigg, 1995)[34]

The wholesale destruction of the family and the misery that ensues can only be achieved through the power of the State, and the problem continues escalating. Family court and these child-focused bureaucracies excel at this diabolical performance, inventing or exaggerating "family problems," which are cited as pretexts for parental government.

"Perhaps the most famous use of this tactic was made by the German Nationalist Socialist Regime, which used the arson attack on the Reichstag in 1933 to pass an 'Enabling Act' permitting Adolf Hitler to rule by decree."[35] This is parallel to the family court judges who rule by court order. You can see the familiar strategy of creating the poison and the antidote in the same laboratory.

---

[34] William Norman Grigg, *Freedom on the Altar: The UN's Crusade Against God and Family* (Appleton: American Opinion, 1995).
[35] Ibid.

CHAPTER SEVEN

THE PSYCHOLOGICAL SEDUCTION OF CHILDREN

Delegated authority is the peaceful transfer of inherent power. And all authority is delegated. Only power can be usurped. When the petitioner files for divorce, the government immediately assumes jurisdiction over the family and ultimately, each member. But it's noteworthy to point out that consent for this extreme power grab is never given by the respondent. Being governed with consent is a principle of freedom.

Without consent, power cannot be transferred peacefully; rather, it must be usurped. Court orders within the confines of family court, strongly indicate that a usurpation took place. Ordering fathers to pay child support, for example, isn't necessary if power was transferred peacefully. We can rightly conclude that no authority is ever delegated to the government through divorce mechanisms.

When a rebellious wife runs to the government for help, power isn't transferred peacefully—she needed the power of government to force her unlawful demands on her husband. This usurpation creates a state of anarchy within the family unit. And without proper authority governing the family, chaos always ensues. The family environment becomes unstable, the safety of its child members erodes, and peace cannot exist until proper authority can be reestablished (Psalm

119:165). Many custodial parents and their children might experience a false sense of peace, but internal peace isn't possible by rebelling against authority.

It's universally accepted that men don't run to the government begging for help. They may certainly file for divorce, but they generally don't seek restraining orders, demand child support, or restrict a mother's access to her children. Why should they need to? The father already has authority. This is where mothers fall short.

The book of Genesis records the family unit as the first government instituted by God. The jurisdiction and authority over the family is delegated to the husband by God (Genesis 3:16; Ephesians 5:22; Titus 2:3-5). This is the law of God, and its violation always results in unpleasant consequences.

A protection order is nothing more than a usurpation weapon. Although it may be available to be used by anyone, it's primarily intended for women to rebel against their husband's authority. However, a protection order is similar to a two-edged sword. It's issued against a father to sever the life support of his children, which is to be collected by the Child Support Enforcement Division.

The other edge of the sword serves the State's interest—a child's mind is a blank slate to be written on. When the State has access to the minds of youth, their mental faculties, over time, begin to deteriorate. Inevitably, the usurpation of court orders accomplishes the opposite of their stated objective.

The Dangers of Protection Orders

Most people think that protection orders (i.e. restraining orders) are intended to protect. In fact, many judges believe their order is protecting, when instead, it's serving a higher purpose. The consequences of protections orders are horrifying when I examine my case.

Less than three months after Judge Driggers issued a restraining order against me, my three older children were diagnosed with Post Traumatic Stress Disorder (PTSD). Additionally, they all could be diagnosed with Parental Alienation Syndrome (PAS). But it shouldn't surprise anyone for the alienator to medically neglect the PAS evaluation. Nevertheless, there's still a plethora of overwhelming cues suggesting that parental alienation is present. As time progressively lapsed with the restraining order in place, my children's alienation also increased in severity.

Addison's progressive accusation is just one example. In her initial interview recorded at the Children's Advocacy Center, she expressed fear of getting in trouble; yet just a couple of years later, she testified in court that she would be murdered (February 27, 2018).

Parental alienation, the most dangerous and cruelest form of child abuse, is the vile assault against one parent's character. Its purpose is to permanently sever the parent-child relationship by erasing all positive attributes of their parent from their memories. (That's a horrifying nightmare, which reminds me of George Orwell's novel, *"1984."*) And the protection order makes this possible.

Deception is the key component to this psychological assault. Over an extended period, a continual dose of deceit and propaganda alters the mind's thinking patterns. This mind alteration technique is demonic by its very nature, but psychiatrists refer to this as a mental illness.

Through the divorce and child custody apparatus, the State repeats this cycle from one generation to the next—deteriorating minds and expanding mental illnesses within our culture. When mentally ill people are unable to think and reason for themselves, they naturally rely on government to plan their life and future for them. As a result, these individuals become loyal to the State. Since they have been recreated in the State's image, they tend to worship the State.

However, there are inherent dangers associated with "government as protector."

- The Government is an institution of force, not a ministry of love. They lack the power of emotional and natural affection. Their force is exercised through laws, orders, and decrees.
- The State's show of force against parental authority conditions the minds of youth to exercise strength against the young and weak to accumulate wealth and power.
- By invading the home and overthrowing the protector, the government is inviting abuse and domestic violence. Other men are tempted to interact with your child due to your absence.
- The best interest of the State is in opposition to the principles of freedom and individual responsibility. Consequently, their parenting decisions are disastrous.
- Protecting your child's mind or shielding them from the negative influences of the culture is out of reach of the government. This is how criminals are created.
- The State has the power to harm your children, but cannot be harmed by your children. The State doesn't have feelings; they simply use police force to suppress bad behavior.

Everyone has heard about tyrannical fathers who beat their wives and abuse their children. Likewise, we're also aware that fathers have abandoned their families and shucked their parental responsibilities. The government would have you to believe it's a common occurrence. That's why they spread the propaganda far and wide—so you'll believe it. And although these two situations do happen on occasion, they're an exception to the rule. These two types of fathers are a relatively small minority. So why label these actions as the general rule among fathers? Because that's what government has been broadcasting for years.

Sadly, family court and their bureaucratic criminals don't protect the God-given rights of each individual family member. Rather, they're all engaged in a lawless system. This explains why protectors are restrained from protecting their children.

But did you know that 17 years before the establishment of the first family court system, the Supreme Court rejected the government's invasion into the family?

"It is cardinal with us that the custody, care, and nurture of the child reside first in the parents, whose primary function and freedom include preparation for obligations the state can neither supply nor hinder." (Prince v. Massachusetts, 1944)[36]

It's worth noting that Supreme Court decisions, which lean more conservative, are commonly disregarded and precedent is ignored. But when the decision is based on liberal ideology, the judicial decree is given the force of law and precedent is upheld.

In politics, nothing happens by accident. If it happens, you can be sure that it was planned that way.

The Agenda of Child Support

Two and a half years after family court abducted my children, the Child Support Division eventually brought child support charges against me. In the November 27, 2018 court hearing, Amy made it seem like I was attacking her (when I requested a custody evaluation) and then implied that defending and protecting the children required an attorney. Therefore, she pleaded with Judge Quintero to enact child support so she could hire herself an attorney.

Only three weeks later (the December 18 court hearing), she insisted on receiving more than $500 monthly so she could pay for household expenses. Yet, lack of financial support for my children didn't exist prior to the State's intervention. So what happened?

I haven't housed or fed my children for five years now; the State has. I have food and shelter to offer my children, along with other ne-

---

[36] Prince v. Massachusetts, 321 U.S. 158 (United States Supreme Court, 1944).

cessities, but the court prohibits their receipt. In other words, the government is robbing my children of the food I supply them, and then blaming me for failing to provide it.

The State clearly has an agenda, and it's not for the well-being of children or families. Their goal is to turn a profit, and they aren't successful if fathers support their children.

However, when family court interferes with the father's responsibility to support his children, the State oppresses the children they claim to free by forcing them to rely on an omniscient, omnipotent, and omnipresent government. Following generations of forcing government dependency upon the people, our government portrays themselves as the "giver and taker of life." Family court is instrumental in replacing revealed religion (dependence on God) with social religion (dependence on government).

When the role of protector is transferred from the father to the government, there's a dramatic shift in the role of provider as a byproduct. The State cannot assume the former without inheriting the latter. Child support shifts accountability back onto the wealth creator. But the father isn't responsible or obligated to accept punishment for the crimes of his ex-wife or the State. This is what child support does.

When your children are dependent on the government through welfare programs and the Child Support Division, this sets a bad example that children are prone to follow—identifying the State as their protector and provider. In later years, this results in a shift of loyalty—from the family and parents to the State.

This strategic maneuver interferes with the parents' Biblical directive. It's immoral for fathers to pay child support, when they should be guiding and training their children (Proverbs 22:6). Conscientious parents teach their children to think for themselves. Independent thinking is an obligation for citizenship and must be taught. That's the difference between a citizen and a subject. The former self-governs, but the latter is subject to their civil government. By attacking the mental faculties, a citizen can be demoted to subject—and subjects can be oppressed. Frank Chodorov describes this process:

> *"The third great immunity is that of the mind, the freedom to think as one wishes. The impairment of this immunity is not easy to detect, for the operation can be conducted in such a way that the victim is never aware of it. It is necessary to look at the methods employed by the government to shape thought, to know that the shaping is being done; when the job is completed it takes a keen observer to realize that people think differently than the way they use to think.*

> *"Thus, the farmer who receives checks for not planting does not realize that his grandfather would have thought the practice immoral; he accepts the taking of gratuities as the regular order of things, as quite proper, because government propaganda has got him into that frame of mind. Free school lunches do not strike the modern mother as an insult, as suggesting that she is unable and unwilling to carry out the responsibility of motherhood; the convenience of free lunches, plus the saving of expense, plus the government's leaflets have changed her way of thinking.*

> *"And so with every activity of government turn Santa Claus by the income tax: a mass of propaganda introduces the new practice and more propaganda justifies it, until the people think as the government wants them to think. Free judgment becomes next to impossible."* (Chodorov, 1954)[37]

In this manner, shifting a child's loyalty from the family to the State is to prepare them to murder on command—an emulation of Nazi Germany.

As a reward, child support enriches the personal checking accounts of those in high places while increasing their insatiable lust for power over others. This exemplifies why your responsibility or child support obligations never address time allowance or physical contact. Child

---

[37] Frank Chodorov, *The Income Tax: Root of All Evil* (New York: The Devin-Adair Company, 1954).

support conceals itself behind cold and heartless monetary provisions since those in power seek totalitarian and financial gain.

However, there are also inherent dangers with "government as provider."

- The power to provide isn't inherent; it must be usurped. Consequently, the State didn't inherit any parental responsibilities. They seize power, but aren't responsible for how that power gets used.

- The financial responsibility is shifted back to its origin. The other parental responsibilities are woefully neglected. The father is held accountable for the government's misuse of power.

- A financial hardship and poverty is created by operating child support as a business, turning over high profits. Cutting the child's life support forces parents to purchase child support services at monopoly prices.

- Child support is strictly monetary to feed an appetite of greed. It doesn't address mental, emotional, or spiritual support. Depriving children of love hinders them from developing intimate relationships. The State is creating its own market demand.

- The State provides a nanny (your ex-wife) to fulfill its initiatives and objectives. Instruction, discipline, and direction to prepare the children for the future are neglected. Your ex is an extension of the State through government dependency.

- Government initiatives promote idleness, greed, selfishness, perpetual adolescence, and irresponsibility. Their objective is to breed dependency and an entitlement mentality. This shift in a child's loyalty prepares them to obey on command.

- The State has the power to steal from your children, but they can't have anything stolen by your children. The State doesn't possess anything that wasn't first acquired by force.

A father, even those who are not the greatest, provides much more than the government ever will. You can produce wealth, but the State can only consume it.

It's well-known and publicized that absent fathers, consequently leads to increased child abuse (government as protector). But to take it a step further, without the father's influence, juvenile delinquency, crime, and violence soars (government as provider). When the State eliminates the father, they steal your child's most valuable provisions. And in the process, your children lose respect for authority and the law. Nevertheless, the love of money and the lust for power are more self-satisfying to these bureaucratic criminals and family court judges.

Remember this: the next time you read a billboard or flier that says, "Protect children, vote 'yes.'" A "yes" vote would put government in charge of protecting children; not their fathers. But as we have already learned, only fathers can protect their children. The government can only harm them. "Protect Children" is a superficial communist slogan. It's collectivism at its core and very hostile to freewill and individual responsibility. All people, including children, are protected when government power is limited to executing wrath on the evil doer. However, no child is safe when government refuses to protect the life, liberty, and property of all individuals, including the child's father.

CHAPTER EIGHT

TAKEN INTO CUSTODY

W hen a person is taken into custody, it always results in a loss of freedom. This is because God instituted government to execute wrath on those who do evil (Romans 13:4), not serve families. Thus, we can rightly conclude that state custody is only reserved for criminals. But how does a protection order serve this purpose?

Protection orders are allegedly issued to protect. But who is being "protected" from whom? Can a hostage-taker get a protection order against anyone who wants to free the hostages? Suppose the hostage-taker binds the hostages and locks them in a dark room. Then goes to court and tells the judge that those hostages are scared for their lives. As a result, the judge favors the hostage-taker to protect the hostages. You might think that's ludicrous. Of course it is.

The term, "hostage-taker," is associated with evil—a bad person. However, if the hostage-taker refers to herself as a loving mother, the phrase sounds more appealing, even though the action remains the same.

Investigating a case based on merit exposes that tactic. But interestingly, protection orders are not entirely detached from their name. They most certainly protect the power of tyrants. And the last thing a tyrant needs is for families to endanger their plans for global governance. The youngest citizen in the lowest class can defeat the strongest tyrant with the Word of God. An intact family is truly a danger to the New World Order.

When the court issued a protection order against me, Amy used the term "fear." She added that she was scared and didn't know what I was capable of. But she couldn't elaborate any further, let alone prove her "fear." Undoubtedly, her fear was irrational and partly due to my masculinity. The other part was primarily based on her own criminal behavior. In essence, she was committing a crime against my children and was scared that I might intervene. Amy, ultimately, produced her own fear, which was used as the rationale for seeking a protection order.

Like a two-way street, protection orders travel both directions. By its very nature, protection orders bind the father and his children. The paradigm of a two-directional order only binds the parties who are absent from the court hearing. It's always initiated by a third party. The father, nor his children, appear in court or request the order. This intent is to pit family members against one another and create conflict. Children turn against parents, and parents against children.

Eventually, the child grows up. Now, how do you think he'll respond when he learns *how* his relationship was destroyed with his father? Will he turn to crime? Will he murder his mother? Only the wicked commit premeditated evil on little children and expect a life full of peace and harmony.

Protection orders are routinely issued to protect the hostage-taker, *not* free the hostages. However, the young hostages are bound with the heavy hand of court orders, and are locked in a dark room—truth is kept from the depths of their minds. Let me explain what this looks like. When a protection order is issued against children, they suffer from two forms of slavery: physical and psychological.

First, they're subjected to an environment under total State control. This is similar to the freedom that prisoners have to move about the prison and engage in certain activities. But without the physical walls, fencing, barbed wires, armed guards, etc. However, the delusion of American freedom is promoted far and wide.

Here's what the enslavement of my children looked like. The State controlled every aspect of their lives and ruled them by decree (court orders). They were housed by the State, fed by the State, and clothed by the State (welfare programs). The State decided what my children would learn, what books they would read, who would teach them, and how long they would be taught (public schooling).

The State's warden, Amy, enacted strict rules regarding who could interact with them. And the people on her "hit list" weren't even named on the protection order. My children were alienated from grandparents, aunts, and other family members who maintained neu- trality or were non-sympathizers to her cause—primarily the paternal side of the family. Grandparents sent cards that contained checks for the children's birthdays, but the checks were never cashed.

Mail, phone calls, and Internet communications were completely severed. Visitors and babysitters were highly scrutinized to ensure they'd render aid to Amy's agenda. However, she amplified her own suspicions since any contact outside of her personal friends and family was presumed to be a spy.

What a terrible way to spend one's childhood; never knowing the love, encouragement, and gifts of their family, or the excitement of a visit from Grandma and Grandpa. But the warden refused to allow it. Sadly, the truth was kept from the depths of their minds. My children were, metaphorically speaking, held hostage, bound, and locked in a dark room.

The second form of restraint is psychological bondage to fear. The freedom to choose goes far beyond material possessions. It encom- passes your internal being—from your beliefs and thoughts to your emotions and conscience. Propaganda suppresses the freedom to use and control your internal faculties.

Manufacturing irrational fear justifies the enactment of a protection order to act as proof of criminality. But fear is a powerful emotion and if used incorrectly, can cause an individual to make self-destructive decisions. Fear is the weapon of tyrants and its purpose is to enslave. Protection orders operate on fear and are very self-destructive. This is because they protect tyranny, slavery, and oppression. Children cannot form functioning relationships living in fear.

I truly abhor the act of child abuse, but in making a comparison, I must acknowledge—the abuse perpetrated by a father is more merciful than the protection offered by the government.

We need to be mindful of Germany's Holocaust. What played out in Germany from 1939-1945 is being replayed in America from 1961-Present Day. The only difference between Adolf Hitler and family court is one of degree. From its inception, family court has steadily followed in the footsteps of Hitler. Germany's physical genocide makes it easy to identify the atrocity against the Jewish people. But America's psychological technique conceals its elements, which ultimately requires family court to move at a much slower pace to accomplish its objective. The distinct methods of employment become irrelevant when the end meets at a single point.

Does it matter if the government...

- Commences physical warfare (Germany) or psychological warfare (America)...
- Targets the Jews (Germany) or targets the fathers (America)...
- Perpetrates physical genocide against the Jews (Germany) or psychological genocide against the children (America)...
- Is controlled by one individual (Germany) or controlled by an elitist group (America)...
- Rules by physical force (Germany) or rules by psychological force (America)...
- Follows one leader (Germany) or follow a process (America)...
- Dictator orders (Germany) or judge's orders (America)...

No! The strategy employed may be different, but the end is still the same. And this is how our government protects children? Family court and their bureaucratic accomplices are training the next generation of children to become American Nazi's. The State needs children —your children—who will murder on command (including any family members who balk at the State's agenda). But your children aren't prepared to commit such an act when they have a warm, loving relationship with you—with their family.

The War on Fatherhood

Children are the seed of their father (Genesis 19:32; John 8:37), and seek their father's approval, not his exile, imprisonment, or destruction. Is it any wonder why the enemies of freedom have waged war against fatherhood? They recognize its value.

Our country's morals and ideals have slowly been poisoned by the government's propaganda campaign for decades. And just like Eve fell prey to Satan's deceptive temptation (She would be like god... Gen. 3:5), Amy fell prey to the State's deceptive temptation (The State would take care of her and the kids forever). Women are far more susceptible to deception than men. That's why the State preys on women.

Fathers bring their children into existence (Proverbs 23:22), *not* their mothers. (Yes, mothers carry the child, but the father impregnates.) This Biblical truth was drowned out by the propaganda pushed from the Women's Liberation movement.

The Principle of Reversal is deployed. To deceive by omission is the most effective form of propaganda, because it neutralizes opposition. It forces people to accept the propagandized statement since opposition doesn't address the untruth. Let me explain...

Feminist Propaganda #1: "These are *my* children!"

The woman carries the child for nine months and nurtures that baby through infancy. So it's natural that she considers the child hers.

Let's face it, without her, there would be no child. But this type of reasoning ignores the science of procreation.

This declaration, however, doesn't elaborate on the father's actions or behavior. It's used solely to imply that your part as father is insignificant. Thereby, it's a display of strength to strip away your parental authority—a power grab. She is essentially transmitting that these are not your children and that you have no authority over them. These women act as if they impregnated themselves.

The parent who lacks authority in the home is the only one who uses it. Mothers don't speak this way towards babysitters, scout leaders, teachers, other family members, neighbors, or anyone else involved in the child's life. Yet, the father makes decisions for his children just like any other adult responsible for his children at that moment, whether a Sunday school teacher or a little league coach.

When the father goes to work, his authority is extended to his wife. She knows she has authority, so there's no need to proclaim it. But upon his return home, her authority is rescinded. This is what causes her to assert her power over him by making this false statement.

Feminist Propaganda #2: "It takes *two* to make a baby."

Now, it's true that neither a man nor a woman can produce a child without the other. But this statement is commonly associated with shifting the financial responsibility back its origin. It's not intended to encourage the father to love, spend time with, or participate in the nurturing role of his children. It's only spoken in regards to demanding money.

The mother who opposes fatherhood is the only one who embraces this statement. She doesn't want the father, only his money. Mothers who were truly abandoned by their husband or boyfriend don't use this statement. They're not against the father; they're only against his actions.

However, this statement falsely implies that you have abandoned your own children and is stiffing your ex with all child-rearing responsibilities. Therefore, the use of this statement is clearly a misrepresentation of the facts since most fathers don't abandon their children.

These two parts of the baby-making propaganda puzzle have an agenda for which they serve. But each piece is designed and its interpretation is crafted to accomplish a different objective, which explains their inconsistencies with one another.

The first statement insinuates that you can't be the father because "these are *my* children," which means "they aren't yours." But the second statement proposes that you have to be the father because "it takes *two* to make a baby," which means "they are yours." These two statements, the child support mechanisms, family court's orders, and Amy's modus operandi have all originated from the same source. They flow from the same fountain. There's a common theme: the usurpation of power but escaping responsibility by shifting blame.

Family court can only possess power over you if it's exercised through your children. This wouldn't be possible if the children weren't yours. Amy and the courts verbally denied this Biblical principle, but their actions identified its validity. "Children belong with their mother," the courts say. But in the next court hearing, child support is established because, "Fathers are responsible to support their children."

If the children belong with Amy, then it's her responsibility to support them. However, if I'm going to be held responsible, then I must be free to choose. This inconsistency should remind us of James' warning, *"A double-minded man is unstable in all his ways."* (James 1:8)

At times, we've heard of a mother who needed to both protect and provide for her children. And sometimes she is forced into that role by the untimely death, incarceration, or lengthy illness of her husband. I'm not trying to minimize the sacrifice of these brave women, who have no other choice. And I'm not making reference to them.

But I've only addressed two types of protectors and providers: the father and the government. Why is that? Because God never delegated that role of protector and provider to the mother—it's not her job. For this reason, an absent father results in an increase in child abuse and government welfare for mothers and their children.

In the case of a young widow forced to rear her children on her own, God the Father will guide and protect her children if she trusts them into His care.

The mother who protects her children does so by allowing the father's natural hedge of protection to surround those kids. Similarly, the mother who provides best for her children allows their father to meet their physical needs. Running to the government for a protection order is a criminal act, and God will not hold them guiltless. Understanding this reality and putting the truth into action is in the best interest of your child.

A Double-Minded Government

Here's one last aspect that's often overlooked, which I would like to point out. Neglect, carelessness, and vandalism are common themes with mankind in regards to the life, liberty, and property of others. We identify this attribute through a plethora of situations: vandalism of rental property by a tenant, carelessness when borrowing someone else's property, neglecting to replace or pay for something you accidentally broke, disregarding the liberty of those around in order to smoke, consume alcohol, listen to loud music, curse, wear provocative clothing, etc.

Wouldn't it be irrational to believe that someone who neglectfully damages and destroys borrowed property would actually provide good care when looking after your child?

So let's consider for a moment. Our government:

- Exempts themselves from the laws they make (CSD is exempt from laws protecting private property. The court is exempt from laws prohibiting the abduction of children.)
- Ignores the laws already in force (Las Cruces police and the prosecutor, Rebecca Duffin, neglected to investigate, charge, and prosecute Amy for filing false police reports, perjuring statements, tampering with testimonial evidence, etc.)
- Neglects to impeach or prosecute their own who violate the law (Judge Driggers, Arrieta, Isabel, and Quintero wasn't impeached for violating my constitutional protections. Detective Guerra was never prosecuted for committing perjury.)

Will the government respect the law that's intended to protect your children?

Human nature does not change. If an individual or governmental agency doesn't respect the life, liberty, or property of the father, then the most effective way to harm him is to go after his children. The government despises fatherhood because of its high value, and so they collectively, and in unison, commit the most heinous crimes against the youngest generation. It's a fantasy to believe that another entity can love, care for, protect, and want the best for your children more than you do.

CHAPTER NINE

THE INVISIBLE ROBBERY

The apostle Paul tells us that it's the love of money that's the root of all evil, *not* the lust for power (1 Timothy 6:10). Yet, both ambition and avarice, as Benjamin Franklin put it, lure men to action. However, when united in view of the same greedy object, the government (and its individual employees in concerted action) will produce the most violent effects. I addressed the government's lust for power in the previous chapter. Now, I would like to turn your attention to the government's root system in this diabolical performance on stage. Their insatiable love of money has burrowed itself deep within the system to operate the individual mechanisms, which are set on a predetermined course.

Roots serve a very important function in life. God's creation provides wonderful examples of the importance of roots. Every person is familiar with the beautiful trees that God has created. Everyone has seen them—whether in a forest, their own backyard, or alongside the road. Trees all have one thing in common: they have roots. Their roots bring them life. Without roots, there would be no life. While standing under a tree, you might walk on some of their huge roots and notice that they branch out in all directions until you can't see them anymore. The roots burrow themselves deep into the Earth. And unless you dig deep, you will never see the tips of the roots. Yet, those roots give the tree life and stability when a storm comes.

The child support system has roots, and just like a tree, you may see where they begin...divorce cases, protection orders, family court...but unless you dig, you will never see how deep they go and how much damage they do. And the roots of the divorce and child custody apparatus is their love of money, not child protection or child support.

As the government gradually increases in size, its roots grow larger and burrows deeper, providing it extra strength to withstand push-back from the people. This ultimately requires a much larger number of citizens to fight back to reduce its size.

Government's ultimate goal is to enrich itself by transferring the wealth from the one producing to those who will not produce. These government employees are growing wealthy on your misfortune. And the lust for money is the root that branches out from these bureaucracies and their accomplice, family court. Their source of life is dependent on the continual flow of money—a feeding tube attached to the heart of America: the family. The child support system is not sustainable since it cannot thrive on its own. It's parasitic. To prevent its demise, laws must prop up the system and executive force must be employed. As a result, the Child Support Enforcement Division and family court produce the most violent effects against men who dare disrupt their flow of money.

It's universally accepted that the State intervenes to protect a child's life. Since the father possesses masculine strength, this al-legedly places their young one in danger. "Better safe than sorry," is the superficial communist adage.

But the State also has taxing power. Therefore, they can force its citizens to support these children in the form of welfare. Although force is present, its execution remains hidden. However, an absent fa-ther is in open view, causing the spread of unfounded assumptions.

"He's not supporting his children," the script goes, "What more proof do we need?"

That line of reasoning is just ludicrous. Different communist lines are repeated depending on the government's agenda. It's as if amnesia strikes every time the government initiates a different action. If a person doesn't have the freedom to control and recall one's own memory, they have fallen victim to mind control.

These shallow arguments don't even prove anything. This is tantamount to a bad guy breaking into your house, murdering your child, and then having you criminally charged for child neglect. That's the absurdity to these superficial statements. This is the exact method employed against me by Judge Quintero.

She defended Amy's position and agenda by interfering with my role as provider. Then asserted that "not supporting your children is a form of child abuse" (Nov 27, 2018). That's absurd. If not supporting children is the same as child abuse, then the judge's interference with that support should be sufficient evidence to impeach and prosecute her.

The propaganda of these scripted lines sways public opinion to favor the State over the family. In this manner, family courts and the child-focused agencies effectively portray themselves as moral and righteous agents (2 Corinthians 11:14)—the *Principle of Reversal*. This false picture demonizes fathers collectively—as well as any opposition, even from women or mothers. The fathers who have an inclination to resist would be depicted as irresponsible, selfish, and even criminal. But is this the case?

Once we examine the facts and look at the evidence, the "inherent" goodness and moral posture within family court, their bureaucratic accomplices, and the child support system collapses under their own weight.

Referring back to my case, the state of New Mexico opted to burden me with $36,534.91 of total debt (enacted on October 17, 2019). I didn't borrow this money or agree to receive any goods or services equaling that amount; nor has there been any conviction under due process of law, which authorized the forfeiture of my property. So how did that figure come into existence? It had to be manufactured— a counterfeiting operation.

In Paul's letter to the Romans, he tells us not to owe anyone (Romans 13:8). God doesn't want His people burdened with debt, because indebtedness paralyzes one's ability to be used by the Lord. But since the debt was counterfeited, it's not an owed amount—that is, unless I deceive myself by accepting that debt as legitimate.

During the court hearing on December 18, 2018, my attorney argued that a custody evaluation had been ordered as a result of Amy's engagement in a pattern of parental alienation. This persuaded John Trujillo, the hearing officer, to suspend this fabricated debt until a custody evaluation could be conducted. (Thanks to Judge Quintero, there wouldn't be an evaluation.)

Child support, whether retroactive or current, is only a decree, not a responsibility; whereas providing directly for my children—without a middleman—is a responsibility (1 Timothy 5:8), not a decree. There's a big difference between the two.

The power of parents to support their children is inherent—it's natural and God-given. However, the power of the State to force child support provisions is usurped. For that reason, an order must be issued, laws must be enacted to uphold the order, and threats must be deployed (outlined in chapter 16).

Although family court and the CSD agency demands obedience, that's not the objective. Rather, complying with the order only begins the process of shifting your thought patterns. The State uses subtle tactics, which coerces fathers to "voluntarily" accept the counterfeited debt called "child support."

Since beliefs control the thoughts, the State attempts to alter what a person believes first. This is accomplished by complying with a child support order. The functions of government, the purpose of family, the role of a father, and the job of a mother conforms to the State's ideology. And over the course of time, it's validated by cultural norms. The internal belief system of an individual has been altered from its original state.

Once complete, the way your mind processes information has changed. You will now think precisely the way the government wants you to think. Your thought patterns, beliefs, language, and actions are progressively conforming to the god of this present world. And born again believers in Jesus Christ are not immune to this form of deception.

If the State hadn't been so brutal and violent towards me and my children, I could've easily been duped. But they overlooked one important aspect. Their aggression at all levels provided me an inside look at their operation. As a result, through my increased understanding and endurance, I gained the courage and strength necessary to resist during these later stages.

After all I'd been through...

- My wife violated our marital contract—betrayal. She withheld my children from me, filed false police reports, and engaged in a pattern of parental alienation.
- The State filed false charges against me. The police raided my home, seized my belongings, and hauled me off in handcuffs. The State's detective committed perjury to the Grand Jury.
- The local newspaper libeled me, branding me in the eyes of the public as a danger to all children. Consequently, my employer terminated me, and my landlord evicted me.
- And if that wasn't bad enough, the government had the audacity to claim that it's my responsibility to pay the state of New Mexico $36,534.91 with a 4% interest rate, in addition to current monthly support and family health insurance.

...What more could they do to me that they haven't already done?

It's clearly evident, that the operators of the divorce and child support machinery are violating God's law and prohibiting fathers, like myself, from exercising their God-given parental responsibilities. Is this not hindering the free exercise of religion—to support your child in a manner consistent with your religious beliefs and conscience?

God commands His people to resist the devil (James 4:7). Yet, no one can resist by honoring child support with God-fearing payments. Obedience to God is synonymous with defiance to tyrants (Acts 5:29).

The Destruction of Human Life Support

After the state of New Mexico threw me out of full-time work, they enacted child support. Unfortunately, my new job was only part-time. The State, however, blamed me for this shift of employment by portraying me as a "deadbeat" for attempting to evade my parental responsibilities. Once again, this is the familiar strategy of creating the poison and the antidote in the same laboratory. The State holds me accountable for their actions and abuse of power.

Contrary to popular opinion, child support isn't calculated based on income. Since the Child Support Agencies are profit-driven businesses, they crafted two methods to increase their revenue.

The technique most visibly recognized is to calculate child support based on "imputed" income. If you earn less money than what the CSD believes you're capable of earning, they impute your income. In other words, the government bureaucrats assign you an income higher than your actual earnings. Then they calculate child support on the income assigned to you.

In their attempt to make the imputed income seem fair and impartial, they claim to utilize several variables (possibly computer algorithms) in their decision. The CSD may ask for level of education, field and skills, employment history in regards to salary, skills, and job titles, and salary reported to the IRS for tax purposes.

On the surface, this sounds reasonable. However, the most important variable isn't considered by the CSD: current economic conditions. Since economic conditions aren't measurable, it should come as no surprise why it's not used in the CSD's calculations.

In America, we live in a mixed economy—a mixture of capitalism and socialism. Informally, it's referred to as, "crony capitalism." That is, the economy is burdened with excessive laws and regulations that businesses must comply with. This can range from minimum wage laws to workplace safety and environmental regulations. The greater the economic burden, the more difficult it becomes finding work at a decent wage.

Nevertheless, this is of no concern for the CSD. It's not their problem if you're thrown out of work, hindered from decreased working hours, or suffered from a loss of pay as a result of burdensome regulations. Imputing income is anything but fair. It's the price to pay for the bad decisions of someone else.

The second technique to increase the profit of the child support business is, as its advocates claim, to "calculate child support based on income." Many states have websites with child support calculators. Hearing officers or support magistrates ask questions regarding an individual's income, expenses, level of education, etc., so they can input the numbers into a calculator.

However, this claim is misleading. The methodology used in the calculations is not based upon income, it's calculated from algorithms. There's a big difference. Let's contrast the two methodologies used.

Banks make decisions on loan applications by calculating based on the income to expense ratio. They might examine credit scores, job history, etc. to decide if a loan should be approved or the maximum loan amount. But when determining the monthly amount that a person can afford to pay back, they calculate based on income to expense ratio. This is the proper methodology. The calculations are visible, and you have the means of performing the calculation if you believe the bank erred.

Child support, on the other hand, is calculated based on algorithms. When a number is input into the child support calculator, whether in-

come, expenses, number of dependents, etc., the programmed algorithms can modify the input before performing the calculation and alter the output after performing the calculation. This methodology is
improper, because the calculations are concealed.

Child support calculations based on algorithms are also applied to
imputed incomes. But by far, the most devastating case is when the
hearing officer or support magistrate won't consider past circumstances. For the recipient of child support to engage in behavior that's
responsible for the obligator's unemployment or lower salary is despi-
cable. That should be enough to disqualify her from the child support
program.

These devious methods, that I can attest to, do more to interfere
with your means of survival than any other program. The government
builds a monopoly to exploit children, protects the monopoly from
competition, price gouges its services, and then imprisons those who
can't afford to pay—all under the banner of child support. Here's a
brief assessment of the actual numbers from my case—complements
of the Child Support Division.

On December 18, I was ordered to pay $400 per month in child
support plus $5.00 per month in medical. The additional $5.00 is
tacked on to the monthly support amount totaling $405.00 per month.
Previously, Judge Arrieta ordered me to pay $200 per month in
spousal support. Total monthly support was calculated at $605. This
sounds reasonable for 5 children, does it not? But only on the condition that I actually abandoned my family and maintained a full-time
job—neither of which were present.

At the time of the court ruling, I worked an average of 31 hours per
week with a monthly take-home salary of $1,170.37. (The job I lost in
Las Cruces was full-time, so I was furious when the State wrongfully
took my job, which forced me into part-time work.) First and fore-
most, God commands that we give back to Him what He has blessed
us with—the first fruits of our labor, a tithe of 10% (Proverbs 3:9).

Finally, support was set at $605.00—a whopping 52% of my actual income.

- 10% — Tithe: $117/month
- 52% — Child & Spousal Support: $605/month

God only requires 10% of my income, but New Mexico expects 52%. That's oppressive, especially since I didn't bring this upon myself. This provided roughly $565 per month for tithe and living expenses, which consisted of:

- Tithe: $117/month
- Lot Rent: $230/month
- Electric: $85/month
- Telephone: $50/month
- Food & Hygiene: $200/month
- Automobile Fuel: $80/month

That's a shortage of $200.00 per month, and this doesn't include incidentals such as auto insurance, auto maintenance, auto registration, driver's license renewal, mobile home property tax, or clothing when the need arises. On top of everything else, they disregarded a fluctuation in pay because of missed days at work due to sickness or other circumstances beyond my control.

Granted, in these circumstances, I wouldn't have been able to support 5 children who lived with me. But it must be remembered that I didn't put myself in this situation—the government did.

During the court proceeding on December 18, my tithe was excluded from my expenses. Since all my other constitutional protections were trampled, it should come as no surprise when my freedom to tithe—classified under religious liberty—was denied. Nevertheless, God commands His children to be faithful in this area. Regardless of what the court system believes, I owe God ten percent of my income. And I certainly don't want to rob God (Malachi 3:8) to pay Satan.

The court asserted that charity towards a church is optional, but "supporting your children is a responsibility." To accept their reasoning, however, is to fall into apostasy. The State's message is loud and clear. They won't tolerate obedience; rather, they demand conformity.

New Mexico is forbidding what God commands. Yet, our society is inundated with comments about the Biblical command to obey the governing authorities. However, the preserved Word of God actually reads in Romans 13:1, *"Let every soul be subject to the higher powers..."* Subjection and obedience isn't the same thing. Similarly, higher powers and governing authorities are two separate entities. These words and phrases should not be used interchangeably (see part 3). Nevertheless, the comments are usually misapplied anyway.

God does expect that we obey those governing authorities; on the condition they do not contradict His commands. God requires *all* governing authorities to judge according to His righteousness, and if at any time they pass judgments that contradict God's righteousness and His Word, we are required by God to resist (Acts 5:29).

But what about the husband's governing authority over his wife (Genesis 3:16)? If she scoots around his authority by feigning herself as a victim, it's silent. During her active rebellion and betrayal, comments about obeying authority are never uttered.

On April 11, when Publix started withholding my wages, I received a pay raise, which increased my monthly average to $1,355.47. But by July, a new edict requiring Publix to enroll me in private health insurance forced me out of work. (I will elaborate below.) So on August 12, I started with Hobby Lobby. My income had increased to $1,943.79, but I had to work an average of 47 hours per week. (This was only a seasonal position.)

My employment wasn't the only thing that changed. New Mexico was quite busy themselves—increasing child support, enacting retroactive support, ordering health insurance coverage. This is what our tax money funds—the invention of evil things (Romans 1:28-32).

To cloud one's judgment, the government continually pushes the communist propaganda that fathers are responsible to support their children.

	Dec 18, 2018 (Court Order)	Apr 11, 2019 (Publix)	Aug 12, 2019 (Hobby Lobby)	Oct 17, 2019 (Court Order)	Feb 19, 2020 (Projection)
Net Income	$1,170.37 / mo @ 31 hr / wk	$1,355.47 / mo @ 32 hr / wk	$1,943.79 / mo @ 47 hr / wk	$1,943.79 / mo @ 47 hr / wk	$1,231.71 / mo @ 32 hr / wk
Spousal Support	($200) / mo	($200) / mo	0	($50) / mo	($50) / mo
Current Child Support	($405) / mo	($405) / mo	($586.19) / mo	($586.19) / mo	($586.19) / mo
Retroactive Support	0	0	0	($121.23) / mo	($121.23) / mo
Health Insurance	0	0	0	0	($400) / mo
Total Demands	($605) / mo 51.7%	($605) / mo 44.6%	($586.19) / mo 30.2%	($757.42) / mo 39.0%	($1,157.42) / mo 93.9%
Approved Income	$565.37 / mo	$750.47 / mo	$1,357.60 / mo	$1,186.37 / mo	$74.29 / mo

Table 4: Income to Child Support Ratio

With several changes, I compiled the raw numbers in Table 4. The first four columns, from Dec 2018-Oct 2019, was the actual income to child support ratio. When my seasonal position from Hobby Lobby ended in Feb 2020, they brought me in as part-time with employer-provided medical benefits. Fortunately, open enrollment wasn't until November. For this reason, the cost of health insurance was the only projection in the last column. All the other figures were accurate.

If you recall, CSD had previously attempted to push through a monthly support of $1,217.00 on June 5, 2018. When it backfired on them, they found an alternate route to impose that amount against me anyway. The projected cost (in Table 4) of health insurance under the Patient Protection and Affordable Care Act for a family of 6 is certainly lower than the actual cost. (Insurance provided by employers is not subsidized by the government, so poverty levels don't reflect cost.)

Although the Child Support Division wouldn't be collecting the full amount, their success is in taking it from me, preventing me from supporting myself. These dollar amounts are to close in relation to be a coincidence. This was strategic.

Since I defied the unlawful order to pay my ex-wife, on October 17, 2019, a monthly amount of $50.00 was ordered to reduce the spousal support that was past due. In addition, retroactive support was tacked in the amount of $121.23 ($116.23 + $5.00). This totals $171.23 per month to pay towards the counterfeited debt of $36,534.91.

Surprisingly, the majority of this amount doesn't even go to Amy or my children. When the CSD called me in response to a letter I mailed to the New Mexico state governor, Michelle Grisham, I was informed that $29,157.00 is what the State is keeping. (The governor passed my letter on to the CSD, but that's where it stopped.)

According to the state of New Mexico, I owe $29,157 in child support; however, none of it supports my children. Another scripted and superficial line is always repeated, "But the State supported your children in your absence."

That statement sounds appealing, but it's flawed. Where did the State get the money to support my children? Obviously, the taxpayers picked up the tab. But that $29,157.00 isn't going back to the taxpayers, it's going into the pockets of government employees and bureaucrats.

That excessive fee has nothing to do with the child or support. This is more like a ransom tactic. In fact, this fee is hidden from public view. When I receive notifications from the CSD, the total unpaid support is printed on the statement, but is only half-itemized. Here's my account summary as of May 16, 2020. Keep in mind that this statement is seven months after the court hearing of October 17, and my wages were being garnish until February.

ACCOUNT SUMMARY AS OF 05/16/2020

TOTAL UNPAID CHILD SUPPORT:	$32,690.36
TOTAL UNPAID MEDICAL SUPPORT:	$65.00
TOTAL UNPAID SPOUSAL SUPPORT:	$4,550.00
INTEREST DUE ON UNPAID SUPPORT:	$1,525.96
TOTAL UNPAID SUPPORT:	$38,831.32

Figure 6: CSD Half-Itemized Statement

Looking at Figure 6, our primary concern is the total unpaid child support figure. The first line item is very explicit by implying that $32,690.36 goes to *support my children*. As you can see, the CSD's fee (hidden ransom demand) is not part of the itemization, only the interest. The public records, however, publishes a completely different amount.

10/21/2019 CHILD SUPPORT HEARING OFFICER REPORT

Rsp Toby Strebe shall pay $581.19/month for on-going child support and $116.23/month toward reduction of judgment of $2,274.78 -$5/month cash medical support -$5/month for payment toward the medical support judgment SPOUSAL SUPPORT -$50/month toward reduction of judgment of spousal support of $5,103.13

Figure 7: Child Support Officer Report

According to Figure 7, the CSD published my unpaid child support amount of $2,274.78 in the public domain. This is over a $30,000 discrepancy—awfully close to the $29,157 ransom demand. The report (Figure 7) and the account summary (Figure 6) may be seven months apart, but keep in mind that my wages were being garnished during four of those months. This isn't a human error or honest mistake. It was strategically planned and maliciously executed.

To further oppress fathers, the CSD also levies an annual interest rate of 4% of the unpaid balance. During the life of this fabricated debt established on October 17, I would fork over an additional $20,529.59 in interest. This totals $57,064.50 of retroactive and past-due support, but only a measly $7,377.91 (Figure 7) ostensibly supports my children.

The State agency has this calculated to be paid off in 18 years, but that's completely detached from reality. All levels of the government —local, state, and federal—are interfering with my means to obtain and hold employment. Dona Ana County continues throwing me out of work, State governors shut down their economies and destroyed businesses in 2020. The federal government burdens our economy by overregulation. Yet, the CSD thinks I can afford to pay them nearly to $60,000 for ransom demands—and then blame me for not having the money.

For closer accuracy, we must include future payments. Since the CSD has demanded a monthly payment of $586.19 for at least 5 years (until my eldest child turns 18), that equals $35,171.40. To sum the current, retroactive, and past-due support, this is a preposterous $92,235.90. This is ludicrous; it's nearing the cost of a house. I couldn't obtain a 30-year loan from any bank.

At this point, I get the impression that the government is intentionally preventing me from paying, just so they can imprison me. Then as people slowly shake their heads at me, I'll get bombarded with another scripted line, "He's a deadbeat dad."

The Child Support Division is obviously part of the conspiracy with an agenda to bring America to her knees. Destroying a father's basic, human life support is strategic. This sets the stage to commit genocide by starvation—an end-run around controlling the food supply.

The Dangers of Government Monopoly

The term "Monopoly," in reference to the economy—not the game, has a negative stigma in today's culture. However, in the unhampered economy, free-market monopolies are actually a good thing. New products and services always enter the market through a monopoly. But before long, competition emerges, and the monopoly dissolves.

Competition is what helps drive prices down, increase quality, and provide more options for consumers. No one can prevent or hinder competition except the government. Throughout American history, the State has a record of protecting monopolies by subsidizing favored companies, requiring competition to obtain business licenses, or prohibiting entrepreneurs from entering into certain industries.

But without competition, businesses charge higher prices, the quality or service provided is poor, and consumers have no other options.

As I have already disclosed, child support is a profit-driven business. The Office of Child Support Enforcement reports their revenues in terms of collections. They even boast about how many "families they serve." A father supporting his children is detrimental to their business.

Within the child support system, an economic transaction is taking place. The father is paying for a service being provided by the CSD. However, there's no competition. The Child Support Division is a government monopoly. Citizens are prohibited from entering into this field to start a business.

Since the CSD is a protected monopoly, they can overcharge fathers for their service. A high quality service entails a father who's involved and supportive of his family. (This is what *fatherhood.gov* indicates.) But the level of service provided by the CSD accomplishes the complete opposite. The father can't even shop around for another agency to handle his child support obligations. Government forces him to pay the extorted rates. And if you haven't noticed, the State promotes fatherhood and helps fund its destruction. This is called a "controlled conflict."

To break the operation of this monopoly down into manageable sizes, let's analyze the State's actions through an Imaginary Grocery Store (IGS). Suppose you were a farmer, but the government commandeered your property. Instead of growing crops to feed your family, you're forced to purchase food at the IGS. The store has a monopoly on food, but at least you can still eat, right?

You have $100.00 in your wallet to spend, so you head to the IGS for the first time to purchase food. As you look around the store, much of the food is rotten and moldy. The aisles labeled with canned food were empty. Dissatisfied with the poor conditions and bad products, you head for the door. As you pass the only cash register, four armed guards block your exit. Then you catch a sign posted by the door. It reads,

"BY ORDER OF THE GOVERNMENT:

You are responsible to provide food for your family through the IGS. Failure to comply will result in disciplinary action."

So it's against the law to refuse to purchase food from IGS? Apparently, those guards are just protecting the store's revenues.

One of the employees approaches you and offers to help you comply with the law and get you on your way. She hands you a moldy loaf of bread and assures you that it's good for your kids. You decide to smell it first and got a whiff of a chemical that you were familiar with from your farming days. Handing it back, you shout, *"That stuff's been poisoned!"* Realizing how loud you were, you quickly glanced in the guards' direction. Then reality set in, you don't have a choice. As the cashier rings you up, she tells you that your total comes to $115.00 for one loaf of moldy and poisoned bread.

Not only is IGS price gouging you, they're selling you a poor quality product. But in addition to its low quality, it's been poisoned. However, since you didn't have the money to make the purchase, the guards hauled you off to jail. You broke the law and refused to purchase bread to feed your children.

The business practices of the CSD are conducted in the exact same manner. After the State commandeers the family—particularly the kids:

- Fathers are forced to support their children through the CSD.
- It's also against the law to refuse to purchase child support service through the CSD.
- The quality of service provided by the CSD is extremely low.
- But in addition to quality control problems, CSD poisons their service.
- The CSD also price gouges for their services.
- All too often, judges and the police stand guard to protect the CSD's profits.
- However, failing to transact with the CSD is against the law, and it acts as a signal to the public of irresponsibility and the refusal to support one's children.

The child support system is 100% total government control. This is Communism! And sadly, far too many have swallowed its poison.

God commands the father to feed, clothe, and shelter his children, *not* purchase childcare from his ex or the State.

I remember when Justice Amy Barrett went through several days of contentious hearings and relentless questioning during her confirmation process as Trump's Supreme Court nominee. On the first day of the hearing, Barrett stated, *"Courts have a vital responsibility to enforce the rule of law, which is critical to a free society. But courts are not designed to solve every problem or right every wrong in our public life."* She added, *"The policy decisions and value judgments of government must be made by the political branches elected by and accountable to the people. The public should not expect courts to do so, and courts should not try."*

So why is family court attempting to solve every child-rearing dispute between a married couple? Several parenting decisions are listed below, which is decided by court order. These include:

- How should the State protect *their* children?
- Who should the State hire to babysit *their* children? (Who should be the custodial parent?)
- Who should the State restrict to visiting *their* children?
- What restrictions should the State have in place? (When should visitation hours be set?)
- Who should the State prohibit *their* children from seeing?
- Who should support the State's children?
- How much support should *their* children receive?
- What medical insurance should cover *their* children?
- Should the State's children be permitted to leave their court's jurisdiction?
- Who will provide *their* children with the appropriate (court-approved) schooling, discipline, and direction?

When the court proposes, orders, and enforces the solutions to these questions, freedom no longer exists, and our government agencies are overstepping their boundaries. Each time the judge's parenting decision is disobeyed, the police state gets involved. This effectively rules the family—including children—at gunpoint.

No one has an inherent responsibility to pay the State, which pockets a portion of your salary and disburses the balance to their rebellious spouse. This money is not theirs to take and distribute. The freedom to own, use, exchange, control, protect, and freely dispose of property is a natural, necessary, and inseparable extension of your

God-given rights. Moreover, property is a means of personal independence and self-reliance. And this was a concept that Jefferson knew well.

> *"I am not among those who fear the people. They and not the rich are our dependence for continued freedom, and to preserve their independence, we must not let our rulers load us with perpetual debt. We must make our election between economy and liberty, or profusion and servitude. If we run into such debts as that, we must be taxed in out meat and in our drink, in our necessities and our comforts, in our labors and our amusements, for our callings and our creeds..."* (Jefferson, 1816)[38]

---

[38] Thomas Jefferson, "Proposals to Revise the Virginia Constitution: Letter to 'Henry Tompkinson' (Samuel Kercheval), 12 July 1816," In *The Papers of Thomas Jefferson: Retirement Series*, ed. Jefferson Looney (Princeton: Princeton University Press, 2013), Vol 10: May 1816 to January 1817.

CHAPTER TEN

THE PRICE OF BEARING FALSE WITNESS

T he last chapter examined the strategic methods executed by the Child Support Division to increase their wealth—the beginning of a child support order against the obligator. But our analysis isn't complete without looking into the end of the child support order favoring the recipient.

Although every divorce case has a different set of circumstances, the underlining principles remain the same. Therefore, I'll elaborate on the State's tactic by using my case and circumstances to provide you a standard of comparison.

To see how the State lures women into the child support machinery, let's first take a look at my ex-wife's household income. This will not be as accurate or as extensive since I do not have access to her current financial records. Instead, Amy's information was acquired through two methods:

- Her verbal testimony during the December 18, 2018 court hearing.
- Knowledge previously disclosed prior to our separation on March 10, 2016.

Keep in mind that this information is several years old and may not reflect current conditions. Amy's financial state may have changed, or New Mexico's welfare laws could have been modified after the publication of this book.

If you remember, Amy's father, John, lived with her and my five children. As a result, I must include his income since he is part of her household. By replacing me with her father as a resident within the house, she also substituted my income for his. The majority of funds coming into the house through an individual resident are ultimately spent on the household in general, especially when the need arises. Thus, his income must be calculated.

John received a social security check each month in the amount of $1,100, and Amy worked part-time at the public school earning $400 per month. (She must have obtained this employment sometime after my expulsion.) She received $500 per month in cash assistance and $750 per month in food stamps. This totals $2,750 per month at tax-payer expense.

This didn't include government-covered healthcare, government-subsidized education, or government housing, which was discounted, costing her only $350 per month. In perspective, this was equivalent to working 40 hours per week with a pay rate of $15.86 per hour, a 100% employer-paid medical coverage, a full-benefits package, and almost a complete tax-free status. (She undoubtedly paid taxes on her school income.)

If we tack on the monthly child support of $581.19 (minus the $5.00 for medical) plus $50 in past-due spousal support, Amy's household income would soar to $3,381.19 per month (or $19.51 per hour). I didn't include retroactive support, because the State is keeping nearly 80% for themselves.

No wonder she left me. Kidnapping children is a very profitable business when the government is on your side. But it's not a free service they provide to mothers. The fathers and children pay dearly for it. That's also how the government makes money on the side. It's their ransom demand of an additional $29,157.00 with 4% interest in arrears.

As the salary of the father increases over time, child support obligations also adjust to ensure the ex receives a larger sum of money. However, upon a salary decrease or loss of employment, for whatever reason, sometimes unexpectedly, the CSD doesn't relent. The child support obligator may petition the court to lower the amount, but this delayed reaction only intensifies their financial burden. If the judge has compassion on the father and approves the petition, the obligator isn't compensated from the time his hardship began.

Some jurisdictions automatically deny any petition by a father who is behind in payments. You might wonder how this applies to retroactive support when the CSD imputes tens of thousands of counterfeit debt onto a father's shoulder. That's solely based on the judge's discretion.

But it should come as no surprise when the State compensates themselves from the time of separation. When Amy filed for divorce and filled out the divorce packet, the date of separation is one of those questions. During this time, a child support proposal is prepared and attached to the packet, which gets served to the respondent.

The date of separation is used to start the child support clock, and the proposed child support is the dollar amount that begins accumulating each month. The monthly amount is not payable to the recipient until child support is officially ordered by the court. But the monthly accumulation of monetary demands, from the date of separation until the date when child support is established, morphs into retroactive child support.

This retroactive support remains concealed until child support is ordered by the court. But once this manufactured debt surfaces, it is payable to the State. Current child support amounts are only payable to the recipient once there's an order. This is the origin of the $29,157.00. And it's growing daily, because they charge interest.

According to the CSD, I'm supposed to pay child support from March 2016 until December 2018. However, Amy and my children get nothing. And I'm supposed to be deceived and believe that this money is supporting my children. That's why it's called "child support," right? To make everyone believe that it [the money] is supporting their children.

The father must keep up with the support payments, even though the payments aren't calculated based on his income. However, if support was based on a fixed percentage, then any change in income, whether from overtime hours or a cut in hours, would instantly reflect the child support payment. And in the process, court appearances would decrease.

Although percentages correct several deficiencies within the child support system, they also create problems for the bureaucrats and judges who desire more wealth than what percentages would allow.

However, the proponents of the child support system purportedly claim that percentages don't work because fathers would intentionally seek lower paying jobs or remain unemployed just to throw off their parental responsibility. This is tantamount to turning down higher paying jobs or not working just to avoid paying taxes. That's just ludicrous.

Only the propagandists and ignorant repeat this fallacious line scripted by the director. Establishing a fixed amount, as we have already observed, is disastrous to the economy, individual freedom, and religious liberty. Ultimately, the CSD's monetary focus is the epitome of promoting child abuse. Propaganda created this problem, and more propaganda justifies it.

Since the services provided by the CSD's don't support children, the term "child support" is a misnomer. It doesn't reflect reality. The ideology behind its designation is to grey the line between child support and supporting your children. Although these two are not the same, they are frequently used interchangeably.

In the case of Blessing v. Freestone, the Supreme Court said this about the child support enforcement program:

> *"But the requirement that a State operate its child support pro-*
> *gram in 'substantial compliance' with Title IV-D was not in-*
> *tended to benefit individual children and custodial parents, and*
> *therefore it does not constitute a federal right. Far from creat-*
> *ing an individual entitlement to services, the standard is simply*
> *a yardstick for the Secretary to measure the system-wide per-*
> *formance of a State's Title IV-D program. Thus, the Secretary*
> *must look to the aggregate services provided by the State, not to*
> *whether the needs of any particular person have been satis-*
> *fied."* (Blessing v. Freestone, 1997)[39]

State child support programs and the enforcement, thereof, are meaningless as a result of their limited geographical jurisdiction. If the state-run program was going to be effective, they required federal assistance. But as the Supreme Court acknowledged, federal intervention in the States' domestic jurisdiction wasn't to help mothers or children; rather, it was to help the State. In other words, if the federal enforcement of child support (Title IV-D of the Social Security Act) was never intended to benefit mothers and children, then the yardstick to measure the state-run program only benefits the State and its bureaucracies.

This is similar to the business strategy of a retail store by measuring their performance in total sales. The managers and its employees benefit by receiving bonus pay.

Tragically, the government's monopoly on child support services tempts the social agents to devise new and profound ways to increase their customer base. Hence, the biggest threat to the State is an intact family. Mothers with children must be lured away, regardless of the harm being inflicted upon the children.

This intricate system, however, has a much larger operation that very few recognize. By enticing women away from their husbands, it allows the State to gain access to and control over the minds of chil-

---

[39] Blessing v. Freestone, 520 U.S. 329 (United States Supreme Court, 1997).

dren—your children, which ultimately empowers the State to control the future.

The price of bearing false witness is greater than anyone can afford. Maybe that's why mothers, like Amy, would sell the souls of their children to the State. The price tag was too high, so someone else must pay.

These indirect and subtle tactics drown out the gospel message of Jesus Christ. The State attempts to replace the gospel of Jesus Christ by promoting the legal obligations that its subjects must fulfill before society. And child support is one such obligation.

However, as a Believer in our Lord and Saviour, Jesus Christ, I have no such obligations. I worship God and God alone. I fear not what the State can do to me, because my God is bigger than the State. Family court and the CSD have no power over me unless God allows it. Every true Patriot and Believer must reject and oppose the propaganda of child support.

Exploiting Children for Financial Gain

During the court hearing on November 27, Amy accused me, and Judge Quintero helped by criticizing me for prospering (covered in chapter 24) while "refusing" to support my children. But on December 18, Amy did more than accuse, she played the role of the victim.

It's noteworthy to mention that I lost nearly everything because of Amy's false accusations, including my reputation and clean background. I was destitute and forced to move back in with mom and dad. In contrast, the State gave Amy anything and everything they could, including my children. She still had her home, furniture, vehicle, welfare income, companionship, etc.

Yet, for some unexplained phenomenon, I prospered and she flunked. Just imagine how furious they were. And their attempt to reason was clearly insane. Amy and the judge equated my "prosperity" to selfishness, trampling my wife, and exalting my desires above the needs of my children. Meanwhile, Amy was depicted as a poor, struggling mother—one who was downtrodden. And her failure was seemingly linked to the burden of my children.

This might explain the court's overwhelming aggression towards me. My prosperity may have led them to the conclusion that I have lots of money, but refuse to share. However, that's only speculation. It wasn't until later that the court was secretly issuing orders against me, pushing my wage garnishments to unbearable levels.

Since family court can't compete with the truth, they resort to suppressing it. But asking the right questions, however, gives us a little glimpse behind the scenes.

- If they're my children, why does Amy have them?
- If she doesn't want the burden, why won't she return them?
- If she wants to keep them, why won't she support them?
- If Amy's possession of the kids results in failure, then shouldn't they be removed for her to succeed?

Family court won't listen to this line of reasoning if they have an agenda. These questions would expose Amy as a greedy, selfish mother exploiting her children for financial gain. By shifting the blame to me, Addison, Kyndall, Tobie, Paige, and Lincoln, Amy's incompetence and failure as a parent isn't revealed. The money valve can stay open and the line unobstructed. The State's worst nightmare is to have an incompetent parent obstruct the flow of money. Children are only a means to an end, no matter who they belong to.

Economically, the child support vehicle and mothers who grab the operating wheel are a much higher cost to society than they produce. They don't contribute in any way. They're parasitic and consume the fruits of someone else's labor. In hindsight, we witness Amy's despotic pattern of mental depravity.

- Addison, Kyndall, Tobie, Paige, and Lincoln have been deprived of their father—his love, his protection, his guidance, his time, his communication, his intimate touch, his financial support, his moral encouragement, and much more.

- I have been deprived of my position of authority, my responsibilities, my residency, my employment, my freedom, my reputation, my clean background, and my children—their love, their time, their respect, their communication, their intimate touch, and much more.
- Our family has been deprived of authority, unity, love, respect, peace, order, and stability.
- Taxpayers and I, specifically, have been deprived of our earnings (the fruits of our labor).
- I was physically restrained and deprived of liberty for a brief period of time (approx. 30 days). Additionally, there was a failed attempt to deprive me of liberty for the rest of my life (prison).
- Above all, the most damning was the suppression of truth and the deprivation of my children's healthy state of mind.

This is such a high cost to bear false witness.

- This isn't love; it's called hate...
- This isn't protection; it's called assault...
- This isn't support; it's called robbery...
- This isn't lawful; it's called criminal.

Make no mistake about it: The lives of your children in the hands of government would never be valued because their only purpose is to generate revenue. The government seeks your destruction; regardless of your political affiliation or ideology.

Enslaving the Recipients

An accusation is a direct attack against the accused. Therefore, a false accuser is, by its nature, an attacker. Contrary to popular opinion, the State doesn't help women escape abusive husbands. Rather, they're setting a trap. The government infiltrates the home, displays friendly signals through their welfare programs, and gains the mother's confidence through the detestable child support program.

By feigning herself as a victim, Amy is unknowingly allowing the government to advance her own destruction. This method is intended to bring down the enemy from within. In 2018, the Office of Child Support Enforcement boasted of having 14.7 million children enrolled into its program.[40] Our government has crushed and enslaved millions of families in America. Yet, no one is fighting for their freedom. Goethe was right, *"None are more hopelessly enslaved than those who falsely believe they are free."*

What happens is that government programs and entitlements, such as social security, food stamps, cash assistance, housing assistance, public schooling, tuition assistance, Medicaid and Medicare, child support, and alimony allows the recipient to spend money they did not earn. They put forth no work effort or hard labor. Individual, economic choices are automatically regulated by the fundamental principle of human effort. Simply put, a person chooses more carefully when it costs them something.

If you recall, my analogy in chapter one fits perfect here. An individual's right [to choose] to purchase a television costing $500 is a packaged deal. But the price tag causes one to choose more carefully.

No one can appreciate anything that's simply handed to them; something that costs them nothing, especially when it's given to them on a regular basis, and all they have to do is spend it. Consequently, any decisions made by the welfare or child support recipient are impulsive, reckless, and wasteful since they are not self-regulated or restrained by their work effort. All too often, the recipients of government handouts travel down the path of irresponsibility and bring up their own children to continue down the same avenue as well.

---

[40] Office of Child Support Enforcement, *FY 2018 Annual Report to Congress* (March 2021), Accessed April 14, 2021 https://www.acf.hhs.gov/css/report/fy-2018-annual-report-congress.

Irresponsible people want freedom to do as they please, but they don't want others to have freedom. They are so self-absorbed, they'll vote for irresponsible leaders who'll take away the freedoms of others to give it to them. The day's coming, though, when their elected officials have removed just enough freedom and consolidated just enough power to turn against the very people who put them in office. Irresponsible people are unable to recognize this dangerous trend because they are only concerned with short-term self-gratification.

Additionally, every one of these government-operated programs removes the individual's freedom of choice. This is the socialist's dream of central planning and economic control. The State chooses how much money the recipient can have, how much food she can buy, where she'll live, what school her children are allowed to attend and what they'll learn, what medical care should be dispensed, etc. Socialism is only a transition to communism. It's never an end in itself.

Amy sold her freedoms when she allowed the government to make these choices for her. She is, ultimately, living like a farm animal. But she doesn't comprehend that farm animals are eventually killed.

Amy's dependency on government keeps her on their leash. Her decisions are nothing more than instincts formed by government propaganda. Her means of survival is held in the arms of government welfare. Her existence is solely for the purpose of increasing power and revenue for government officials. And she'll be suppressed and thrown away when the government has no more use for her. An unhappy life sold into slavery, oppression, and moral bankruptcy—packaged and wrapped up under the child support program.

CHAPTER ELEVEN

THE SUBVERSION OF INDIVIDUALITY AND PROPERTY

W hen the term "rights" was shifted from the choice to the object, the concept of property rights altered as well. People began to associate property exclusively with external and tangible items—objects which can be bought and sold. But property consists of much more than what's visible to the naked eye. It encompasses your internal being such as your conscience, religious beliefs, traditional values, ideas, opinions, talents, mental resources, creative powers, intellect, and emotions. Property is an indispensable attribute linked to your individuality. To destroy individual freedom, the first step is to disassociate property from the internal being.

James Madison was a contributor to The National Gazette of Philadelphia, a short-lived newspaper, and he published his article titled "Property" on March 27, 1792.

"This term [property] in its particular application means that dominion which one man claims over the external things of this world, in exclusion of every other individual.

"In its larger and juster meaning, it embraces everything to which a man may attach a value and have a right; and which leaves to everyone else the like advantage.

"In the former sense, a man's land or merchandise or money is called his property. In the latter sense, a man has a property in his opinion and the free communication of them.

"He has a property of peculiar value in his religious opinions, and in the profession and practice dictated by them.

"He has a property very dear to him in the safety and liberty of his person.

"He has an equal property in the free use of his faculties and free choice of the objects on which to employ them.

"In a word, a man is said to have a right to his property; he may be equally said to have a property in his rights..." (Madison, 1792)[41]

Madison quoted Sir William Blackstone in his first paragraph. And Blackstone referred to Genesis 1:28 as the foundation for property rights.

"There is nothing which so generally strikes the imagination, and engages the affections of mankind, as the right of property; or that sole and despotic dominion which one man claims and exercises over the external things of the world, in total exclusion of the right of any other individual in the universe. And yet there are very few that will give themselves the trouble to consider the original and foundation of this right...

"But when law is to be considered not only as a matter of practice, but also as a rational science, it cannot be improper or useless to examine more deeply the rudiments and grounds of these positive constitutions of society.

"In the beginning of the world, we are informed by holy writ, the all-bountiful Creator gave to man 'dominion over all the

---

[41] James Madison, "For the National Gazette, 27 March 1792: Property," In *The Papers of James Madison*, ed. Robert Rutland and Thomas Mason (Charlottesville: University Press of Virginia, 1983), Vol 14: April 1791 to March 1793.

Earth, and over the fish of the sea, and over the fowl of the air, and over every living thing that moveth upon the Earth.' This is the only true and solid foundation of man's dominion over external things..." (Blackstone, 1765-69)[42]

We are inclined to observe civil violations over our visible and tangible things, but the invasion into our inner being is often overlooked. Although the government has no jurisdiction over such matters, the most effective tactic in gaining control or possession over your external and tangible property is through aggressive policies, orders, or laws, which targets your internal being.

But when property is restricted to external and tangible objects, it separates revealed religion from your conscience and moral responsibilities before God. The substitution imposed is social religion based on pluralism, toleration, and your legal obligations to society.

The divorce and child support mechanisms—social agencies, courts, laws, policies, procedures, and orders—are very aggressive and inhumane. This machinery invades your inner being and deprives you of several of your internal property characteristics—the most sacred being your conscience. And the overwhelming evidence is conclusive.

Protection orders, child support, and restricted contact through visitation hinders an individual from freely exercising their religious beliefs. It removes their moral responsibility before God and replaces it with legal obligations to society. For example:

Maybe your deeply held religious belief is that a father has a moral responsibility to bring up his children in the nurture and admonition of the Lord (Ephesians 6:4). But your legal obligation is to pay child support instead of bringing them up. You cannot exercise the latter without forfeiting the former. This is because your beliefs control your thoughts, and your thoughts control your actions. It's not possi-

---

[42] William Blackstone, *Commentaries on the Laws of England* (Oxford: Clarendon Press, 1765-69), Vol 1.

ble for you to act in a manner contrary to your beliefs. Consequently, the fulfillment of these legal obligations demands that religious beliefs and moral responsibilities must conform to the State.

Here are several examples of the State's invasion into religious liberty, moral responsibilities, and internal property.

- Fathers are to discipline their children (Proverbs 13:24; 19:18; 22:15; 23:13-14; 29:15, 17; Colossians 3:21; Hebrews 12:5-11).
- Fathers are to educate their children (Proverbs 1:8; 22:6; Deuteronomy 6:6-7; 11:19; Isaiah 54:13; Ephesians 6:4; 2 Timothy 3:16; 3 John 1:4).
- Fathers are to provide for their children (1 Timothy 5:8; 2 Corinthians 12:14).
- Fathers are to protect their children (Psalms 127:3; Proverbs 14:26; Nehemiah 4:13-14; Matthew 18:6; Mark 9:42; Luke 11:21-22; 1 Timothy 5:8).

Additionally, the State also invades the religious liberty, moral responsibilities, and internal property of children. They, too, have a requirement to fulfill before God.

- Children are to hearken unto their father (Proverbs 17:25; 23:22).
- Children are to obey their father (Deuteronomy 21:18-21; Colossians 3:20; Ephesians 6:1; 2 Timothy 3:2; Romans 1:30).
- Children are to honor their father (Exodus 20:12; 21:17; Deuteronomy 5:16; Matthew 15:4; 19:19; Mark 7:10; 10:19; Luke 18:20).

To freely exercise these religious beliefs and traditional values—none of which harm the life, liberty, or property of another—the government must not interfere. The requirement to fulfill these moral responsibilities and Biblical obligations requires physical contact without limitations or restraints. But what's performed in the various aspects of the divorce industry?

- Protection orders sever all forms of contact.

- Visitation limits and restricts physical interaction.
- Child support substitutes moral responsibilities with legal obligations.

These activities, which receive nearly unanimous support from every level of government and praise by the majority of citizens, intrude your internal being, violate the most sacred property you hold, and subvert your individuality. The fulfillment of these legal obligations must first require a change in your beliefs to shift your thought patterns. Once your thoughts have changed to conform to the legal requirements, your actions to obey will automatically follow.

What's happening is that you're being coerced to conform your internal being to that of the State and accept its substitution as valid and just. Your internal property, connected to your individuality, is no longer yours; it belongs to the State. As the State molds you into their image and their likeness, you lose your individuality. And without individuality, there can be no accountability. You and the State become one. And any resistance of this intrusion is met through the barrel of a gun.

Without government intervention, each person is held accountable for how they utilize their internal property. This accountability is visible with the inequalities of external property. It's an intricate system. *"The nature of external inequities or differences in the ownership of property, results from the exercise of diverse, individual faculties, which is the source of unequal distributions of property. Put another way, the unequal distribution and possession of property is a direct consequence of individual deployments of internal property."*[43]

The divorce and child support mechanisms are intended to absolve mothers of the consequences of misusing and abusing their own internal property. When any mother seeks child support, the same superficial scripting gets repeated. They don't have enough money to sup-

---

[43] Gai Ferdon, *A Republic If You Can Keep It: America's Authentic Liberty Confronts Contemporary Counterfeits* (Chesapeake: The Foundation for American Christian Education, 2008).

port their children...They need help...They can't do it alone...It's not their responsibility...on and on and on. Yet, more often than not, the father appears to be doing just fine. This difference is based on how each individual operates their internal property (Matthew 25:14-30).

Mothers requesting support are usually the ones who file for divorce and demand custody of the children in the process. This mother, like Amy, is misappropriating her internal property. She could have filed for divorce and left the children with their father. She could have remained married and kept her children. She could have stayed separated and shared the parenting responsibilities with their father. All three options were abandoned for her to embrace a destructive decision. Therefore, she brought her own financial troubles upon herself. The unequal distribution of her external property is based on the law of sowing and reaping (Galatians 6:7).

Only the mothers who misuse and abuse their own internal property are the ones who seek child support. Mothers who are doctors, lawyers, CEO's, and those making six figures a year don't run to the Child Support Division begging for help. Their prosperity resulted from the wise deployment of their internal property.

In addition, mothers who are content with what they have don't seek more in the form of child support. Child support *only* appeals to the covetous and greedy, which explains why it's overwhelmingly dispensed to mothers who abandon their husbands and kidnap their children.

A Dehumanizing System: Cogs in a Machine

Earlier, I mentioned that without individuality, you cannot have accountability. This is the State's formula for success. This explains why officials and anyone occupying high governmental offices are rarely held accountable. When crimes of this magnitude are committed against you, your child, or a loved one, no one can be prosecuted because no person committed the act. You become a victim of the process, not an individual. But the process (or system) usually consists of several hundred or thousand individuals all working in unison towards a common objective.

Now imagine this government process as gears, which operate the child support system. Everyone should be familiar with gears since they are used in tons of mechanical devices, from car engines and transmissions to VCR's and grandfather clocks. They perform several important functions, but one is to keep the rotation of two axes synchronized. Working together, the device (or child support system) runs accordingly.

One individual gear turning on its own can't operate the system. Similarly, removing just one gear causes the entire system to malfunction. Gears are only effective if they work in sync. Numerous governmental positions and their occupants are acting as individual gears within the child support device.

Breaking this down, let's suppose you were arrested for the lies your ex-wife told so she could keep your children. When you're transported to the jail, several people are involved with booking (processing) your arrival. The arresting officers leave and go on their way.

Those who work in the jail (jailers) also book robbers, murderers, etc. This job function is a vital role of government, and not a criminal act. However, your circumstances are different. You may have been arrested without probable cause; the oath or affirmation could have been perjured.

Without the jailers, you couldn't be unlawfully detained. Although booking your arrival is *not* a crime, the jailer is unaware that he's aiding others in the commission of a crime. Government is using him as a pawn to fulfill their agenda. But in the process of his daily tasks, you and your children are being harmed.

The actions by each government employee are relatively small, thus increasingly making it difficult to take legal action against anyone. The catastrophic damage, which is overwhelmingly established, isn't the accomplishment of one person, but rather, a collective group of hundreds (or even thousands) working in unison. Since this scheme cannot be attributed to anyone in particular, the father becomes the scapegoat.

These government gears host numerous other systems within the United States, not just child support. These include entitlement and welfare programs, the education establishment and public schooling, the medical establishment and pharmaceuticals, etc.

The problem is the process, *not* the individual. The divorce and child support mechanisms are not designed to build up the family and reconcile differences. Its purpose is to destroy America's foundation by murdering the family as an institution, while clearing the individuals who are responsible of all accountability.

Due to the nature of the process, well-meaning citizens, Patriots, and Christians who join the ranks of the government are unable to reverse the direction of the gears. Politically, it's acceptable to criticize anyone who operates within the machinery, as long as the device or process is approved. The individuals who represent the gears are just fools being exploited by their government. The only remedy is to abolish the process—a system most Americans embrace.

Anyone familiar with the Biblical account of the Tower of Babel should easily recognize that God detests this type of unity (Genesis 11:1-9). There's a vast difference between individuals helping one another in love and a large collective group of persons working together as one unit to advance a destructive cause.

The Freedom to Fight

Freedom in America produces a false hope to many people. Freedom can be defined as the power to act for oneself. If one is free to choose where to shop and what to buy, but not free to mount a defense in court, refuse vaccinations, own firearms, or live a life according to their religious convictions, then does an environment of freedom truly exist? Our government masterly and artfully creates a false sense of freedom.

Just some food for thought, off topic: If freedom in America is only an illusion, then what's our military fighting for? Large standing armies have always been a danger to liberty. They may start off with good intentions, but always turn against the very people they vow to protect. Even the current operations of our standing army is vastly different from America's earlier wars for freedom, such as the American War for Independence, the Barbary Wars, and the War of 1812.

The enemy has waged war against fathers, children, and the family to annihilate all remaining aspects of freedom and to enslave the entire human race. This war is being fought within the divorce and child custody apparatus.

Our government violates the God-given rights of all its citizens, just like the British Crown, back in the eighteenth century, violated the God-given rights of the colonists. This is a repeat of our past, so we can take great comfort in learning, knowing, and understanding American history. Our founding fathers resisted their government and eventually prevailed. We are no match for our monstrous government, which consumes everything in its path. But then again, George Washington's rag-tag soldiers were no match for the professional soldiers of Great Britain.

If you or a loved-one are going through a very similar ordeal as I have, understand that the State will continue to assault your freedoms and wage war against you and your children for years to come. However, the freedom to fight back is a gift from God. The choice to resist is freely made, but the choice to comply is compelled. Free, individual choice requires the absence of court orders (compulsion).

There are many similarities between the American War for Independence and your fight for freedom. George Washington came up against a more powerful enemy, which resulted in several losses, including Fort Necessity, Fort Washington, Georgetown, Long Island, Monongahela, and White Plains. Nevertheless, George Washington is known for his ability to rally his troops and sustain their morale throughout the war. Against all odds, Washington's victory was not achieved through military might, but rather, through knowledge and Divine intervention.

By putting his knowledge into action, he thwarted the British plot to inflate the currency and crash the economy. He also prevented the fall of West Point at the hands of Benedict Arnold. George Washington is a man of courage and never thought about surrendering.

Your divorce battle might differ from mine, but the principle remains the same. We have come up against a more powerful enemy. Therefore, suffering losses is expected. And in my case, these included: the denial of a custody evaluation, the enactment of child support, the theft of my wages, the end of three jobs, as well as the counterfeiting of over $92,000. Nevertheless, the fight isn't over because I haven't surrendered.

You have no power to defeat the State through physical strength. Since the State's weapon is propaganda, you must fight with truth. Victory is only achieved through knowledge and understanding (chapters 12-15). However, you must put the truth into action (chapter 16).

Maintaining a high morale is an important aspect during your fight (chapter 19). On many occasions, the outcome will disappoint you, but don't ever allow your disappointment to turn into discouragement. The worst thing you can do for your children is to think that because you can't do much, you don't do anything. Never abandon the fight. That's the ultimate defeat—the surrender of your freedom of choice.

I fight for truth, justice, and freedom. Not for me only, but also for my children. Addison, Kyndall, Tobie, Paige, and Lincoln are enslaved, and they don't possess the knowledge and courage to resist. They aren't free to receive spiritual, psychological, and emotional support, which requires a parent to put forth effort. I can't afford to surrender to the enemy—the price is too high, and the souls of my children are too valuable.

The State only focuses on physical provisions. But Jesus tells us to take no thought for our lives because everything we have comes from God (Matthew 6:25). Their tunnel vision on monetary and physical provisions is clearly misguided. Don't fall into the same trap. This fight is to free my children from a life of slavery; child support has nothing to do with it. The Lord knows what we need to sustain life, and once you are adopted into God's family, He will care for you accordingly. If God is our provider, why does the government establish child support?

My income, which is earned through honest, hard, and productive work, is for the prudent and responsible person. Through my own work effort, my financial choices are naturally regulated. I understand my financial limitations, and so with wise shopping habits, I stretch my dollar. Yet, I still prospered and received God's blessings.

Our freedom, passed onto us as a sacred trust, is only for the virtuous and moral person. The weight of freedom is not measured by one's own financial state or assets, but by one's power to choose. The State can, and oftentimes will, reduce you to a state of poverty. Yet over time, you have the ability to acquire fresh property. But once you surrender your freedom to the family court tyrants, it will never be restored. It's a fantasy to comply with court orders while still fighting to regain your freedom. Once the money begins flowing, the State will never relinquish its power. Liberty once lost is lost forever.

"Your description of the distresses of the worthy inhabitants of Boston, and the other sea port towns, is enough to melt a heart of stone. Our consolation must be this, my dear, that cities may be rebuilt, and a people reduced to poverty, may acquire fresh property: but a constitution of government once changed from freedom, can never be restored. Liberty once lost is lost forever. When the people once surrender their share in the legislature, and their right of defending the limitations upon the gov-

ernment, and of resisting every encroachment upon them, they can never regain it." (Adams, 1775)[44]

Don't sacrifice your freedom of choice through ignorance and your cowardice to face the truth. It's better to die in freedom than to live in slavery. Choose freedom and resist the divorce and child support machinery.

---

[44] John Adams, "Letter to Abigail Adams, 7 July 1775," In *The Adams Papers: Adams Family Correspondence*, ed. Lyman Butterfield (Cambridge: Harvard University Press, 1963), Vol 1: December 1761 to May 1776.

PART THREE

PREPARING FOR COMBAT

CHAPTER TWELVE

RECOGNIZE THE BATTLE LINES

Many dress up in a robe of authority. Others speak as one who has authority. Some may even announce their authority. And all have followers echoing their authoritative status. However, appearances can be deceiving. Not everyone is who they appear to be. Our culture is saturated with false authorities. We are constantly surrounded them. And a false authority poses the greatest risk to American freedom.

The manipulation and misinterpretation of the rights of mankind, the rule of law, and the role of government (discussed in chapter 1) is the model by which false authorities operate. By conceiving new ideas, which oppose God's order and design, they embrace false doctrine, superficial slogans, and evil schemes. This facilitates the dismantling of our foundation.

"If the foundations be destroyed, what can the righteous do?" (Psalm 11:3). There is a profound assumption within that verse—namely, the righteous have a duty, a God-given agenda, and a cause for which they serve. They operate on the strength of eternal foundations. If these foundations go missing, even God's people are helpless (2 Chronicles 7:14).

Proper interpretation and the need for understanding are crucial if you are to lay a solid foundation. Only then, will you possess the strength and courage to endure adversity. In the Old Testament, the Bible records examples of righteous people who disobeyed government edicts and received God's protection. Two prime examples are:

- The account of Shadrach, Meshach, and Abednego—The king decreed that all were to bow down and worship his golden image. When the three Hebrew children defied his order, they were thrown into the fiery furnace (Daniel 3).

- The account of Daniel—The king decreed that no one was allowed to pray to any God or man, except him. Although Daniel knew about the order, he went into his house and prayed anyway. Consequently, he was thrown into a den of lions (Daniel 6).

These Old Testament saints possessed the strength and courage to resist government orders because their foundations were firmly in place. They properly interpreted the Scriptures and understood the importance of resisting government overreach. Their disobedience to government orders resulted in the repeal of an unjust law and a positive shift in government policy (Daniel 3:28-29; 6:25-26).

These two Biblical examples, out of several others, indicate that politics and God's Word are naturally intertwined. America's Founders understood this. That's why they used the Bible to judge political actions. In today's culture, an emotional appeal has replaced Biblical knowledge. But we can still find humor in God's Word when He addressed Job on speaking without understanding. *"Who is this that darkeneth counsel by words without knowledge?"* (Job 38:2).

I have pointed out several superficial slogans in regards to destroying the family and hurting children. Yet, everyone who speaks them darkens counsel by words without knowledge. Any Biblical or constitutional arguments to refute these shallow statements are usually met with hostility. This is because those superficial phrases don't have depth; they're spoken from the emotions.

Every so often, some slick person proposes a Biblical or constitutional interpretation that appeals to their emotional beliefs. But when you are confronted with different interpretations, meditate on Jefferson's philosophy.

> *"When an instrument admits two constructions, the one safe, the other dangerous, the one precise, the other indefinite, I prefer that which is safe and precise. I had rather ask an enlargement of power from the nation, where it is found necessary, then to assume it by a construction which would make our powers boundless. Our peculiar security is in the possession of a written constitution. Let us not make it a blank paper by construction."* (Jefferson, 1803)[45]

Let's examine the difference between a legitimate authority and a false authority. This understanding is imperative because people are easily taken in by false authorities. Holding a certain position, obtaining a particular education, or winning a specific election casts one in the light of authority. This view assumes that those individuals possess a greater amount of knowledge than everyone else, thus their ability to reason is far superior. However, there are facts that nobody can know apart from Divine revelation (1 Corinthians 2:14). Due to man's fallen nature, people will reason with preconceived ideas, but *"the end thereof are the ways of death"* (Proverbs 14:12).

Today, the distinction between power and authority has been eroded. Just as light dispels darkness, the truth must be brought to light to expose deception. This thought may appear revolutionary, but it's founded upon the authority of Scripture. There are two elements of authority that we need to be aware of. First, there is a position of authority (Romans 13:1). Second, there is the possession of authority (Romans 13:4). Do not confuse the two. They are not one and the same.

---

[45] Thomas Jefferson, "Letter to Wilson Cary Nicholas, 7 September 1803," In *The Papers of Thomas Jefferson*, ed. Barbara Oberg (Princeton: Princeton University Press, 2014), Vol 41: July 1803 to November 1803.

CHAPTER THIRTEEN

BATTLE LINE 1: THE POSITION OF AUTHORITY

"*Let every soul be subject unto the higher powers. For there is no power but of God: the powers that be are ordained of God. Whosoever therefore resisteth the power, resisteth the ordinance of God: and they that resist shall receive to themselves damnation.*" (Romans 13:1-2)

In Paul's letter to the Romans, he is referring to a position of authority. Paul uses the term "higher powers," because the individual who occupies this higher position will inherit strength. But even those holding a position of authority are still subject to a higher power—the utmost power being held by the Creator of all life.

These powers are inherent—innate or naturally inseparable from the position. Inherent powers allow the occupant to perform their duties and fulfill their obligations, which isn't possible outside of the position. Therefore, we can rightly conclude that these powers are associated with the position, not the occupant. The Office of the President, for instance, is the higher position, while the President is the individual who occupies that position. The context of Paul's term, "higher powers," attaches the inherent power with the higher position.

Each time Paul uses the word "power," he's referencing the inherent power associated with the higher position. Those are the only powers (inherent power) ordained by God. An ordinance is an authoritative rule or law, so to ordain would be to enact or establish by authoritative decree. And God's authoritative law has been published in the most widely recognized book known as The Holy Bible.

It's important for Paul to tell us this, because other powers and higher positions will rise up that aren't from God. And anything not of God is of the devil. Paul wants us to discern between the inherent power of God's positions of authority and the usurped power of Satan through false positions.

After properly rendering verse one, verse two opens up with much more clarity. Paul wants us to know that when a person resists the inherent powers that are attached to God's higher positions, they will receive damnation. However, this doesn't apply when a person resists usurped power or higher positions from the devil. These false positions are empowered by the ruler of darkness. So when our government at the local, state, or federal level, exceeds their constitutional limitations and Biblical jurisdiction, their power is not ordained of God—it's not inherent power; it's usurped power.

Here's an illustration of positions of authority ordained by God and the inherent powers associated with those positions.

- Head of the Family: Power to educate, guide, nurture, and make choices for children, represents his family, makes decisions for the family, etc.
- Pastor of the Church: Power to deliver God's message to His people in a sermon or Bible lesson, oversee the operations of the church, etc.
- Police Officer: Power to search, seize, and detain with appropriate warrant, etc.
- Bench of the Magistrate/District Court: Power to check police power by signing warrants, oversee criminal and civil cases, maintain order in the courtroom, and judge accordingly.

- Jury of your Peers: Power to acquit and to nullify unjust law within a case.
- Seats of Congress: Power to vote on legislation, enact law, confirm Supreme Court justices, declare war, impeach high officials, etc.
- Office of the President: Power to sign/veto legislation, execute the law, nominate Supreme Court justices, command the forces during a declared war, repel invasions, etc.
- Bench of the Supreme Court: Power to judge disputes/controversies, maintain order in the courtroom, and judge according to the law.

This list is not all-inclusive, but it exemplifies a position of authority and several of its inherent powers. These powers are exercised naturally and can be discharged without hindering liberty or violating freewill. Notice how there isn't a single power that you can exercise unless you hold that position. Let's not forget that we still have "higher powers" ordained by God at the local and state levels.

Neutralizing the Church and Christian Responsibility

This may appear foreign to those who read a different translation of the Bible. Most other translations use the term "authorities" or "rulers" to replace "higher powers." This is, of course, very problematic, since it's a misrepresentation of Paul's (or more precisely, God's) intent. Here are a few examples of Romans 13:1:

- "Let everyone be subject to the governing authorities..." NIV
- "Let every person be subject to the governing authorities..." ESV
- "Obey the rulers who have authority over you..." CEV
- "Everyone must obey state authorities..." GNT

Each of these translations replaces the inherent power connected to the position of authority with the occupant holding the position, which rewrites the author's original intent. In fact, here's the entire verse from the New Living Translation:

> *"Everyone must submit to the governing authorities. For all authority comes from God, and those in positions of authority have been placed there by God."* (Romans 13:1 NLT)

The word "those" is not referencing the power held within the position, it's addressing the occupant—a person. Even the Nazi leadership in Germany was just obeying the higher authorities over them. They were just obeying Adolf Hitler since he was in a higher position.

How can Congress, the President, or judges obey the rulers over them? These higher authorities are governed by the Constitution, but the Constitution cannot enforce itself. The translators of this passage make reference to human authority—a mortal being holding an office. Yet, no human position would ever be high enough to satisfy the requirement of these verses. On the other hand, the "higher power" translation subjects everyone to God's authority under a human system. The subtle rendering error with these translations has neutralized government opposition—helping pave the way for a one-world government. Coincidence? You decide.

Nearly all modern translation methodologies utilize dynamic equivalence (or a thought-for-thought translation method). Dynamic equivalence is a dangerous translation method because it allows the translator to manipulate or misinterpret the language and modify original intent. However, the King James Bible uses formal equivalence (or a word-for-word translation method), which helps preserve the original text. There's much more which can be written about translation methods, the accuracy of formal equivalence, the manuscripts translated from, and the inerrancy of the King James, but that is beyond the scope of this book. If you're interested in learning more, I will include a couple of good books within my *Additional References* section.

During America's settling era, the Pilgrims aboard the Mayflower carried the Geneva Bible, an English translation full of John Calvin's commentaries. Shortly before America's settlement, King James I authorized the Bible to be translated in the English language in 1604. The translation was completed in 1611 and dominated American culture until an explosion of alternate translations emerged.

So the two most widely used translations of the Bible during America's Founding era were the Geneva and the King James Bible. The text of Romans 13:1 is identical in both translations. Our Founder's were never taught unconditional obedience to the King of England. They were resisting the King's usurped power, not his inherent power.

The newer and more modern translations surfaced following America's descent into progressivism. So it should come as no surprise when most other translations slant towards Political Correctness to neutralize the civic and political responsibility of God's people. The King James Bible is, by far, the most politically incorrect version available.

The Rise of False Positions

Not every position established and given power by Legislative action is ordained by God. God warns us of false prophets (Matthew 7:15), false teachers (2 Peter 2:1), and false apostles transforming themselves into ministers of righteousness (2 Corinthians 11:13-15). So it's reasonable that God would also warn us of false positions of authority (Romans 13:1). These positions must have an outward appearance of godly authority, if they are to deceive the populace into submission and obedience.

Let me illustrate the rise of false positions and the danger they pose to a free society with a short novel. Although this story is fiction, its principle is not detached from reality. This is how the State proposes solutions to all problems within society.

The End of School Bullying

It's another dreaded day at Battlefield High School for 14-year old Nathan. After the short two-day weekend, he begs his mom not to send him back to school. Bullies constantly target Nathan and a number of other students. Some days, Nathan wonders if his enemies at school are more numerous than his friends at church.

The school administrators only discipline when the bully is caught in the act, which happens to be about 1% of the time. Nathan and his mom have plenty of options to choose from. These free choices include:

- Nathan is free to resist or flee from the school bullies.
- Nathan is free to group together with other students to provide themselves a stronger defense or possible deterrence for being bullied.
- Nathan's mom is free to remove her son from the hostile school environment.
- Nathan's mom is free to home educate her son or place him in a private school.

Unfortunately, Nathan and his mom don't entertain the thought of freedom. They both want him free from bullying, but they don't believe they're free to change his environment. This is why these choices never enter their mind. Since Nathan and his mom are in psychological bondage to the State, their ability to make a decision is paralyzed. But after giving their dilemma some thought, their enslavement to the State leaves them no alternatives but to turn to the State for a solution.

So Nathan's mom and a number of other parents file complaints with the local school district. They want to compel the school district to intervene and stop the bullying because their children are getting hurt. In response, the district proposes to the schools that they should create a new position to handle the issue. The district will provide direct funding for each school that accepts their solution. That person, whom we'll refer to as the Bullying Investigations Officer (BIO), will be responsible to investigate school bullying and put a stop to it. Nathan and his mom are now satisfied that the school is getting involved and school bullying will soon end.

For the BIO to effectively perform his job functions, he needs access to student circles and conversations where teachers are generally not privileged. He needs to blend in with students undetected. So a student becomes the perfect candidate. To stop the bullying, he must be given enormous, unchecked power. (To limit or check his power might obstruct the strategy he implements to end the bullying.) But his power would be exercised through the school administration. Therefore, he would automatically be exempt from any investigation since he is the investigator. Who do you think would fight for that new position: Nathan, who just wants to be left alone, or the bully, who likes the power over Nathan and other students like him?

The students at Battlefield won't get to vote for the occupant who will hold that new position. The school staff will appoint the best candidate. For a short time, the bully begins complying with school rules and offers his assistance to the faculty. After a short while, other students start noticing that he's become a "teacher's pet." His campaign to school staff is private. The bully projects himself as one who will crack down on bullying and declares his love for truth, justice, and a safe environment for all. His rhetoric succeeds, and on a busy Friday afternoon, the school bully is called to the principal's office where he is appointed to the new anti-bullying position. (This appointment is conducted in the shadows while all the students are distracted since they're focusing on their homework and upcoming exams to free up their weekend.)

A few weeks pass by and some of the students gradually notice that the bullying is increasing and their freedom to escape is deteriorating. The bully and his friends use the newly created position to increase their wealth by stealing lunch money.

Not long after assuming his position, the Bullying Investigations Officer, accompanied with his two assistants (friends), corner Nathan in the bathroom. He orders Nathan to pay for the investigator's service of providing a safe environment.

Nathan refuses, so the BIO's two assistants shove him backwards and pin him up against the wall. Becoming impatient, the BIO threatens to harm him if he doesn't comply. But Nathan doesn't have any money; he packed a lunch. Without warning, the two assistants start pummeling him with their fists. Nathan throws his arms in front of his face to shield himself from the blows, and the boys kick his feet out from under him. Nathan hits the tile floor hard as a solid kick to his stomach knocks the air out of him. Curling up on the floor, he tries to protect himself from further assault while he attempts to catch his breath. The investigator walks out, returning a moment later with the school security officer.

The officer helps Nathan to his feet and escorts him to the clinic to be examined by the school nurse. He's given an ice pack before visiting the principal's office. The principal listens to the charges brought against Nathan, and then reasons that the BIO had every right to defend himself against an attack. So the principal gives Nathan a ten-day out-of-school suspension for resisting authority, initiating a fight, and assaulting another student.

The investigator petitions the principal on Nathan's behalf since this is his first offense. Thus, Nathan's sentence is reduced to a three-day suspension and a Saturday detention, but a second offense would result in school expulsion and criminal charges filed for assault. Then the security officer calls Nathan's mother to pick him up from school, since he isn't allowed to even finish out the day. As Nathan sits down in the office to wait for his mother, he wonders why he never got to share his side of the story or speak a word in his defense.

The bullying at Battlefield High gets so bad that students start skipping school to avoid the bullies, but the authorities catch them and charge them with truancy. A handful of smaller ninth-graders stick together for their own protection. But when the school administrators receive the BIO's written report of these youngsters operating as a gang, the children are suspended and labeled as bullies.

To avoid trouble, many students simply give up and pay the extorted fees to the school bully for "his service" to protect them from bullying. Not only do these students go hungry every day, but they now hate school. The student victims also despise their parents and the school staff for aiding in this brutal behavior. Grades plummet and some children stop caring about life. The BIO's provocation caused one victimized student to begin entertaining the thought that since his dad has a gun, he can always stop the bullying himself.

As the bully's wealth increases, he uses a portion of his proceeds to buy supporters. Only a couple of months after his ascension to the newly-created, anti-bully position, opposition arises to demand his removal. However, his supporters like the flow of money they're receiving, so they launch a campaign against the victims and their families to discredit them. They are slandered, smeared, and accused.

The majority of students in Battlefield High doesn't know who to believe and are completely ignorant of the situation since they aren't targets. To oppose the bully requires them to engage in the fight—and fighting can lead to harm. To remain neutral and avoid fighting requires an apathetic attitude towards the victims, which actually helps the bully remain in power. Therefore, the bully investigator had far more proponents than opponents. Through all this chaos, no one realizes that it was the school district and school administrators who created the war zone.

Nathan and the other bullied students eventually accept the notion that they only have peace by complying. Unfortunately, compliance is not realistic since the bully is prejudiced, demands are based on whim, and his will changes from one day to the next. What applies to one student doesn't apply to another (a subjective environment). What's demanded one day is prohibited the next. This creates chaos and confusion. The new false position of authority is the very destruction of freedom. As freedom goes, so does peace. Once peace is gone, there can be no safety.

The position of the BIO performed the complete opposite of its stated objective. The only accomplishment of the new anti-bullying position was that it barricaded the avenue of escape for the bullied students. They were no longer free to resist, flee, or group in opposition.

Have you identified the parallel to the divorce and child support machinery?

- The local school district is a representation of our federal government.
- The school security officer represents the executive branch (e.g. the police).
- The principal represents the judge who presides over divorce and family law cases.
- The BIO position represents the State's social agencies (e.g. CAC, CPS, CYFD, CSD, etc.).
- The school bully is a representation of the rebellious spouse.
- The friends of the BIO/school bully symbolize the media, psychologists, therapists, counselors, family law attorneys, Guardian Ad Litems, and others who are biased, entirely complicit, and helpful with the government's agenda.

And all together, this conspiracy barricades the avenue of escape. Similar to Germany's holocaust, there is no escape and no one you can trust.

Packaging False Positions

The rise of artificial positions are conceived and packaged in secrecy by an elite—the rulers of darkness. They justify the existence of a new position using an element of deception that's designed to neutralize opposition. But the stated purpose for its existence is collective and masquerades behind vague language. Ask yourself the following questions to help discern between false or genuine positions of authority:

- Is the occupant of the position accountable to the people or to the legislators?
- Are the powers associated with that position enumerated and clearly defined? Are the enumerated powers made readily available to the public?
- Is the position consistent with constitutional principles? In other words, are the powers limited, disbursed, balanced, and checked?
- Can the occupant of the position exercise his power within the confines of state statutes and constitutional limitations?
- Do the powers authorize the occupant to protect the rights of all individuals?

If you cannot answer "yes" to all questions asked, then no authority was ever delegated to the position(s) in question. Establishing positions through legislative action is only valid if the legislature has constitutional and Biblical authority. False positions, such as CAC, CPS, CYFD, and CSD, have no authority. Their power is not inherent. It's obtained through usurpation.

The ascension of phony positions was the leading stratagem to misconstrue the word "authority." Don't be fooled, but power and authority are separate entities. Power is strength; whereas, authority is the legal power or right to command or to act. Occupants of false positions believe they have legitimate authority, and all their power, they claim, is inherent. However, God's Word trumps their beliefs.

The assertion leveraged by proponents of these false positions claim that their rise was in response to a social necessity. *"Child abuse,"* they say, *"was an epidemic, so new agencies had to be created to handle the situation and protect children."* The propagation of such an argument is an emotional appeal but lacks historical knowledge. A thorough examination of history clearly reveals that government is continually the predecessor to America's social ills, such as easy divorce, rebellion among wives, child abuse, absent fathers, poverty, illiteracy, mental illnesses, etc. Government's actions are intended to produce a reaction in the people. *In other words, our government initiates the cultural shift. It does not respond to it.*

From the numerous phony positions involved with the invasion into my family, the most damning was family court. Contrary to popular opinion, family court preceded wide-spread child abuse and absent fathers. It was not a response to a social problem—it was the creation of a social problem.

But each time the government orchestrates an epidemic, which did not previously exist, it's common for old terms to be resurrected but reassigned with new definitions. This strategic maneuver blinds the people to prevent them from recognizing the government's role. For instance, the well-known term, "fatherless" is one which hoodwinks the great majority of citizens, Patriots, and Christians alike.

The term "fatherless" has been around for ages, but the context in which it's used has recently changed. The Bible records the term "fatherless" 43 times, and in 31 of those instances, it accompanies the word "widow." This is an indication that the man, a husband and father, is no longer living. Webster's 1828 dictionary defines fatherless as being, *"destitute of a living father."* Therefore, we can be certain that in its original and proper context, a *fatherless home* is actually *"a home destitute of a living father."*

Today, our politically correct society employs the term "fatherless" in reference to an absent father, without an explanation to why the father's absent. By shifting it into a new context, the word's definition is being expanded, which increases vagueness. The most common recognition of the phrase "fatherless home" implies, "a home without a father." This definition, however, lacks clarity since it doesn't explain why the home is fatherless. This phrase can equally apply to the father who died protecting his children as well as the father who abandoned his children. These two separate, but completely opposite, circumstances are now lumped into the same category.

The modern use of the term "fatherless" does not accurately describe reality and is, therefore, misleading. This is because it's most commonly associated with an absent father, but is rarely spoken in cases where the father is no longer living. This prank pulled over on humanity is seriously flawed. This error only applies to the word "fatherless" when it refers to an absent father. It's not applicable when utilized within its original and proper Biblical context.

By applying the word "fatherless" to a home or to children with an absent father, the term exempts the role of the mother from the equation by placing the emphasis on the father. Thus, it insinuates she never filed for divorce, requested a protection order, petitioned for sole custody, sought child support, or withheld the children from their father.

So if the mother is exempt and the child isn't to blame, fault has to shift to the only person remaining. Hence, a fatherless home, under its new definition, cunningly suggests that fathers are guilty for abandoning their families as well as any marital problems which led to it. The mother and children are only victims—the politically correct victimhood mindset. This is vastly different than the Biblical use of the term "fatherless."

Family Court: A False Position

As family court emerged to forcibly create single-mother homes and abolish the family unit, undoubtedly, the old Biblical term was resurrected and inserted into a new context to shift the government's criminal actions onto the father. The subtlety of family court is, however, camouflaged behind God's higher power—the judiciary. Family court was never ordained by God. Thus it holds no legitimate authority. All of their power and court orders are usurped, not inherent. The existence of family court has deceived many.

"Is there a way to determine if this particular court is God's higher power held by wicked men or if it's not a higher power at all?" Great question! I believe there is.

Juvenile court, the precursor to family court, was conceived through deception—the false interpretation of *Parens Patriae*. But the early juvenile court system is where the seeds of family court were sown. Ironically, the inception of juvenile court coincides with the emergence of the 'progressive' movement, which rejects the Biblical role of government.

Family court emerged in 1961 and was framed inconsistent with constitutional principles and Biblical law. Power was consolidated at its conception, and it was not limited, disbursed, balanced, or checked. Due process, which requires a jury to protect the innocent, was abandoned.

Family court handles cases involving "family law." However, this law is only an illusion. First, law is passed by legislatures, and judgments are passed by judges. Secondly, the judge's rulings are inconsistent with Biblical principles since the family is already governed by law (Psalms 19:7-11) and a ruler (Genesis 3:16; Ephesians 5:22). Thus, we can rightly conclude that "family law" replaces God's law, and court orders overrule God's orders.

Family court's standard is subjective. Every judge must create his or her own standard, and then choose how to apply that standard depending on the subject brought before them (i.e. applying and enforcing a rule selectively). The nature of family court accumulates all the powers in the hands of one: legislative, executive, and judiciary. But James Madison wisely warned, *"The accumulation of all powers, legislative, executive, and judiciary, in the same hands, whether of one, a few, or many, and whether hereditary, self-appointed, or elective, may justly be pronounced the very definition of tyranny.* "[46]

Family court actually falls outside the structure of the judicial branch. First, the court is not bound by standard judicial practices (e.g. hearsay is admissible, cross examination is quashed). Second, there isn't a higher court to appeal the decision. The only way to have a fresh opportunity to present your case is through the judge's reassignment, retirement, or death. Thus, unjust rulings may provoke the aggrieved individual towards violence since there are no alternatives for peace.

In this realm, one person rules with the consolidation of total and unlimited power over an individual and their family. This is the establishment of a dictatorship in America, completely contrary to our God-ordained representative government. And similar to Adolf Hitler, family court judges are committing genocide against the family unit. They only target the family for extinction. Bachelors and bachelorettes are left alone and not subject to their governing force.

As we have already identified, family court is not part of the judiciary. It masks itself behind the judiciary. This false portrayal is so deceptive that it can actively use the arm of the executive branch to force compliance to unlawful orders.

The deceptive appearance of family court easily persuades well-meaning police officers to break the law unaware. The most common misunderstanding is the discernment between lawful and unlawful warrants. An inherent power of the judiciary, ordained by God, is to check the power of the police—*not* issue warrants.

The police possess an inherent power to enforce God's standards of right and wrong, but due to man's fallen nature, the police cannot be trusted. Therefore, the law restrains them from physically detain-

---

[46] James Madison, "No. 47: The Meaning of the Maxim, Which Requires a Separation of the Departments of Power, Examined and Ascertained," In *The Federalist, The Gideon Edition*, ed. George Carey and James McClellan (Indianapolis: Liberty Fund, 2001).

ing anyone (unless they witnessed the crime) or seizing private property without probable cause. But to prove it, law enforcement officials petition the court with an oath or affirmation in support of their probable cause. If the judge determines that the police are using their power correctly, he signs a warrant. An arrest warrant only removes the restraints of law placed on the arresting officers. This is the only valid and lawful warrant.

This lawful and godly procedure is all scrubbed in family court. Fathers who don't comply with family court edicts, regardless of the circumstances, are treated all the same. Since no statue has been broken, family court judges only issue arrest warrants to impose their will. The court is petitioned by either the recipient of child support or the child support bureaucracy, not law enforcement. The nature of these warrants and their procedure are unlawful on four counts:

- Family court judges are illegitimate and don't possess authority to sign warrants.
- There was no probable cause that a law or statute had been violated.
- Law enforcement didn't petition the court with an oath or affirmation in support of their probable cause.
- The power of the police isn't being checked.

"But isn't failing to obey the judge contempt of court?" Ah, another superficial and scripted line. Let's not darken counsel by words without knowledge. The phrase "contempt of court" has recently shifted to act as a catch all. Without a crime or wrong-doing, "contempt of court" charges must be attributed to justify an arrest and incarceration.

Contempt of court only applies when an individual disrupts judicial proceedings within a courtroom. There are certain rules inside a courtroom for the purpose of maintaining order. If a person continually interrupts or doesn't let others speak, gets physical with anyone, or ignores any other verbal order the judge issues to maintain order, the person can be charged and arrested for contempt of court.

When this happens, keep in mind that everybody becomes a witness, the court proceedings are recorded, and the arrest is made on the spot by a police officer who witnessed the unruly behavior. (There's no arrest warrant.) This is a closed case. But once a person exits the courtroom, all of those circumstances disappear.

Contempt of court is solely used to maintain order in the courtroom, *not* to maintain social order. So when a judge issues an arrest warrant for "contempt of court," he or she is actually ignoring the fact that there's been no contempt and there are no witnesses. In essence, the judge denies an individual of due process by charging them with contempt of court in order to make it a closed case, so a defense isn't possible.

Suppose you paid the Child Support Division your monthly support amount, but a crooked bureaucrat pocketed the money. Since the payment was never applied to your account, the CSD assumes you didn't pay, so they petition the court. They show valid proof that no payment ever applied to your account. With this evidence, the judge assumes that you defied his order, so he issues an arrest warrant against you. But for the warrant to appear valid, he charges you with "contempt of court." But this is not a charge you can defend against. "Contempt of court" charges are automatic verdicts of guilty. You don't have an opportunity to provide bank statements or receipts that show you paid.

"What about cases in civil court?" Okay, so let's say you were found guilty of injuring another person in some way, and so the judge orders you to pay restitution. If you fail to comply with the judge's order, you're summoned back to court. You are permitted a defense. Maybe you paid the person, and they're lying about it. So here's your chance to prove it. But if you're found guilty for failing to comply with the judge's order, the judge might sentence you for a certain amount of time in jail. You would be arrested on the spot. There's no arrest warrant.

What should the police do if they are handed an unlawful warrant to execute? They have a duty and responsibility to interpose on behalf of the citizen and refuse to enforce the warrant, irrespective of what the public says or what the government wants. The State always demands unconditional obedience, regardless of the crimes committed in the execution of those demands.

The subtle invention of juvenile and family court was specifically crafted for the government invasion into private life, the take-over of the child, and the overthrow of God's ordained power. Its success is the result of the entire world being deceived (Revelation 12:9). Just because they look like judges, dress like judges, talk like judges, and sit on the bench like judges doesn't make them judges. Judges presiding over family court cases are only impostors, because they occupy a false position of authority.

Family court serves only one purpose: to throw you out of your position of authority so they can sit on your throne, rule over your kingdom, enslave all of your subjects (children), and steal all of your kingdom's wealth. When your enemy deceptively infiltrates or violently conquers the high position within your jurisdiction, your empire will collapse. Understand this: family court and their hateful bureaucracies aren't your friends nor are they friends of your children. Their hatred for families and children are so intense, they seek and destroy one family after the next. They're your enemies and your children's worst nightmare. Following their conquest, the usurper might possess power that you once held, but they lack the possession of authority that you still hold.

CHAPTER FOURTEEN

BATTLE LINE 2: THE POSSESSION OF AUTHORITY

For he is the minister of God to thee for good. But if thou do that which is evil, be afraid; for he beareth not the sward in vain: for he is the minister of God, a revenger to execute wrath upon him that doeth evil." (Romans 13:4)

Paul's focus shifts toward the occupant of the position by characterizing the "minister of God" as the prerequisite to possessing authority. Only an individual can be a minister of God; not a position. Webster's 1828 dictionary defines minister as, *"Properly, a chief servant; hence, an agent appointed to transact or manage business under the authority of another..."* Paul wants us to know that a ruler only possesses authority if their actions are managed under the authority of Scripture.

The apostle repeats himself twice (vs. 4-6), and he does so for emphasis. To be a minister of God, an individual must be in subjection to God's law himself. Otherwise, his or her actions are conducted under the power of Satan—these rulers possess no authority because they're ministers of the devil. And Jesus actually refers to the devil as their father (John 8:40-44).

The devil protects and reserves his false positions for his ministers. This is because he executes his power through them. On the rarity that a child of God manages to slip through and occupies a false position of authority, he must either allow the devil to work through him or suffer the loss of his position. He cannot serve God and Satan.

But the devil's ministers work overtime to infiltrate and occupy God's positions of authority. This is full-blown war. The devil and his servants are, metaphorically speaking, charging with guns and swords to kill anyone who stands in their way. They want power and they want it bad. But occupying God's positions doesn't mean the occupant possesses authority. Without authority from God, the power they execute is from Satan.

The Delegation of Authority

Webster's 1828 dictionary defines authority as, "legal power or a right to command or to act." Therefore, all authority is delegated. The delegation of authority is the peaceful transfer of inherent power. Inherent power transferred from an individual without their consent is usurped power.

From the beginning of time, God delegated authority to the individual—the power to govern oneself (Genesis 2:16). When the individual extends his authority to civil rulers through elections, that official becomes a representative. Representative government originated from God (Exodus 18:13-27), not America's founders. The concept of representation is known as "the consent of the governed." The individual is not governed without their consent. The power to govern oneself is paramount to all authorities in civil government.

When an individual extends their authority to a representative, the ruler is elevated to a position of authority. The only authority that can be extended is the authority that God has delegated to that individual. If a person, acting on their own, has no authority to behave in a certain manner, that action cannot be delegated to the government.

For example: God has delegated to each individual the authority to protect his property from intruders. Therefore, this authority can be extended to his representative. The representative can pass a law to protect private property from intruders. If a person breaks the law, the executive enforces the law's standard, and the judiciary judges the lawbreaker according to the law. But the delegation of this authority revolves around the law passed by the representative, who is only exercising the God-given right on behalf of the individual. This is the inherent power, which originated from God and is executed by His ministers.

Since God has delegated no authority to the individual to steal private property, this power cannot be extended to the representative. So anytime the legislature passes some law that violates the God-given rights of an individual, the transfer of that power is not delegated, it was usurped. And usurped power always originates from the devil and is enforced by his ministers.

"But what if a government employee or official is using their position to accomplish a good deed?" This question may sound appealing, but it makes the assumption that the governmental action, from the means to the end has already been established as "good." Therefore, it shifts focus off of the means to achieve the end.

For instance, feeding your children is a good deed and something God requires from parents (1 Timothy 5:8). But suppose you rob a bank, kill a couple of people in the process, and then use the money at the grocery store to feed your children. The means you applied to achieve feeding your children were bad. You broke several laws State law and God's law. Government actions considered "good" only focus on the end, but ignore the means to achieve the end.

Since God forbids mankind from taking, by stealth or by force, what belongs to another (Exodus 20:15), He delegates no such authority to the individual. No person, acting on their own, has any authority to extract child support payments. Therefore, this power cannot be delegated to the government. Government force was never ordained by God to support children. This is beyond the State's jurisdiction.

The ministers of God serve one purpose and one purpose only: *"to execute wrath upon him that doeth evil."* Attention to detail reveals that ministers of God don't prevent someone from doing evil. Anything preventative is a violation of an individual's right to choose (e.g. crime prevention). Civil rulers are only supposed to execute wrath after the evil act; not before. This method of execution is known as "crime deterrence."

Each individual possesses the authority to deter crime and intervene, when necessary, to stop evil. So a group of individuals, such as a neighborhood, can freely work together to exercise their right to deter crime and evil acts, just so long as they don't prohibit another person from freely exercising his or her right to choose—even if that individual chooses evil. Once the person freely makes his choice and begins committing evil, citizens can now exercise their individual authority to intervene. The authority of crime deterrence can be extended to the representatives. The government's Biblical responsibility to execute wrath is the most effective crime deterrent method available.

"But the harm has already been done. Isn't it better to be safe than sorry?" This is another question that appeals to the emotions. What if I perceive that my neighbor is going to harm me in the future? So to protect myself and prevent this future hostility, I break into his house and kill him. That's not self-defense. It's murder. The "playing it safe" mindset evokes aggression and violence.

When you ask the wrong questions, you'll arrive at the wrong answers.

Packaging False Authorities

Higher crime originates from the government in two ways: (1) government refuses to execute wrath on those who do evil (the Biblical method of crime deterrence), and (2) government actively provokes others to perpetrate evil (through aggressive laws, policies, and orders). The school victim in our story was deliberately provoked by those with power to commit evil.

This analysis is pertinent to our understanding since God's ministers only deter crime. And to possess authority, one must be a minister of God.

The "better safe than sorry" or "playing it safe" are superficially scripted lines. This is the heart of crime prevention methods. Family court employs this method when ruling in the "best interest of the child" and "protecting children as their first priority." In theory, they want to prevent child molestation, so they issue a restraining order. This isn't a past crime, or else the perpetrator would be brought up on criminal charges and convicted. Rather, they perceive this as a future crime; thus, the State restrains the father from future contact.

The future, however, can only be predicted or prophesied, not proven. This lack of proof, however, creates a problem for the State. Since the government is "divine" and all-knowing, they feel strongly about the father's criminal tendencies. But to justify their actions in "protecting your children," the State must fabricate a story and manufacture evidence. They seek to catch the father red-handed, and in this manner, he won't have a chance to harm his family. Strangely, it appears that nobody gets hurt, except the father and his children.

This crime preventive measure, however, produces a lesser known side-effect that I have not yet discussed. By terminating the loving relationship between father and child as a mere precaution, the child won't understand why he's gone, where he went, or why everybody is saying that he's a bad guy. The child only knows one thing: the person they love is missing.

Their father doesn't come home. The child is inundated with comments about his father's faults, the misrepresentation of those faults, and the distortion of his father's actions.

So their emotions of hatred, anger, resentment, and bitterness are kindled by the government's invasion into his home. These negative and harmful feelings smolder inside the child well into their adult lives. The child doesn't actually understand what's happening to them or who's doing it. But after some time, they'll actually possess false memories about being abused, molested, or raped. (This is the poison of propaganda.)

The child will begin to think they know what's going on when in reality, they don't. Their false memories and lack of understanding is exploited by the perpetrator and government. These negative emotions, however, function as proof that a crime was committed —even when there were no negative emotions at the time of termination.

As the child ages, his or her negative emotions, which are still smoldering, become more visible. They have difficulty focusing, remembering events, and their ability to reason or think critically erodes. Their grades in school drop, and they'll become withdrawn. They'll have troubles developing intimate and meaningful relationships, which leads to poor choices and bad behavior. They'll tend to hang out with the wrong crowd, which often results in drug and alcohol use and abuse as well as teen pregnancy.

Of course, any psychologist will tell you that these are signs of child abuse and neglect. But the devil's ministers hold high positions to safeguard and shield the destruction of children. This is why the crimes perpetrated by the mother are projected onto the father. If he becomes the scapegoat, then the infliction of child abuse by the perpetrator will not be stopped, but rather, furthered.

Consequently, children may live as if life has no purpose—no true meaning or value. Jesus equates anger with murder (Matthew 5:21-23), but the Bible also equates hatred with murder (1 John 3:15). Both, anger and hatred are conditions of the heart. Nobody commits murder without first harboring anger and hatred within their heart. The government's crime prevention actions are intended to foster anger and hatred within your child's heart. Therefore, we can justly conclude that the government's invasion into your home is extremely violent, by its very nature.

Even if the child grows up and never commits physical murder, they'll use words to hurt others and tear them down. That's the method Amy used against me and my children. That's what my children are learning to do. Their behavior will be mindless, because their words and deeds are without thought or reason. And sadly, they won't be able to stay married. They'll start living like an animal—unable to govern themselves. Then sooner or later, when a combination of their choices confronts the perfect environment, violence erupts. It's like dumping gasoline onto a smoldering fire. The divorce industry is producing its own market.

False Positions House False Authorities

The actions of many government bureaucracies, such as the CAC, CPS, CYFD, and CSD are done in secret. These agencies (and many others) serve to provoke by executing aggressive laws, policies, and orders. The function to execute laws is reserved for the executive branch of government. This is why these agencies are part of the executive branch and overseen by the state Governor.

In any case, being provocative explains why their deeds are hidden. Why wasn't I given the opportunity to speak with the CYFD before they published their verdict against me? I didn't even know that a report had been produced until I was waylaid in court almost two and one half years after the report's publication date. There was no misunderstanding. It wasn't an honest mistake. It was strategically planned and executed with malice. The report didn't surface sooner because it was only ammunition. Similar to a sniper, my ex-wife wanted to shoot at just the right time—not to early and not too late. CYFD is only a weapon manned by cogs in a machine—ministers of the devil.

CAC is just as secretive with their operations. Every story has two sides. And it's natural for the story teller to slant the story in their favor. So why wasn't I allowed to share the other side of the story with the CAC? Similar to the position of the BIO in our novel "The End of School Bullying," the CAC dresses in regular clothes to blend in with the community, but their actions are conducted in secret.

The proponents of CAC levy false claims that these professionals have training in child relations and forensic interviews that the police don't have. Yet how can these "professionals" perform their job functions with only one side of the story? The CAC's alleged "forensic training" doesn't replace experience, practice, or public interaction during the performance of their duties. Contrary to the CAC, the police are visible, are easily recognizable in their uniforms, and interacts with the people they serve on a regular basis. This is vastly different than government agencies like CAC who perform their tasks in the dark.

During my New Mexico case, one of the children interviewed by CAC exclaimed adamantly that none of the accusations against me were true. With an uncooperative child, the CAC paused the recording. Eight minutes later, the recording resumed, and that little nine-year-old boy *changed his entire story!* Now he accused me. What happened during those eight minutes? Was he threatened? Was he bribed? Was he accused? Who was present in addition to the interviewer? How come the defense couldn't be present to ensure the integrity of the interview? No one outside that room will ever know, but this is the very definition of a dark conspiracy.

Later on, when my attorney interviewed that boy, he went back to his original story and asserted that there was no sexual impropriety. Around the same week, but on a different day, he also interviewed my eldest child. But what I find striking is that the prosecution was present. Why weren't we afforded the same level of privacy? Because their interview tactics were devious, and they wanted to ensure we weren't attempting to sway her statements or rekindle the bond I had with my daughter before all this began. Otherwise, she could be the one to change her story when they least expected it. Ultimately, they implemented double standards.

If the CAC intends to manipulate language or practice the art of verbal engineering, the defense cannot be present. The last thing they want is to get caught framing an innocent man for a crime that never occurred.

My ex-wife had no understanding that the CAC and CYFD, as well as the other agencies and family court, placed her life in severe danger. To prevent me from committing a future crime against my own children, they were attempting to provoke me to commit evil against my ex-wife instead. Although, Amy is blinded to this reality, God still demonstrated His goodness to her. What could have happened to Amy if she had married someone else? Only God knows.

Our government agencies are professionals at provoking others to commit evil and create crime. How many school shootings are the result of family court rulings and their bureaucratic accomplices from years prior? Undoubtedly, America's increase of crime is a direct result of government intervention into private life. Crime prevention is already a failed experiment. To return to a safe environment, we must employ the Biblical solution of crime deterrence.

Crime deterrence is visible and effective at protecting the innocent. The police interact with residents of their community on a regular basis. They are easily identified by wearing uniforms. Even young children see them and recognize the police as the good guys who protect people from the bad guys. Hence, real child abuse should only be reported to the police. As the police investigate, they'll hear both sides of the argument from both parties. They can obtain evidence from both sides (evidence of guilt or exoneration).

If the abuse appears solid, the suspect will be criminally charged. The prosecutor will prosecute. The court proceedings allow the suspect to cross-examine his accuser, present evidence, and call witnesses in his defense. The jury renders a verdict. And finally, the judge passes judgment.

The police and the justice system are in view of the public. Investigations and the prosecution of an individual is not withheld or done in secret. Both sides (the accuser and the accused) can stay informed. They can see what's happening and present their arguments. And if the defendant feels the court erred in its proceedings or new evidence emerges following his conviction, he can always appeal his verdict to a higher court. When nothing is invisible, crimes are easier to expose while the innocent are protected.

If you'll remember, in my case, I dealt with a corrupt detective and a prosecutor who was ambitious to prosecute but reluctant to exonerate. This system can handle a certain level of corruption and still protect the innocent.

This criminal system is how wrath gets executed against those who do evil. But what happens if this system isn't being used to prosecute the guilty? If you recall, Amy filed several false police reports, committed numerous counts of perjury, engaged in a pattern of parental alienation (the most severe form of child abuse), and even tampered with a witnesses testimonial evidence by threatening to murder (chapter 3, February 27, 2018)—*all criminal offenses*! Yet the system isn't being used as God intended.

The criminal justice system is often used to condemn the innocent with little or no regard to the truth of the crime committed. Consider how many men in recent years have been freed from prison for a crime they didn't commit. Freed after serving 15 years…20 years…25 years… And once they have a patsy to take the fall for the crime, the guilty go free. Why do judges, prosecutors, and police officers want criminals free in our society? Often times, they're engaged in criminal behavior themselves. There are honest judges, prosecutors, and police officers who strive to protect the innocent and do their very best to convict the criminals. But the corrupt officials will not prosecute the guilty. And the further our nation strays from the truth, the more corruption will spread through our justice system. When crime isn't being deterred, it will only increase.

Our American justice system has been in place since the beginning of our Republic and has worked quite nicely to maintain a low crime rate. So there's already a system to protect children. The CAC and CYFD claim to "protect" children, but refuse to protect the innocent. Their words are inconsistent with their actions. How can they protect a child, while refusing to protect the innocent? This is the difference between crime prevention (government's solution) and crime deterrence (God's solution).

But when one plots to commit evil against another, wouldn't they despise a system that protects their victims? As a result, these criminals must bypass our judicial process so their victims cannot be protected, and they do not find themselves being prosecuted through a criminal system which they detest.

We can rest assured that our rulers who have delegated authority from God deter crime only. These are the true ministers of God.

All others holding God's position of authority may possess its inherent power, but they lack any legitimate authority from God.

To decrease crime and protect America's children, a good place to start would be to dissolve the CAC, CPS, CYFD, CSD, and family court in all 50 states. Any refusal to abolish these agencies is nothing short of the perpetration of crimes against children. Period!

False Authorities Infiltrate God's Positions

False positions of authority are always occupied by false authorities. And the power of false authorities is always usurped. However, false positions cannot rise on their own. Satan must infiltrate God's positions and execute its inherent powers to establish a false position with usurped power. This is important to recognize because Satan is under God's authority.

Rulers who occupy God's positions inherit the inherent powers associated with their position, but unless they're a minister of God, they don't hold any legitimate authority.

The devil's ministers steal God's higher positions through deceit and fraud. (A minister of God doesn't obtain a higher position in this manner.) Once the wicked rise into God's positions, they turn against the very people who put them in office (Proverbs 29:2). This is most effective by using the inherent powers to create false positions that usurp the freewill of the people. Nevertheless, the end result is always the same: global domination and the enslavement of humanity.

To reiterate: The possession of legitimate authority is strictly reserved to the rulers who manage their actions and perform their duties under Biblical authority. No ruler possesses God's authority when they exceed their Biblical jurisdiction.

Family court is a false position of authority, concealed behind God's higher position, the judiciary. But family court was established by legislative action. It did not and could not rise on its own.

God ordained the state legislative branches as His higher power. That position is accompanied with an inherent power to vote on legislation. Casting a vote (any vote) for the Standard Family Court Act is an inherent power. But was the passage of this act within their Biblical jurisdiction? To rephrase, were the members of the legislature performing their duties under Biblical authority when casting an "Aye" or "Yea" vote for the Standard Family Court Act?

The text of the Standard Family Court Act would violate numerous Biblical and constitutional principles, such as the consolidation of power and establishing a court to rule the family contrary to the government of the family that God already set up. The very text of the act can answer our question. No legislator possessed authority to cast a "Aye" vote.

"Doesn't the legislature have authority to establish new courts?" Of course they do. This authority has been delegated to them by the Constitution. The federal Constitution authorizes Congress to establish inferior courts from time to time (Federal Constitution, Art 1, Sec 8; Art 3, Sec 1). The New Mexico Constitution (Art 6, Sec 1) also delegates this authority to its lawmakers. Every state Constitution delegates this authority. This constitutional authority also conforms to the Biblical example found in Exodus 18:13-27. Establishing new courts doesn't go beyond their Biblical jurisdiction. However, the operations of family court does.

The underlying purpose for legislatures to establish inferior courts is to account for the increasing population. A population increase will cause a rise in disputes and controversies with a greater need for more courts to handle the case load. So we can rightly conclude that state legislatures do possess authority to establish courts, but their authority is limited to *inferior courts*.

"Is family court an inferior court?" The definition of "inferior" is to be lower in position—subordinate. Thus, an inferior court is a lower court that is placed beneath another court. Also, inferior courts must adhere to standard judicial practices and protocol. If they stray from the rules, an appeal can be made to a higher court, which has the power to overturn any judgment from an inferior court. So if a lower court wants their judgments to stand, they follow strict guidelines.

Family court, as we have already determined, does not conform to this model. Since family court is not an inferior court, their establishment falls outside the boundaries of legislative authority and Biblical jurisdiction. The ministers of the devil never created this court to dispense justice, but rather, to murder the family unit. God established the family with a built-in government, and therefore, family court is unnecessary.

Overthrowing God's Authority

The family unit is already governed by the husband (Genesis 3:16). He's the head of his wife and has the final say in all family matters (Ephesians 5:23-24). The head is a representation of the decision-making process through logical reasoning. The man may extend his authority to his wife as is necessary and proper for maintaining the home, child rearing, or other duties. But in all circumstances, she's subject to him (1 Peter 3:1, 5).

The women's liberation movement rejects this Biblical doctrine. They claim that if men possess power over their wives, then women are oppressed. Based on collectivist principles, this is class warfare, which is overwhelmingly initiated by women. This feminist ideology never presents an argument, just superficially scripted lines. But they never comment about the free choice women make when entering into a marital contract.

But how does one "free themselves" from the bondage of marriage? They must turn to the State, but by doing so, they are not actually freeing themselves. The State is a social apparatus of compulsion and coercion that induces people to abide by the rules of life in society. It has a monopoly on violent action. So by inviting the State into the home, the wife violently throws off the freedom to be loved and cared for and willingly shackles herself to the chain of dependency and the weight of control.

But if she isn't married to her husband, she'll be married to the State. If she isn't governed by her husband, she'll be governed by the State. If her husband isn't her head, the State will be her head. If she isn't in subjection to her husband, she'll be in subjection to the State. By transferring the power from her husband to the State, she is actually sacrificing her freedom and replacing it with oppression.

Historically, the husband always stood in between the State and his family. He represented his family. He handled all the legal issues. His wife and children weren't subject to the governing force of the State. (This is why women weren't allowed to vote in the early days of our Republic.)

When the husband died, friends, family, or the church rushed in to take his place. They understood the danger she and the children faced without a husband. (This was prominent during the apostle Paul's day under the rule of the Roman Empire. America didn't face this problem because of its Biblical foundations and the decentralization of governmental power.)

When government force is used to replace the husband, the woman is not freeing herself, but rather, she's enslaving herself. Social freedom can only be found within the confines of a Biblical marriage.

As the feminist ideology creeps into the home, it divides the unity between a husband and his wife, which drives an increase in family disputes. The individual who is governed must rebel against higher authority if the home is to be divided. Therefore, to pit husbands and wives against each other, the government must pursue the female. Failure of leadership doesn't divide the home, but rebellion against authority does.

Now don't misunderstand me. I'm not saying that men never do anything wrong. I have witnessed husbands and fathers mistreating their wives and children, and it grieves me. But failing to govern your family properly isn't the same thing as division. If the husband is a drunk, fails to provide for his family, or neglects his wife, it's true that he's failing as the head, but it's not a division.

On the other hand, if he makes a decision in which his wife disagrees, and so she goes against him to do what she thinks is right, the home is now divided. He's going one direction and she's going another. But whether she's right or not is irrelevant. She has a moral responsibility before God to yield to the authority of her husband and allow him to make the decision. Her refusal to submit to the higher power is what divides the home.

Since the husband, ordained by God, has the final word in the home, then family disputes, in all reality, don't exist. A family dispute is nothing more than a rebellion—a defiance against God's authority in the home. But by changing the definition of rebellion and calling it a "dispute," justification has been made to create a new court. This is important because the purpose of a court is to handle controversies and disputes. So by creating disputes through the redefinition of a word, a special court has to be established to hear these "disputes."

The passage of the Standard Family Court Act was more than just an assault against freedom; this was an engagement against God's social order and His law. More than 50 years later, people are crying for peace, but there is no peace. The very machines created by our state legislatures to bring about peace (e.g. CAC, CPS, CYFD, CSD, family court, etc.) do more than any other governmental entity to destroy peace.

The family cannot exist without a ruler. This is why the abolition of the family only requires removing the father. By pitting the wife against her husband, the State produces a state of anarchy. This is accomplished by tempting or wooing the wife with easy divorce (no-fault legislation), government-created rights (women's rights), and appealing entitlements (welfare and child support). The government-created chaos within the family then leaks into society creating the illusion that mankind cannot govern themselves and must be controlled to maintain social order. So family court, in their "infinite wisdom," is restructuring society to create the perfect world—a world where God doesn't exist. But where there is no God, there can be no peace.

Single mothers and their children becomes the perfect, unsuspecting avenue of approach. By offering numerous rewards, the temptation is overwhelming for many wives. The more aggressive she is, the greater her reward. By rejecting her husband's rule, she is ruled by the State without her consent. And the children's minds are just blank slates for the government to write on and impose its New World Order.

A mother holding the position of authority isn't necessarily violating God's law. God is more concerned with how the position is acquired, not who's holding the position. Mothers who usurped the power of their husband lack the legitimate possession of authority. (This family structure no longer exists.)

However, single mothers who have lost their husbands due to circumstances beyond their control have inherited the position of authority. (This family structure is still intact.) There was no conquest for power and they were not made single by choice. Her authority has been delegated to her by God.

The mother who inherits her position has the power to reject the State's control. But the mother who usurps her position is forced to accept the State's control since overthrowing her husband requires the power of the State.

Amazingly, the possession of authority (ministers of God) actually strengthens the occupant holding the position of authority. This is not an additional power. It just strengthens the powers that the ruler already possesses because their source of strength is God. God's strength threatens the State's New World Order, so the legitimate authority over the family unit must be extinguished, and a false authority must rise up.

The mother who ascends to replace the father may possess the inherent power within the position she's holding, but she lacks the additional strength granted to those who actually possess authority. In other words, God has rejected her as ruler over the family and children. To compensate her weakness, she must utilize the power of the State to impose her will. But to tap into the State's power, she must play the role of the victim. The source of her strength is Satan.

Distinct Jurisdictions of Authority

It is important to note that Romans 13 is directed towards civil government, not family government. Although there are many similarities in regards to the position of authority, we also observe some slight differences with the possession of authority.

The smallest governmental structure—the family—is the only unit where God specifically delegates authority to the husband (Genesis 3:16; Ephesians 5:23; Titus 2:3-5). Contrary to popular opinion, God does not delegate authority to the woman, nor does she possess equal authority or rule in the home. Genesis 3:16 tells us that the husband will rule over his wife, and Ephesians 5:23 clearly states that the husband is the head of his wife. If he's the head and she's to be in subjection to him (1 Peter 3:1), how can she possess equal authority?

The Biblical command for children to obey their parents (Ephesians 6:4) rightly includes mothers. And God wouldn't give such a command if she didn't possess authority over the children. However, there's a difference between the husband's governing rule over his family and the wife's authority over his children.

Remember, all authority is delegated. So the husband can extend his authority to his wife to watch over and care for his children during his absence.

The *American Left* loves to claim that this Biblical structure of the family enslaves and perpetrates violence against women. But this claim is completely detached from reality. A female is not ruled by force. She is ruled by consent. This consent is the marital contract. If she disapproves of this Biblical structure, she is free to exercise her right to remain single.

On the flip side, a woman's conquest for equal rights, equal authority, and equal strength actually necessitates she rule a man by force and without his consent. In other words, she accuses him of the very action she is guilty of herself. These feminists are enslaving and perpetrating violence against men and their children by violating the Biblical family structure.

Since God delegated authority to the husband, he retains his possession of authority unless there is a voluntary termination, forfeiture, or death. These actions can include abandonment, writing of divorcement, giving away custody, or a criminal conviction—grounds easily provable under the fault-based divorce system.

Now, we often see husbands and fathers who aren't in subjection to God's law themselves, but that still does not negate the authority delegated to them. This is not a question of possessing authority, but rather, the wielding of authority. A man always possesses authority over his family, but he exercises his authority when he conforms to the laws of God, and he exceeds his authority when he contradicts the laws of God.

The similarities between family government and civil government, in relation to the position of authority, are as follows:

- Inherent power is accompanied with the position of authority, not the possession.
- Occupying the position of authority naturally increases power; losing the position decreases power.
- Rising into the position of authority by conquest (force or deception) is strictly to gain power or wealth at the expense of others.
- Holding the position of authority does not automatically grant the possession.

The contrast between family government and civil government, in relation to the possession of authority, reveal the following:

- Authority delegated to the husband (family)—Authority delegated to God's ministers (civil).
- Authority can be inherited (family)—Authority is strictly reserved (civil).
- Retains possession of authority, even if he loses his position (family)—Loses possession of authority if he loses his position (civil).
- Authority is extended *from* the ruler (family)—Authority is extended *to* the ruler (civil).

Family court may have the power to overthrow the father out of his position of authority; nevertheless, they're powerless to strip away his possession of authority. Fathers who possess authority over their children but aren't occupying the higher position naturally results in a loss of power to exercise their authority.

Family court, their judges, and their orders are illegitimate and unlawful. Freedom from enslavement requires an act of resistance. And in the words of Patrick Henry, *"Is life so dear, or peace so sweet, as to be purchased at the price of chains and slavery? Forbid it, Almighty God! I know not what course others may take; but as for me, give me liberty or give me death!"*

CHAPTER FIFTEEN

THE COURAGE TO RESIST

Don't confuse resistance with rebellion, because it's not the same thing. These words should not be used interchangeably. According to Webster's 1828 dictionary, rebellion is *"open resistance to lawful authority."* The key phrase is "lawful authority." Therefore, it would be impossible to rebel against family court. However, resistance literally means *"to stand against; to act in opposition or to oppose."*

The act of resistance is grounded in the absolute truth of God's Word. We are commanded to resist and also to comply. Resisting when you should be complying, and complying when you should be resisting can have devastating consequences. So it behooves us to learn the difference and apply these truths.

In our culture, resistance is a term that's applied inconsistently. It's usually based on the individual's perception of right and wrong at that very moment in time, which can easily be swayed by inventing new phrases or redefining old words. Its relativistic interpretation changes with the wind. This is why lawful resistance leaves a bad taste in many mouths.

But regardless of what other people think, God still requires proper resistance. If your resistance is lawful and conducted in the power of Christ, God will bless your efforts.

In James' epistle, he writes, *"Submit yourselves therefore to God. Resist the devil, and he will flee from you."* (James 4:7). The devil can approach us through several different avenues. He can access us directly through our thoughts and emotions. He can gain entry through our televisions, internet, and smart phones. He can pass through others who have contact with us, such as our family, friends, neighbors, and even preachers. He can even reach us through government officials and court orders. Through all circumstances, God commands us to resist him, regardless of the route he takes.

Jesus was tempted three times by the devil, but resisted each time (Matthew 4:1-11). And we're suppose to follow in the footsteps of Christ (Matthew 16:24; John 8:12). If you read this passage, you'll notice that Satan quoted Scripture on the second temptation. Christ wasn't resisting His own Word; rather, He was resisting the devil.

It's Biblical for fathers to support their children. In fact, that's part of God's design and social order. However, refusing to pay child support is not the same thing as failing to support your children. Defying a child support order, isn't resisting the Biblical principle of child support; rather, it's resisting the temptation of the devil. Satan just perverts the Bible and God's social order to tempt us.

Again, we find in Paul's letter to the Ephesians, he tells us to *"Put on the whole armor of God that ye may be able to stand against the wiles of the devil."* (Ephesians 6:11). "To stand against" is to oppose, to resist. Resistance is, therefore, not an outward expression; it's self-defense. But to defend yourself, you must gird your loins about with truth.

In Bible times, people wore tunics which would reach down to their ankles. This made it difficult to go into battle. To gird up your loins meant that you would hoist all the fabric above your knees. Then gather the extra material in front so that the tunic was snug against your backside. Pull the fabric between your legs to the rear. It would feel much like a diaper. Gather half the material in each hand and wrap them around your legs, bringing them to the front. Finally, you would tie the two handfuls together. You now have the maneuverability to fight in battle.

Since this warfare is spiritual, you gird your loins with truth. Paul then proceeds to tell us about the different parts of the armor and how to put them on. I urge all of my readers to study Ephesians 6:10-18.

The lack of knowledge and understanding neutralizes well-meaning citizens. And sadly, those who aren't fighting try to discourage others from fighting. But don't let that stop you from employing lawful and Biblical resistance. The darker your circumstance, the brighter God's Word appears.

American citizens have been taught from early childhood to respect and obey the law, so the concept of resistance represents defiance and rebellion to anyone whose loins aren't girt about with truth.

Tyranny always starts with the censorship of truth. It's easy to point towards visible sources of censorship, such as Facebook, Twitter, CNN, NBC, New York Times, Washington Post, etc. But how often have we been guilty of the same thing?

Take these topics, for example, where the wrong side is embraced, and the truth is censored:

- False: Abraham Lincoln was one of the greatest presidents in U.S. history. Truth: Lincoln was a tyrant who imprisoned political enemies and destroyed America's voluntary union.
- False: God put George H. W. Bush in the White House (implying that's he's righteous in God's sight.) Truth: George H. W. and his son were members of a secret society known as "The Order of Skull and Bones." The society controls American politics and works to overthrow God's influence in America.
- False: Our service members are fighting to protect our freedoms. Truth: War is a pretext to steal our freedoms. The United States created the enemies she fights. Perpetual warfare is the goal, not national defense.

The censorship of truth always originates with the higher echelons of government. Following the generations that have been presented with only one side of the story—the false side—whether in school textbooks, newspapers, magazines, radio, or television outlets, thinking patterns among the populous have changed.

Alternate thoughts and differing viewpoints give you a standard of comparison. But without the freedom to share the truth (or receive the truth), resistance, in many minds, equals defiance and rebellion.

Misconceptions about Biblical Resistance

Prior to discussing your right and obligation to resist, I would first like to address two misconceptions about Biblical resistance.

The first misconception is found in Romans 13:2, *"Whosoever, therefore resisteth the power, resisteth the ordinance of God: and they that resist shall receive to themselves damnation."*

Keep in mind that the "power" Paul is speaking about is inherent power executed under God's authority. James commands us to resist the usurped power enacted under Satan's deceitfulness (James 4:7).

The devil is a very powerful spiritual force, so it's important to discern truth (inherent power ordained by God) from error (usurped power seized by Satan).

Any governmental law, order, or policy that violates the Word of God is from the devil. Hence, it should be resisted, even if the name of the action has changed. This name change always originates from the devil. Just take these examples:

The government might say, *"You're not stealing, you're garnishing wages."* That's a lie from the pit of Hell. Without a lawful conviction under judicial proceedings, garnishing wages is theft.

What about, *"You're not kidnapping children; you're protecting them from their father."* That's another lie from the pit of Hell. Without a criminal conviction in a court of law, taking children from their father is kidnapping.

Paul's not speaking about the devil's power, he's talking about the inherent power that's associated with God's higher position from verse one. God's standards to resist must meet at least one of the two criteria. One, the position cannot be God's higher position. (Tip: If the position houses collectivist principles, then it's not God's.) Two, the power cannot be an inherent power. (Tip: If the power is used to compel or force action, it violates freewill and is, therefore, not inherent.)

Note: All inherent power is attached to God's higher positions. But positions not from God don't possess any inherent power. Their only power is usurped.

A proper interpretation of the preceding verse (detailed in chapter 13) reveals an interesting fact from the second verse. To receive damnation, you would have to resist God's higher power, which are the inherent powers associated with God's position of authority. By resisting the inherent power (e.g. resisting arrest), you would be resisting the ordinance of God. By contrast, resisting false authorities or resisting power which in *not* inherent with God's position of authority would then be excluded from God's damnation.

Interestingly, Paul uses the word "resist." His other epistles tell wives to "submit" (Ephesians 5:22), children and servants are to "obey" (Colossians 3:20, 22), and he advises the aged women to teach the young women to be "obedient" (Titus 2:3-5). Yet, Paul uses a different word with regards to citizens or subjects in relation to their civil authority. Why?

Submission is the act of allowing an individual to make decisions; whereas, obedience is the act of complying with those decisions. Submission and obedience can only apply to individuals, not power. Power is strength, and only strength can be resisted. This understanding reveals that Paul only warns us against resisting God's inherent powers, *not* the occupant of His higher position.

Paul's statement is conditional. If any person resists God's higher power (the inherent powers associated with His position), that resistance is a resistance of God's ordinance and they shall receive damnation. By parity of reason, if any person resists Satan's powers (false authorities and usurped powers), that resistance is not a resistance of God's ordinance and they shall not receive damnation.

Paul's focus in verse 2 is on the inherent powers established by God, not the occupant of his position. Paul doesn't shift focus to the occupant until verse 3.

Peter tells us to submit to rulers who are sent by God for the punishment of evildoers (1 Peter 2:13-14). Well, a minister of God (Paul's term) would certainly be sent by God (Peter's term). Therefore, the righteous occupants of God's position of authority are the only rulers we must submit to.

The issue is settled; Scripture is clear.

- Do not resist the inherent powers attached with God's position of authority.
- Submit only to rulers who are the ministers of God—sent by God to punish evil.

Proper and lawful resistance entails this understanding between the position of authority and the possession of authority.

Now that we have arrived at the proper interpretation of Romans 13:2, which provided us with much more clarity, it's time to turn our attention to the second misconception about Biblical resistance found in Mark 12:17, *"...Render to Caesar the things that are Caesar's, and to God the things that are God's..."*

A common theme among the church is that every action government demands are things that actually belong to government. As if government will never ask for the things that are God's. This thought, however, is only from man's imagination; it's fantasy. Wouldn't it be nice though to live under the perfect government, with perfect rule, and perfect justice? But history validates that government has a tendency to demand the things that are God's. You don't have to read very far into the Old Testament to see that.

If government commands you to refrain from owning a Bible or speaking about God, should you render that commandment to the government and just give God your thoughts? The truth is that resistance to unlawful authority originates from God Himself. This resistance is not taking from government what belongs to them. Rather, it's giving God what belongs to God. The devil just uses government to take what belongs to God. That's what we resist.

But examine Jesus' statement in Mark 12:17. His response was to a question asked by the Pharisees. But in reading this passage, the Pharisees' motive behind the question is often overlooked. Their intention was "to catch Him in His words." So they asked Him, "Is it lawful to give tribute to Caesar, or not?" If Jesus said "yes," He would have elevated Caesar above God. If He said "no," He would be advocating rebellion against the Roman Empire for people not to pay their taxes. And they could arrest Him (Mark 12:12-17). The Pharisees didn't care if tribute to Caesar was lawful or not. They only wanted to catch Him in His words. So the question about taxation was only a means to achieve their end. But Jesus' response wasn't about taxation. He only used the picture on the coin to make his point.

Jesus never answered their question. Instead, He responded with *"...Render to Caesar the things that are Caesar's, and to God the things that are God's..."* But notice how He didn't tell them what things are Caesar's and what things are God's. The Pharisees were religious leaders. They knew the law and the Old Testament Scriptures. But pride stood in their way from honoring God.

What's less obvious, but just as important, is that Jesus' response also reveals that God has placed limitations on civil government. Government can't have everything it wants because there are things that are God's. Nor does government have the inherent power to take the things that are God's, especially since God gave government their power in the first place. Hence, it becomes our moral responsibility to resist the State when they demand the things that are God's.

We are God's creation and under subjection to God's law and His social order. Therefore, God's Word becomes the final authority to determine the things that belong to government. Since government never instituted itself, government has no voice.

Choosing Your Battles Wisely

Resistance is an obligation and civic responsibility when the government commands what God forbids or forbids what God commands. However, there are circumstances when resistance becomes one option out of several choices. The government is a master at graying the line. They'll impose a tyrannical order on the populous, which the people can easily execute without harming the life, liberty, or property of others. But these demands aren't enforcing God's standard; rather, they only serve to control you by removing your freewill.

Mask mandates is a prime example. The Bible doesn't give clear direction if we should wear masks or not. However, my position wasn't from the divisive nature of the mandates; rather, it was firmly planted on the foundation of freewill. Regardless of your position, I'm sure we can agree that wearing a mask doesn't violate the freewill of another.

When government grays the line, it becomes vital to pick and choose your battles wisely. But a word of warning: never allow the strength of your opponent to intimidate you from engaging in or defending your battle position. Failure to heed this warning can have devastating consequences.

During the widespread panic over Coronavirus, several state governors issued orders shutting down businesses and churches. Many small business owners didn't choose their battles wisely; their choice was based on the intimidation by government and irrational fear propagated by the media. Tragically, many of these businesses went under.

In contrast to businesses, church leaders didn't have an option to resist. They had an obligation and commandment to resist. By closing Houses of Worship, the government was forbidding what God commands in Hebrews 10:25, *"Not forsaking the assembling of ourselves together..."* Yet, nearly every church in America accepted the devil's reasoning, "You're not forsaking the assembling of yourselves. You're protecting yourselves from the virus. Plus, God commands you to obey the governing authorities." These are lies from the pit of Hell.

I chose to resist the tyrannical mandates during the Coronavirus. My freedom is more valuable than the enslavement of mandates and the irrational fear of the virus. Courage provides the strength to stand against tyrants, and the peace of God casts out fear. This is the purpose of choosing your battles based on principle, not on the strength of your opponent.

David defeated the nine-foot giant named Goliath (1 Samuel 17) when he was just a boy. His decision to battle Goliath was based on principle, not on Goliath's strength and intimidation. David's victory was the result of choosing his battles wisely. This doesn't mean that every time you resist unjust laws or policies, you'll win. But you'll never win if you never fight. And if you never fight, you'll always lose. And your children or grandchildren may end up in slavery.

When God told the Israelites to engage in battle and take the land of Canaan (Numbers 13-14), they refused. Their decision was based on the strength and intimidation of their opponent. Their enemy was stronger, bigger, and more powerful, so they were afraid to fight, even though God was on their side and had sent them into battle. Unfortunately, the consequences of their decision cost them dearly and haunted their children for 40 years.

If the government makes a demand, whether through law, policy, order, or a face-to-face confrontation, which infringes upon your freewill, it's crucial to weigh the cost of the fight against the value at stake. Let me rephrase this: you must decide whether it will cost you less to fight than the loss of surrender. If the cost is greater than the value, the fight is not worth it. On the flip side, if the value is higher than the cost, you must engage in battle. Your battle is simply resistance—a self-defense mechanism.

If I placed my case from New Mexico on the balancing scale, the value had more weight than the cost. My freedom, my survival, and the souls of my children were at stake. So getting arrested and going to jail for "disobeying a tyrant" is a small price to pay. The value is much higher than the cost of resisting. This was a battle I chose to fight, regardless of the strength of my opponent.

Your circumstances may vary from mine. Your ex-spouse may be less aggressive. Your case may be mild compared to mine or maybe worse. Your scenario and environment may be different. But in all situations, it's important for you to weigh the cost of the fight against the value at risk (Luke 14:31-32). In addition to its Biblical principle, this will help you choose your battles wisely.

A Standard of Comparison

Lawful resistance is the means of non-compliance, and proper resistance entails a Biblical understanding of authority. Where should we draw the line? What should be done when government crosses that line? These types of questions haunt Americans because they appear unanswerable. Without a solid understanding of proper authority and the mode of resistance, we ask the wrong questions.

Government seizes the opportunity and exploits the ignorant populous, which gradually expands their power until the entire nation is consumed into a totalitarian State.

"Totalitarianism is much more than mere bureaucracy. It is the subordination of every individual's whole life, work, and leisure to the orders of those in power and office. It is the re-

duction of man to a cog in an all-embracing machine of com-
pulsion and coercion. It forces the individual to renounce any
activity of which the government does not approve. It tolerates
no expression of dissent. It is the transformation of society into
a strictly disciplined labor army – as the advocates of socialism
say – or into a penitentiary – as its opponents say...It holds the
individual in tight rein from the womb to the tomb. At every in-
stant of his life, the "comrade" is bound to obey implicitly the
orders issued by the supreme authority. The State is both his
guardian and his employer. The State determines his work, his
diet, and his pleasures. The State tells him what to think and
what to believe in. Bureaucracy is instrumental in the execu-
tion of these plans." (Mises, 1944)[47]

This warning was issued by Ludwig von Mises back in 1944, prior to the rise of the divorce and child support bureaucratic machinery.

Resistance is the only method by which to prevent totalitarianism. (The Soviet Union Gulag and Germany's Holocaust are prime examples of totalitarianism.) History provides a standard of comparison. We can compare the actions of our government with the actions of governments in the past. In this manner, we can see the road we're traveling and what waits for us at the end.

The most powerful resistance requires placing your trust in God. Those who claim to trust God, but don't resist a tyrant are living a lie. However, individuals who trust God when they do resist, are the ones who move the very hand of God.

Suppose, for instance, there are 1,000 people who are resisting family court edicts, and only ten (1%) have placed their trust in God. Those ten individuals will enjoy the peace and presence of God in the face of anarchy. The government system, however, stays in place and tragically, the other 990 will be crushed and enslaved.

Now, let's suppose there are one million people resisting family court tyrants, and 50,000 place their trust in God. God will fight the

---

[47] Ludwig von Mises, *Bureaucracy* (New Haven: Yale University Press, 1944).

battle for the sake of the 5% involved. And if God fights against Satan's court, then the divorce and child support machinery, which is unsustainable, would collapse from within. The other 95% resisting as well as the millions who don't resist would receive God's blessings because of the 5% involved.

In the first scenario, God aided the ten who called on His name and trusted Him during their resistance. In the second, God fought the warfare and defeated the devil's system, benefiting all who have been sucked into it. This is precisely how the American War for Independence had been won. Colonial history reveals that there were enough colonists and clergymen who relied on Divine Providence when they resisted the British Crown.

How do I know that this is God's method? Here are a few passages in Scripture, which provides a glimpse into the mind of God.

Matthew 18:18-20 states, *"Verily I say unto you, Whatsoever ye shall bind on Earth shall be bound in Heaven: and whatsoever ye shall loose on Earth shall be loosed in Heaven. Again I say unto you, That if two of you shall agree on Earth as touching any thing that they shall ask, it shall be done for them of my Father which is in Heaven. For where two or three are gathered together in my name, there am I in the midst of them."*

The words "you" and "ye" are both plural in the second person. But there's a distinction, so they should not be used interchangeably. "You" is an objective pronoun, which functions as the object of a verb. "Ye" is a nominative pronoun, which is the subject of a sentence and also performs the action in that sentence.

Matthew 18:1 tells us that Jesus is addressing His disciples when He says "you." But then He swaps to "ye" informing His disciples that He is talking about all of them, and they all are to perform the action—bind (or loose) on Earth. In the next verse, Jesus repeats Himself but reveals God's requirement of two disciples.

Most of you have probably heard the phrase, *"There's power in numbers."* When we all work as individuals, we can accomplish so little (or nothing at all). But when there is a firm reliance on Divine Providence in the midst of concerted action, God will bring down the system used to destroy America's families and children. If you want God's aid, you have to surrender your life to Him.

Let's also consider First Corinthians 7:14. *"For the unbelieving husband is sanctified by the wife, and the unbelieving wife is sanctified by the husband: else were your children unclean; but now are they holy."* The unbelieving spouse and children fall under God's hedge of protection as a result of the spouse who believes in the name of Jesus. This doesn't mean that harm doesn't come your way. It only means that Satan cannot harm you without first asking for God's permission (Job 1:6-12).

The most effective way to crawl under God's hedge of protection is to accept Christ as your personal Lord and Saviour so you can be adopted into His family. But this hedge is extended to unbelievers within the home. It's extended to unbelievers within the doors of a godly church. It's extended to unbelievers living within a godly nation. It's also extended to unbelievers who help God's people fight a godly warfare. That's because these unbelievers receive the overflow of God's blessings while here on Earth only because of God's children.

On a side note: Unbelievers who perish are instantly separated from all that's good. They go to a devil's Hell, where they shall await trial before a Holy God. For an individual to receive an inheritance in Heaven, they must be born again.

Remember, when people refuse to resist ungodliness, whether inflicted on them or not, by their government or its agencies, their end while here on Earth is utter destruction. History is full of examples of these atrocities. But when people place their trust in God and resist a tyrant, God is moved, and His power miraculously aids in the defeat of an overwhelming and oppressive force. A powerful example of this history is the American War for Independence.

If we contrast America's diabolical family court system with the long train of abuses and usurpations by King George III, we find a remarkable discovery. This provides us a standard of comparison. The Declaration of Independence lists 27 charges against King George. I chose ten that parallel to our divorce and child support machinery. Can you find more?

- "He has refused to pass other laws..."—State legislatures refuse to pass laws to strip judicial activism in family court, such as reinstating fault-based divorce or placing them under a higher court.
- "He has dissolved Representative Houses..."—State legislatures have dissolved the jury, which is the last line of defense for the innocent.
- "He has obstructed the Administration of Justice..."—State legislatures obstruct the administration of justice by empowering social agencies. The federal Office of Child Support Enforcement obstructs the state's administration of justice.
- "He has made judges dependent on his will alone..."—Family court judges make other government agencies, private businesses, and individuals dependent on their [the judge's] will alone. For instance, an employer garnishes wages.
- "He has erected a multitude of new offices, and sent hither swarms of officers to harass our people..."—State legislatures have erected a multitude of new bureaucracies and sent hither swarms of bureaucrats to harass our fathers. (e.g. CAC, CSD)
- "He has combined with others to subject us to a jurisdiction foreign to our constitution..."—The legislature, executive, judiciary, and administrative agencies on state and federal levels are combined to subject the family to the court's jurisdiction, which is foreign to our state and federal constitutions.
- "For protecting them, by a mock trial, from punishment..."—The State protects the accuser from punishment by attributing their crimes onto the shoulders of the accused. If the accused

triumphs, the crimes of the accuser are protected under the guise of "good faith."

- "For imposing taxes on us without our consent."—After driving fathers from their homes, family court imposes child support on them without their consent.
- "For depriving us in many cases, of the benefits of trial by jury."—Fathers are deprived of the benefits of trial by jury. Their parental rights are being terminated without trial by jury. Tens of thousands of dollars are being imputed without a trial by jury. They can face repeated arrest without a trial by jury.
- "He has plundered our seas, ravaged our coasts, burnt our towns, and destroyed the lives of our people."—Family court has divided our families, invaded our homes, ravaged our relationships, plundered our fathers, and destroyed the lives of our children.

In God's power and strength, the colonies resisted the British Crown, and God poured out his blessings upon them. The colonists understood the difference. They weren't resisting God's higher power, but they resisted the devil's power in God's authority.

CHAPTER SIXTEEN

THE FREEMAN'S RESOURCE

W hat motivates you toward action? Is it the freedom to choose? If you're going to resist, your actions must be righteous and lawful. Your words must be chosen with great care, especially when defying a tyrant. Let's examine lawful and proper resistance. But for beginners, remember this simple principle: you are only responsible for your actions.

The tyranny of governmental force is summed up by two types of actions: (1) the government takes by force, or (2) the government compels by threat of force. Let's examine each type.

When any person, holding any position, in any class takes what doesn't belong to them without the voluntary consent of its owner, they are stealing. Theft has two main avenues, stealing by force or stealing by stealth. In criminal law, the former is called "robbery" and has traditionally been accomplished by the sword (or the barrel of a gun).

In present-day America, government theft of private property is primarily conducted by stealth. The invisibility of stealing prevents intervention to protect one's property. This subtle tactic persuades the majority that no theft has occurred, contrary to reality.

This strategy is employed when the government devalues the purchasing power of the dollar, which causes inflation and rising prices.

However, government uses two mixed tactics—compulsion and force —to garnish wages. On the front end, your employer is being compelled to withhold taxes or child support from your salary. On the back end, well, you can't intervene to protect your property.

But tangible property is not the only thing that can be stolen. During Colonial times, liberty was understood to be free from physical restraint. Stealing liberty by force occurs when the police execute an invalid warrant from family court. But it's also a common occurrence when an arrest warrant is issued through perjured statements or deceit.

Liberty can also be stolen by stealth. This is the taking of an individual's freedom to control and use their internal faculties. Such actions include protection orders to abduct children and mind control through propaganda.

Throughout history, governments were commonly recognized for using physical tyranny against their people. But when our Founding Fathers curbed this tyranny, our government found an alternate path. It's the avenue of stealth.

It matters not whether the action is physical force or stealth. You aren't responsible for the actions of government officials. State-sanctioned criminals don't ask permission.

So how do you resist when you don't have the ability to intervene? You can file lawsuits, petition your state legislatures, or replace your politicians at the voting poles. Other peaceful options include publishing a book, contacting the media to expose the criminals, or writing a letter to your police chief, sheriff, employer, and state official requesting for their intervention on your behalf. You can start your own business, sell on Ebay (However, I personally recommend Bonanza.), or seek employment under the table to prevent further theft.

This mode of resistance is accomplished without violating the life, liberty, or property of others. It is non-aggressive and does not compel. Proper resistance is only a self-defense mechanism.

The second type of tyranny is compulsion. When government compels, it's always accompanied by a weapon. The gun may not be visible, but it's in their arsenal. The government threatens and intimidates to force compliance with its mandates. But in the event that you refuse to surrender, the only way the State can make good on its threats is to pull the gun. In America, this is accomplished by utilizing the police state—signing false arrest warrants, suspending your driver's license to involve the police, etc.

Compulsion, however, serves a different purpose. It demands worship. Obediently executing and following higher orders elevates the State above the individual. People begin to look up to the State for direction and guidance. They'll pledge their allegiance and loyalty to the State. But the end goal of compulsion is acceptance and approval, not obedience. Obedience is just a means to the end. This is the worship of a false god.

Government compels in several areas where individual choice should reign supreme. Just to name a few: compulsory school attendance laws, child labor laws, child support orders, anti-discrimination and equality laws, mask mandates and shelter-in-place orders during Project COVID. Tragically, forced vaccinations by deceit and stealth have been going on for several decades, but forced vaccinations at gunpoint are nearing the horizon.

This humanist worldview of government compulsion takes many different forms, which includes legislative acts, executive orders, judicial orders, and administrative (bureaucratic) regulations and policies.

Some food for thought: the Federal and every State Constitution created only three branches of government. So why do we have a fourth branch of government—the administrative branch?

Compulsion is made effective by the threat of force, not by force itself. Force can never be the fulfillment of a compulsive act. It can only be used as an instrument of punishment if the threat of force fails. Compulsion requires "voluntary" submission.

No one (including politicians and judges) have the authority to force you to do something you don't want to. But it's one thing to be compelled when your action only affects you, such as mask mandates.

It's a totally different matter when you are being compelled to violate the life, liberty, or property of another, such as garnishing wages from your employee, making a false arrest, or bribing a mother to force her child to perjure court testimonies.

Think about that. If you are only responsible for your actions, why would you allow a tyrant to choose your actions for you, especially when those actions would harm a fellow citizen or neighbor?

People comply because they believe it's the right thing to do. But compliance is the acceptance and approval of the State's decisions. You cannot oppose theft in principle, while obeying judicial orders to steal, whether it's called child support, wage garnishments, tax withholding, or anything else. This is government worship. Compliance with government is the essence of breaking the law. When government compels, proper resistance is the refusal to comply.

Child support is a compulsive act, and its justification is leveraging the communistic propaganda piece that "Fathers are responsible to support their children." But for you to be held accountable, you must be free to choose, not compelled. You aren't responsible for the actions of the State. If you're not free to choose how to support your children, then you're not responsible to support them at all. Freedom and responsibility go hand in hand. You can't have one without the other.

To accede to family court edicts is to embrace their ways as your own. This is government idolatry, and therefore, an act of resistance is not only the rightful remedy, but it's also a moral obligation. The State is powerful enough to take everything you have by force, except your devotion. This must be voluntarily given. This is the end goal, which child support is intended to accomplish.

The State assumes the role of God. It "creates rights" in exchange for free stuff, but at the expense of free choice. It "gives life" through the child support program and a plethora of welfare programs. It "provides liberty" by permitting one person to freely inflict a burden upon another. And finally, it "owns all property" by imputing child support, manufacturing debt, and controlling the dollar's purchasing power to operate its god-like machinery. These four attributes are contrasted to a common theme during our Founding Era: Our rights come from God, and government was instituted to secure those rights of life, liberty, and property.

Without a shadow of a doubt, the forerunner to child support is Franklin Delano Roosevelt's Economic Bill of Rights, which changed American politics forever. As the freedom of individual choice was replaced with the "freedom" to satisfy individual greed, the expense incurred was one of worship. As your provider and protector, the government believes themselves to be "entitled" to your devotion and worship.

Welfare and entitlement programs are available to you, even if you don't use them. Laws and regulations are in place for your benefit, even if you don't need them. The State has established themselves as your god, and without consent, they expect and demand your loyalty and worship.

Resistance, however, is the means of rejecting the State as god. Your refusal to worship government will result in persecution, since those higher powers are operated by the rulers of darkness.

Propaganda establishes child support, and more propaganda justifies it. The mechanisms of our child support system are completely based on plunder and compulsion. There isn't one lawful act that takes place. Judges presiding over family court cases possess no authority to judge, nor do they possess any power to execute their judgment.

Lawful Resistance to Compulsion

All family court power is exercised by compelling others. This is vastly different from the inherent powers of God's positions. Many states, along with the federal government, have adopted various methods to compel influential citizens, which stand between the government and their target.

The most effective method of getting to you is by going through others. This is how family court operates—the same strategic method used by Satan—a satanic design. The Genesis account reveals how Satan went through Eve to get to Adam (Genesis 3:1-6). Then by going through Adam, he could get to Cain (Genesis 4:8). Through Cain, he got the city of Enoch (Genesis 4:16-17).

Government agencies and family court begin their assault by charging through children and their mother (the young and weaker vessel) to pit family members against one another. After the conflict has commenced, family court shifts gears by going after the strong and powerful who hold positions over the father and his assets. Coincidence? I think not. Strategically planned? Absolutely!

They will now strike through your employer, your bank, the license bureau, the credit reporting agencies, the IRS, and the police. If you flee, they'll pursue you by enlisting other state and local governments.

The distribution of propaganda through court orders is powerful enough to instill fear and turn any person against you. Essentially, through wage garnishment orders, the government makes you a liability to your company (even if your actions speak otherwise). Your boss and the future of the company might be harmed if they don't follow government orders. So the payroll department must inflict pain on you for the benefit and health of your company.

The suspension of your driver's license would turn you into a criminal overnight. In America, you don't need to break the law to be a criminal. Somebody else has the power to make you a criminal, even when no crime has been committed.

Propaganda, threats, intimidation, and fear are the underlying factors in which the child support system is carved. And it's manifested through the following resources, all of which are at the court's disposal:

- He can suspend your driver's license.
- He can garnish your wages.
- He can report your delinquency to the credit bureaus.
- He can confiscate your federal and state tax refund.
- He can seize any and all assets you hold with a title.
- He can clear any and all bank accounts linked with your name.
- He can issue an arrest warrant for you.
- He can incarcerate you for 30 days without a criminal charge. (This would create a domino effect. You could lose your job or get evicted from your home for non-payment.)
- He can restrict your access to your children or terminate your visitations all together. (Thus, he's actually terminating your parental rights and bypassing the procedural process.)

These threats of force are intended to instill fear in you. But has it ever dawned on you that the judge doesn't have the power to execute these threats? He requires the assistance of other people to execute his decree. This is the same method employed by dictators, such as Hitler.

For example: The judge orders your employer to garnish your wages. He commands your financial institution to transfer all funds to the State. He issues an edict to the police to have you arrested. He compels the Department of Motor Vehicles to suspend your driver's license. What would happen if everyone resisted, because they understood the judge to lack the appropriate authority? This illegitimate judge would be stripped of all power by the citizenry. God's inherent powers cannot be stripped this way.

We aren't speaking about a judge who is ruling over a civil or criminal case. We are addressing a judge who is attempting to enslave you. You haven't been convicted of any wrong doing, nor have you violated any state statute, but that's beside the point. You wouldn't be allowed to vacation, take some time off from work, or get sick without the State's permission. Doing so could unintentionally result in a monetary delinquency and one or more of those previous threats could be executed against you.

If your employer doesn't pay you enough or work you plenty of hours, you would be compelled to seek a second job (or risk jail). This is so the judge could reap the fruits of your labor. Is this not slavery? These illegitimate rulers are the ministers of the devil. And we're commanded to resist them (James 4:7).

It's a common misunderstanding that since the State is more powerful than the individual, any resistance is futile. The State triumphs by deceiving you into thinking that you've been defeated beforehand, and so any resistance is ineffectual and just brings you unnecessary suffering. This stealthy tactic grays the line between cause and effect.

The State and those around you might exclaim that your suffering is the effect of your resistance. But nothing could be further from the truth. Since the infliction of pain preceded your refusal to comply, your suffering became the cause of your resistance.

Family court's compulsive orders are instrumental in demanding your unconditional surrender. Since resistance is only a self-defense mechanism, defying court orders is the defense of your life, liberty, and property. But at the end of the day, figuratively speaking, when the State fails to secure your devotion and shackle you in the chains of slavery, you have won the battle.

But the State doesn't care about only one battle, because they are relentless. They will attack you again and again and again. But you must fight, and you must win. Win enough battles, and you defeat the State.

Defeating the State, however, doesn't mean that you'll get your children back. It doesn't suggest that everyone involved with your case will be prosecuted and convicted. It doesn't imply that the divorce and child support machinery will collapse. And don't expect the judge to step from behind his bench, kneel down, hand over his gavel, and proclaim, "I surrender. You win!"

The State's objective is to remove your freedom of choice and compel worship. But if they fail to achieve their goal, they have lost. That's what it means for the State to be defeated. If enough people, collectively, defeat the State in this manner, then in the process, children may be returned, people may be imprisoned, the flow of money would be severed, and the child support mechanisms may collapse.

Family court's aggression (e.g. wage garnishments, suspension of driver's license, arrest warrants, etc.) is only an attempt to force you to surrender. Thus, your resistance becomes more powerful than the State's aggression. The State actually has an uphill fight against those with the courage and willpower to resist. But your continual resistance and fight for freedom is a long-term investment. Don't throw it away as a result of short-term persecution. Only the strong-willed can live to fight another day.

Unfortunately, America's destruction will be brought about by citizens and businesses who comply with the State. Publix's and Hobby Lobby's compliance is the result of propaganda. This is a prime example of businesses and leaders resisting God's higher power, so they can obey false authorities. Your employer may have the power to steal the fruit of your labor, but they can't force you to retain employment with them. You still possess the freedom to resist and stop further payments to the State.

Family court's enslavement is inhumane. Fighting against the elements or wild beasts for survival has more dignity than the slavery imposed by family court. That's because you're not faced with the hatred that's filled man's heart.

However, there's still a choice you must make. You can either fight and endure persecution or surrender and become enslaved. It's a packaged deal. If you choose the former, you retain the power to fight for freedom. By choosing the latter, you've given up the fight and sacrificed your freedom without any hope of ever getting it back.

Economic Consequences of Obedience

A strong and healthy economy benefits all citizens. Jobs are plentiful, wages are higher, prices are lower, resources are available, and competition thrives, giving consumers more choices. But what happens to the economy when the recipient and obligator of child support reside in separate states? Child support orders are only issued against individuals who create wealth. The child support recipient, family court judges, and the Child Support Division only consume the wealth created of a productive member of society. That's parasitic.

When private businesses transfer the wealth created in the economy of one state to that of another state, they aren't only harming you, but all the residents within that state. The wealth created in the economy of Georgia, for instance, cannot be spent and re-circulated back into the Georgia economy when it's being sent to New Mexico. Instead, it will circulate into the New Mexico economy. This inevitably decreases the wealth of Georgia's economy which sets off a chain reaction. Less wealth equals fewer jobs, lower wages, reduced hours, higher prices, etc. Wouldn't this harm all citizens and businesses within that state? Of course, when this problem is equally distributed among all citizens within the state, people are unable to see visible results.

Resistance is the only thing required to dismantle the entire child support scheme. Yes, it would be nice to have laws repealed and agencies abolished, but if our state legislatures refuse to act, we the people can nullify child support laws and defund these agencies ourselves, effectively bypassing our state governments. The people retain the power to deter crime, reduce poverty, and increase their wealth by leveling this illegal system of mobocracy and plunder. But for this to become reality, the people must possess two valuable virtues: (1) to respect the life, liberty, and property of others, and (2) to possess understanding and the courage to resist.

Ending on a positive note, we don't need the recipient of child support, family court, or their bureaucratic accomplices to sever their flow of money. All we need is unrelenting resistance. If Americans just ignored unlawful court orders, the system would collapse on its own. Remember, it's not sustainable and can only thrive by sucking the life out of the family.

Let's use an analogy: Suppose you were paying the monthly electric bill of another person (an enemy who seeks your destruction). Since you're paying the bill, you're the one who's actually keeping their power on. But if you refuse to pay, at some point in the future, their lights will go out. Now granted, the power outage would not be instant. It may take several months, so you would have to be patient.

The majority of people who support this process have never been sucked into the system, nor are they financially supporting those who operate this machinery. The child support mechanisms only harm those who keep it alive.

For simplicity, let's say that we have a total of 100,000 people, and there are 30,000 sucked into the system. Only 30% of the population is keeping the process in business. It matters not if the other 70% fully approves of the system. Without their funding, they have no voice. If the 30% being harmed by the system severs the flow of money by defying court orders, the system would collapse.

The moral of the story: It doesn't require a majority of people or government officials to help. All we need is the majority of those being harmed to act courageously by peacefully resisting—the act of non-compliance.

If more Americans understood the need to resist their despotic government, freedom would survive, poverty would decrease, and the crime rate would decline. God created the individual with the unique ability to choose, and then gave him the right to use that ability (Genesis 3:6). The moment you surrender your right to choose is the moment you've lost your freedom to obey God. You possess an inherent power to make choices over your own life, and you must not be intimidated by any form of danger to submit to the arbitrary acts of false authorities. I, for one, will not purchase my life at the price of chains and slavery. Will you? Resistance is the only viable option.

PART FOUR

PLANNING YOUR STRATEGY

CHAPTER SEVENTEEN

PROTECT YOURSELF

L et's look at some practical ways that forces the State to fail in their endeavor. This is broken up into three categories. Since marriage—in the physical realm—is the point which separates your old life from your new life, this chapter will address the unmarried. It offers some pointers in finding a future spouse who will help keep the State out of your home. This way, you won't find yourself in a bad situation.

The next chapter, *Minimize the Damage*, offers some practical advice for the married person to minimize the damage of the State's involvement. This isn't fail-proof, nor does it mean you'll come out on top. But you may have a higher probability of surviving the fallout.

The chapter after next, *Endure Adversity*, suggests ways to help you remain positive after the State's assault against your family. You need to keep busy in healthy and productive ways because idleness always precedes self-destructive behavior.

The most effective method to protect yourself against the State's intrusion is safeguarding your life prior to marriage. If you fail to adopt safety procedures before marriage, then you must resort to identifying high risk behaviors and taking appropriate action to minimize the damage after marriage. But if you fail to act quickly and appropriately to minimize the damage, you're in for a hard and rough life. But don't lose hope; you still have a chance. Let me show you.

Enjoy a Personal Relationship with Jesus Christ

Family court and their criminal mafia is only a taste of what the future holds. But if Christ returns today and raptures out His children, the world will be on the brink of its 7-year tribulation period. The criminal-run family court is helping pave the way for the reign of terror, which is to come. But following the Lord's return, God's mercy will come to an abrupt end, and He will pour out His wrath on this world like no one has ever experienced. When Christ comes back, He is taking out all true believers—those who have placed their faith, hope, and trust in Him. *Those who know Him personally. But whether you're young or old, nobody is guaranteed tomorrow. Nobody lives forever.*

If you were to die today, where would you spend eternity? I know you've heard about "people dying and going to Hell." And you likely think, "How can a loving and merciful God send people to Hell?" But you probably haven't heard that Hell was never made for people. God made Hell for the devil and all His demons (Matthew 25:41). He made people to be with Him. He had no intentions of people ever going to Hell. So what happened?

Sin entered the world. Sin is a transgression against God's law. *"Wherefore, as by one man sin entered into the world, and death by sin; and so death passed upon all men, for that all have sinned."* (Romans 5:12) That's why there's death in the world. God made us to live forever. But the penalty for sin is death, and it couldn't be changed! But God is omniscient, so even before He created man, He had a plan to save the world from Hell.

God is perfect and has perfect standards. He made mankind perfect. When sin entered into the world, we were no longer perfect, but that didn't change God's standards. He still requires perfection. So someone has to die to pay the penalty for our sin. *"And almost all things are by the law purged with blood; and without shedding of blood is no remission."* (Hebrews 9:22)

But for us to shed our own blood (the death penalty) for our own sin is to be tormented for all eternity in everlasting fire. And God doesn't want anyone to go to Hell. And no one else could die for our sin because God requires a perfect sacrifice. So God implements His perfect plan. *"For God so loved the world, that He gave His only begotten Son, that whosoever believeth in Him should not perish, but have everlasting life. For God sent not His Son into the world to condemn the world; but that the world through Him might be saved."* (John 3:16-17)

Jesus died to pay the penalty for our sin. *"For as by one man's disobedience many were made sinners, so by the obedience of one shall many be made righteous."* (Romans 5:19) We have absolutely no control over being born into sin, but we do have control over how we respond to Christ's sacrifice. Although He died for the sins of every person ever born into this world, not everyone will go to Heaven.

Eternal life through Jesus is a gift. *"For the wages of sin is death, but the gift of God is eternal life through Jesus Christ our Lord."* (Romans 6:23) Eternal life is a gift that you must receive.

Have you ever given someone an expensive gift that you *really* wanted them to have and there was no way they could afford to buy it? What if they had refused it? "Oh, no, I can't accept this." For whatever reason, *they won't take it*. Would that gift have benefited them in any way? No. You paid for something specifically for them that they could never buy for themselves, and they refused to take it.

Well, Jesus' death on the cross is just like that. He paid for something that you're not able to pay for. This gift of salvation is for you. But what if you refuse to accept His gift? Then you can't be saved from Hell? If you don't accept this gift, it does you no good. Christ's death on the cross does not benefit anyone who doesn't accept it.

Are you ready to accept God's gift? You must first realize that you are a sinner. God is our lawgiver and sets the standard by which we must follow. This is where we all have fallen short. We have failed to live according to God's law. *"For all have sinned and come short of the glory of God."* (Romans 3:23)

Second, you must recognize the payment for your sin. Violating God's law brings judgment upon yourself. And the payment for your sin is death. *"For the wages of sin is death..."* (Romans 6:23a)

Understand this, God's love towards you is so great that, even though you are a sinner, Christ died as a payment for your sins. *"But God commendeth His love toward us, in that, while we were yet sinners, Christ died for us."* (Romans 5:8)

His death is a gift to you, so you can live eternally. *"...but the gift of God is eternal life through Jesus Christ our Lord."* (Romans 6:23b) However, if you refuse to accept His gift, your sin still needs paid for. And the price you'll have to pay is Hell (eternal damnation).

To receive God's free gift of salvation, you must *"...confess with thy mouth the Lord Jesus, and...believe in thine heart that God hath raised Him from the dead..."* Only then, *"...thou shalt be saved. For with the heart man believeth unto righteousness; and with the mouth confession is made unto salvation."* (Romans 10:9-10)

If you prayed and asked Christ to save you, I would love to hear about it. You may contact me at the following email address:

STRIKINGDOWNTHEHOME@PROTONMAIL.COM

Seek an Equally-Yoked Partnership

"Be ye not unequally yoked together with unbelievers: for what fellowship hath righteousness with unrighteousness? And what communion hath light with darkness?" (2 Corinthians 6:14).

In Paul's letter to the church at Corinth, he uses the term "unequally yoked" as a picture, which was relevant to the culture of that time. When America was primarily farmland during the nineteenth century, this picture was visible then.

A farmer preparing to plow his fields or perform some other strenuous activity takes two animals, usually oxen, and yokes them together. A yoke is a wooden device for joining together a pair of draft animals, especially oxen. It ordinarily consists of a crosspiece with two bow-shaped pieces, each enclosing the head of the animal. The team of oxen pulls the combined weight together, but only if each animal pulls its own weight. If one animal is weaker than the other, the team is unequally yoked and cannot effectively complete the task.

Unequal yoking has always been prohibited. The text of Deuteronomy 22:10 reads, *"Thou shalt not plow with an ox and an ass together."* Because of their unequal size and strength, if an ox and donkey are yoked together, the yoke will weigh heavily on the stronger animal while choking the weaker. In addition, the animal with the longer stride moves ahead while painfully dragging the other along by the neck. They would not be able to pull smoothly or painlessly together and little work would get done.

Unequal yoking is in reference to partnerships, whether a marital, business, or some other relationship. Any form of partnership should consist of two individuals, each pulling their own weight, yet working together, pulling the combined weight in unison. If the enemy can prevent equal yoking, he will gain the upper hand. The partners will turn against each other, as opposed to working together to defeat the common enemy.

Our enemy, the devil, prevents equal yoking through the tactic of infiltration. There are three points of entry, also known as access points, into your internal being. Since access points are the most vulnerable, your enemy attempts to infiltrate them, so they must be heavily guarded. These access points are known as your spiritual identity, spiritual legacy, and spiritual goals. This spirituality applies to everyone.

Your enemy disguises themselves to gain entry into your internal being. The most common disguise is an emotional attire. In other words, they appeal to your emotions—fear, guilt, pity, pride, envy, anger, bitterness, etc. Other disguises can include beauty, personality, wealth, power, etc.

When a person approaches your access point, you should be on guard. Only allow entry to friendly forces. These friendly forces (or partnerships) share the same spiritual identity, value the same spiritual legacy, and pursue the same spiritual goals. Let's look closer at each access point.

Your spiritual identity is your worldview. How do you view the world? There are only two worldviews: Biblical and Humanist. The Biblical worldview is the only identity that can be shared between partners since *"...strait is the gate and narrow is the way..."* (Matthew 7:14). Humanism, however, is any direction that opposes God's way as it is clearly defined in Scripture. And without clear and defined guidance, each Humanist travels a different direction. Therefore, no two Humanists can actually share the same identity.

When two people enter into a partnership with completely different worldviews or humanistic thoughts, their words, behaviors, and emotions don't align. Initially, this doesn't appear to be an issue, but it quickly becomes one as the challenges of life arise. In the difficult moments of child rearing, sickness, persecution, suffering, and loss, it's imperative that a couple stand on a unified foundation. This foundation is their faith in Christ.

Your spiritual identity should be a reflection of the character of Christ. A couple who shares this identity will pour those virtues into their marriage, pulling their weight together as one team. As a result, a mutual vision flows through their spiritual identity. An equally-yoked partnership wants to leave behind the same spiritual legacy of truth and love. They work together to make an impact on the world for the kingdom of God. These values don't happen if one or both parties in the relationship possess a humanistic worldview.

Faith in Christ with a humanistic worldview is a dead faith. If both partners are believers in Christ and have been saved from Hell, but one of them holds to the humanistic government-created rights and entitlements, the partnership is unequally yoked, since only half the relationship will uphold Biblical values.

This doesn't just affect the individual—it affects the marriage, children, and effectiveness of the gospel in the entire family. This is why choosing a spouse is such a weighty decision, to be done prayerfully, carefully, and with the wisdom of God.

Equally-yoked partners pursue the same spiritual goals. They want the same spiritual things. Their inspiration for life comes from the Holy Spirit within their hearts. Unequally yoked couples are short-changed, and the team cannot form unified goals toward which to strive.

When both parties place God first in their own hearts, individually they each draw nearer to God. As they're drawn to God, they'll draw closer to one another. The Spirit of God empowers them to accomplish work they never could have accomplished on their own. One of the blessings of an equal marriage or business relationship is that the work is easier when someone is pulling beside you.

This doesn't mean that the person you turn down is bad, but there's a peace in knowing you're in a partnership with someone who is your spiritual teammate. You'll be pulling the same weight, at the same time, and in the same direction.

Search for a Politically-Yoked Companion

This section is not distinct from its previous counterpart. If a partnership is unequally yoked in politics, they cannot be equally-yoked in spirituality. But since religion and politics are generally viewed as separates, I decided to add this political section.

First, we must address what makes something political. According to Webster's 1828 dictionary, politics is "the science of government." Therefore, political would be pertaining to civil government or its administration. Any person can study history and reach a valid conclusion that non-political activities from the past have now become political. How is this happening?

When civil government is restricted to foreign affairs and the national defense, handling disputes and controversies, and deterring criminal behavior, politics is limited in scope and doesn't create two sides. However, if government intervenes in a non-political area of private life, that activity is now politicized.

Making anything political is naturally divisive as it creates two sides—proponents and opponents. Most people are unconcerned about the private affairs of others. But once those affairs are politicized, it now affects all people and becomes a public issue.

The more areas of life that government consumes, the more divided the nation becomes. This division causes more arguments and fights to ensue. So the people will respond in the only way they know how"I don't talk about politics." The idea is that if no one talks about politics, then there can be no disagreements. Without disagreements, we can coexist in peace and harmony. But this thought or belief is a lie from the pit of Hell.

Comments like this have a much deeper implication than what's portrayed. Robert Higgs pointed out that *"virtually nothing remains untouched by the myriad influences of governmental expenditure, taxation, and regulation, not to mention the government's direct participation in economic activities."*[48] The only person who avoids talking about politics has their mouth duct taped shut.

---

[48] Robert Higgs, *Crisis and Leviathan: Critical Episodes in the Growth of American Government*, Twenty-Fifth Anniversary Edition (Oakland: The Independent Institute, 2012).

Not surprisingly, the people who claim to keep their distance from political conversations are generally supportive of government intervention. They're being dishonest with themselves and with you. They speak and engage in politics quite regularly when it aligns with their ideology. They just don't want to hear alternate views that challenge their fantasized beliefs.

The problem with government intervention is that someone is always harmed in the process, even if the injury is relatively small because it's distributed among the populous. Can you live peacefully with someone who's attacking you? No. That's why there's division. The proper response isn't to avoid political talk, but rather, to girt your loins about with truth. That's where political dissent arises from. It's a self-defense mechanism.

Nevertheless, political turmoil makes presenting the truth more difficult and dangerous than it ever has been in American history. Every American citizen or resident of our nation engages in political activities, but the majority of people deny it by avoiding political discussions to ostensibly keep the peace. Just take these examples:

- How can a church avoid politics while maintaining a 501(c)(3) tax-exempt status?
- How can a business refrain from politics while offering a military discount, withholding income taxes from their employees, charging sales tax to their customers, or enforcing court orders?
- How can any resident within our country abstain from politics while obtaining a marriage license, filing for divorce, owning land, possessing a driver's license or State ID, working for the local, state, or federal government, filing yearly taxes, paying sales tax, or receiving government aid, entitlements, or benefits?

Because our lives involve activities promoted or sponsored by our government in one form or another, as Americans, politics revolves around every aspect of our daily lives. Yet, the political aggression is, and always has been, one-sided. It's an assault against those who contradict America's new State ideology of cultural Marxism, most commonly referred to as *"Political Correctness."* This phrase entered into the English language in the late 1700's, but has undergone several shifts in meaning. By the early 1970's, the term "politically correct" was redefined to refer to language that surrounds controversial issues that the American Left believes to be socially acceptable.

For instance, supporting the war oversees is necessary for our freedoms, but opposition to the war constitutes bashing our service members. Approval of government entitlement and welfare programs is deemed caring and compassionate, but exposing the dangers of these programs is hateful and selfish. The origin of man is a science if it's evolution, but considered a religion if it's creation. When women rule the home, it's classified as equality, but when men rule the home, it's argued as oppression.

Friedrich A. Hayek was ahead in his time by 25-30 years when he addressed this structural change in language:

> If you have never *"...self-experienced this process, it is difficult to appreciate the magnitude of this change of the meaning of words, the confusion which it causes, and the barriers to any rational discussion which it creates. It has to be seen to be understood how, if one of two brothers embraces the new faith, after a short while he appears to speak a different language which makes any real communication between them impossible.*
>
> *"It is not difficult to deprive the great majority of independent thought. But the minority who will retain an inclination to criticize must also be silenced."* (Hayek, 1944)[49]

This humanistic technique unconsciously directs your path to the new god you are to serve (Romans 12:2). This transference of loyalty to the god of this present world is what divides a home and destroys a marriage. Humanism, in the form of Political Correctness, results in

---

[49] Friedrich Hayek, *The Road to Serfdom* (Chicago: University of Chicago Press, 1944).

the government invasion into your home, the abduction of your children, theft of your property, flagrant violations of your individuality, and the loss of your liberty. Yet, this dangerous ideology tolerates no expression of dissent. To protect your life beforehand, you must know your enemy and their tactics. You must be equally-yoked in the political arena.

There are 360 degrees in a circle. Humanism encompasses 359 degrees—anything is acceptable except the Bible way. To be equally-yoked in politics, both partners must travel through the strait gate and follow the narrow path of the one Biblical degree.

Guarding yourself and shielding your home, which protects those innocent children of yours, is absolutely crucial. Your future spouse will not avoid politics despite claims to the contrary. It's often overlooked that for the State to get to the man, they must go through the woman. Seizing children requires access through one parent. Increasing government dependency to create loyalists is attained through single mothers who throw off their husband's rule. Abolishing the traditional family to restructure our culture is ultimately performed through the female. This is a satanic method (Genesis 3:1-6).

For this reason, the State exhausts their time and resources at taxpayer expense, attempting to woo women away from their husbands with nicely paid rewards and benefits. This means you (if you're a female) or your wife (if you're a male) will be very susceptible to propaganda and under politically correct pressure to fall into temptation. Equally-yoked partners guard their hearts against the State's ideology.

By remaining vigilant, you can answer the following questions to get a clearer understanding of what side of the fence your hopeful, soon-to-be spouse thrives on. Since men generally suffer in greater numbers from the State, I will address these questions from the perspective of a male protecting himself from feminist thought. However, if you're a female, this still applies equally to you. Just substitute the masculine for the feminine nouns and pronouns.

- Does your girlfriend prosper when she makes her own choices, or does she rely on the choices of someone else to succeed? — *freedom to choose v. central planning*
- Does your girlfriend heed your advice, or does she pursue a consensus instead? — *individualism v. collectivism*
- When you and she disagree with a solution to a problem, does she use logical reasoning and provide an analysis to help you understand her position, or does she rely on "woman's intuition?" — *reasons for herself v. follows the crowd*
- When your girlfriend is faced with a dilemma, does she present solutions, which involve only herself, or would she pressure others to remedy the problem? — *freedom (acting for oneself) v. tyranny (imposing one's will)*
- Does your girlfriend take responsibility for her own actions, or does the problem always appear to be someone else's fault? — *accepts responsibility v. shifts blame*
- If you make restitution for an unintentional mistake, does your girlfriend accept your payment, or does she remind you of your mistake and hold it over your head, as if your payment was not enough? — *justice v. revenge*
- When you make a mistake, does your girlfriend give you the benefit of the doubt, or does she find fault in you? — *trust v. betrayal*
- When there is a misunderstanding, does your girlfriend ask you questions for clarification, or does she make assumptions? — *searches for truth v. embraces propaganda*
- Does your girlfriend correctly interpret your behavior and speech, or does she twist your actions and words out of context? — *truthful witness v. false witness*
- Does your girlfriend enjoy giving more than receiving, or does she mainly focus on receiving? — *contribution (production) v. entitlement mentality (consumption)*

- Will your girlfriend initiate (or freely engage in) political conversations with you, or does she avoid political talk? — *reveals political worldview v. conceals political ideology*
- Does your girlfriend read with the purpose of increasing knowledge and understanding, or does she read, watch television, or access the Internet strictly for pleasure? — *discernment between truth from error v. susceptible to propaganda and deceiving oneself*

If the other person consistently demonstrates the former action, you'll know she cherishes freedom with greater responsibility. To the contrary, the latter actions indicate that a person has troubles with their behavior and is unable to make wise decisions. This type of person lacks the qualities necessary to govern themselves, but don't expect them to let you govern them; the State has deeper pockets. These people are signs of disaster.

To avoid the State's intrusion into your life, you must be equally-yoked and holding fast to a Biblical worldview of government. Faith in Christ is not the same thing as a Biblical worldview. It's possible to receive salvation, but embrace the humanistic worldview. This happens by accepting the devil's superficial slogans. A dead faith neutralizes your moral responsibility before God. It doesn't move the hand of God. It prevents you from defending your life and those under your charge. A dead faith is a useless faith.

An equally-yoked partnership consists of a living faith. Each partner remains steadfast with the original language of classical liberalism while rejecting the language of Political Correctness. In addition, each partner thrives within an environment of freedom with greater responsibility (limited and decentralized government) while rejecting an environment of State intervention (total government). An equally-yoked team pulls together, each by pulling their own weight.

CHAPTER EIGHTEEN

MINIMIZE THE DAMAGE

T he three steps from the previous chapter are just as vital to apply after marriage as it is before. However, if you're already locked into a marriage, don't make any impulsive decisions. You can still answer the questions from the last chapter, which can potentially warn you of your risk level should divorce ever show its ugly head.

Remember, if you don't share an identity (Biblical worldview), a mutual vision (a legacy of truth and love), and pursue the same spiritual goals as your current spouse, exiting the marriage can actually invite the State's invasion, and this is especially true if you have minor children together. Every divorce has only two results: minimum State intervention or maximum State intervention.

- Minimum intervention is solely the order that dissolves the marriage and nothing more.
- Maximum intervention is when the State assumes jurisdiction over each individual. It gives itself the power to establish parental custody, visitation guidelines, financial support, restraining orders, etc.

Maximum State intervention would be your main concern due to the gross violation of your civil liberties and the denial of your constitutional protections. Once you understand the danger of your spouse's political worldview and her adaptation of cultural Marxism, you must recognize the signs of false allegations. Your prediction can help minimize the damage. False allegations usually arise in high-risk situations or events, *not* out of the blue. These situations can include:

- Filing for separation or divorce.
- Anticipating or currently involved in a custody battle.
- Petitioning for a transfer of custody.
- Altering visitation schedules.

Prior to your involvement in one or more of these events, there's subtle indications within the context of your marriage that's indicative of futuristic false allegations. By taking action ahead of time, you may help reduce or even eliminate false allegations. Does your spouse repeatedly display any of the following points during or throughout your marriage?

- Exhibits symptoms related to Borderline Personality Disorder in her behavior (spelled out in chapter 2), regardless if there's a medical diagnosis.
- Adapts the new language of Political Correctness.
- Undermines your authority or endorses the child who challenges your authority.
- Negligently makes false accusations against you (blames you when things go wrong).
- Makes poor parenting decisions, such as refusing to maintain a bedtime schedule, poor nutritional diet, inconsistency with discipline, etc.
- Disciplines in anger, *not* in love or constantly yells at their children.
- Asserts being in charge, making decisions, or ruling the home (applicable towards wives). This includes decisions the husband is not allowed to make without approval from his wife.
- Displays an "always right" attitude and continually makes use of hearsay or intuition as proof.

- Conveniently forgets recent events, but ostensibly possesses a superb memory for the intricate details of past events.
- Acts in a manner that suggests she doesn't trust you or is suspicious of you.

If your spouse has displayed any of these points consistently, then you should watch out for any behavioral changes. This change can be either over cooperativeness and friendliness or non-negotiable and aggressive. This may be a prelude to false allegations. So you must remain vigilant and prepare to strike first with the eight points that follow:

Document Everything—Create a chronology timeline of events. Take notes on what your children say (especially if it's out of the ordinary), anything your spouse says that's rash or unusual, and whether or not there are other people in the picture. Record the conversations, if you're able. (If your state is a one-party state, the recording may help you later on. If not, the recording can still help you keep accurate notes and documentation.)

Have an Eyewitness Account—If possible, have an eyewitness present at all times while you're with your child or your spouse to corroborate your testimony. Don't be alone with either of them if you are suspicious about your spouse's actions or potential actions.

Visit Expert Ph.D. or M.D.—If your child appears to be psychologically, emotionally, or physically abused, take your child to an independent expert Ph.D. or M.D. before you take them back to your spouse. This could alert you to factors in the child's home environment of which you are unaware.

Hire an Attorney—If you have reason to believe that you're headed for a bitter divorce and custody battle, hire an expert attorney, beforehand, who is familiar with Parental Alienation cases and can identify the signs of false allegations of child abuse. Research attorneys throughout the country, and find one who will litigate in your best interest, *not* the child's best interest. An honest attorney understands that the child's best interest is always ruled by law, not deceit.

Since child abuse is a criminal matter, any arguments made in family court become invalid. Circumventing the judicial process, criminally playing the role of the victim, and conspiring with government employees automatically disqualifies the unfit and deceitful parent from child custody. An attorney with this mindset is more valuable than the one who believes that the courts are just trying to protect your children.

File for Divorce—This next point is very sticky for me because I detest State intervention, so exercise extreme caution prior to implementing this point. If divorce is on the horizon, file first and seek an ex parte order granting you temporary custody effective immediately. This can shield your children from the toxic influence of false allegations and Parental Alienation.

Purchase a Custody Evaluation—If you manage to get temporary custody, then obtaining a custody evaluation is much easier. The evaluator must also specialize in Parental Alienation. This will help alleviate your spouse from shifting his or her abusive behavior onto you by accusing you of alienation.

Close All Accounts—Close all joint accounts and cancel credit cards. It will cost you every cent to fight the allegations (or to protect yourself from the allegations).

Remain in the House—If you do not have temporary custody, remain in the house as long as possible. If the house was purchased and is in your name, resist any order to vacate your own property unless you can transfer the house into your spouse's name (or have your name removed). If, on the other hand, you are renting and prefer to vacate the premises, ensure you notify your Landlord in writing. You don't want to be held liable for non-payment or damages to the property. Remember, once you leave, your spouse will have full control over the children, and the process of programming your children's innocent minds, if it hasn't yet, will begin.

These eight points are not fail-proof and doesn't guarantee protection from government persecution. But if you strike your spouse first, you have a higher probability of surviving the fall-out and protecting the minds of your children.

CHAPTER NINETEEN

ENDURE ADVERSITY

O nce your spouse has total control over your children and false allegations begin making their way into police reports and recorded interviews, your defense and the safety of your children are transferred into the hands of government officials. The majority of false allegations don't end with a conviction in criminal court. (But tragically, some do.) This is because criminal court was structured to protect the innocent, unlike family court. For this reason, I will only be speaking within the confines of the family court system.

Once you are falsely accused, the government will either favor the accuser or uphold the law—but they get to make that decision. The State will determine if you're allowed to argue a defense, call witnesses, cross-examine, or submit valid evidence. The State, not a jury, will render the verdict, as well as deciding what grounds will be used to obtain your conviction. The State may freely decide that your actions are irrelevant to a conviction, but rather, your genetic make-up might be all the proof they need. In other words, your life, liberty, and property are at the sole discretion of the government. However, their decisions are usually determined by what's more profitable to them. Is your freedom profitable or is it your slavery? Is upholding the law profitable or is it favoring the accuser?

When everyone turns against you—your spouse, children, relatives, friends, neighbors, employer, landlord, pastor, etc., life doesn't seem worth living and all hope is lost, you need a boost of confidence—some encouragement. Psychological strength is imperative at a time like this, because you need hope in a hopeless situation.

Adversity is essential to your maturity and growth, but only if you can endure through it. Your outcome will differ from mine, but with God's help in the midst of adversity, you'll endure. Adversity is not your enemy. And through endurance, you'll go places that you wouldn't have gone otherwise. So I'd like to share with you the necessary steps to help you endure adversity.

If you are not thrilled about certain aspects or don't consider it a habit, then you need to make a serious change to enable you to overcome the challenges you'll face down the road. This is because enduring adversity only becomes reality through work, not pleasure. (Any pleasurable activity which keeps your mind preoccupied, or mind-altering substances like drugs and alcohol, doesn't help you endure the problem; it only conceals it.)

Phase 1: Encourage Yourself in the Lord

Anyone forced into the circumstances that I've had to endure is faced with a tragedy that no one should go through alone. But your real enemy is the devil. He is the mastermind behind the operation of this entire conspiratorial system. If you encourage yourself in the Lord, you can never be defeated (1 Samuel 30:6). But first, you must be adopted into God's family. It's imperative to realize that you are not strong or wise or good enough to keep yourself from the perils of this life or the next. You need someone stronger, wiser, and more knowledgeable than you. You need Christ.

If you haven't done so, I'd encourage you to read step one from chapter 17. I show you how you can know for certain that you have a home reserved in Heaven. Once you've accepted God's plan of salvation, the Spirit of God comes to live within your heart. This is the most important decision you'll ever make in your lifetime, so make it today.

Once Christ lives within your heart, you now have the power to encourage yourself in the Lord. Do so today. This is accomplished by memorizing Bible verses and talking with your Heavenly Father. To find relevant Scripture to memorize, read the Bible daily and select verses that comfort you. Here's a few to get you started:

- *"Trust in the Lord with all thine heart; and lean not unto thine own understanding. In all thy ways acknowledge him, and he shall direct thy paths."* (Proverbs 3:5-6)
- *"Thy word is a lamp unto my feet, and a light unto my path."* (Psalm 119:105)
- *"But seek ye first the kingdom of God, and his righteousness; and all these things shall be added unto you."* (Matthew 6:33)

Phase 2: Trust the Lord

"Trust the Lord" is a common and universal phrase; however, no one ever tells you what trust looks like. When you've been bound and gagged by the State, you feel so helpless. But don't fall for this lie. Trust isn't just sitting back and waiting for God to orchestrate some event upon your life? That's not trust; it's called idleness. Trust is a reliance on God's integrity, veracity, justice, and friendship. There's an element of action, which accompanies trust. If there's no action, it's because there's no trust.

Trust entails purposeful action, not mindless behavior. Action with purpose can be either direct action or indirect action. Direct action is carrying into action, while indirect action is the act of resistance.

If you trust that God will reunite you and your children, then your first and most important action is to bathe your request in prayer. Don't just make your request known to God, but pray often and earnestly that God would intervene in your circumstances. James 5:16b says, *"The effectual fervent prayer of a righteous man availeth much."* But be specific in your prayer. Don't generalize! Ask Him for wisdom and guidance as you desire to act according to His will.

Next, start preparing to receive your children. If you trust God to intervene, then you'll prepare yourself in every way possible—emotionally, mentally, spiritually, financially, and physically.

For example, preparations can include securing a residence with multiple bedrooms and furnishing those bedrooms. Is your dining room table big enough? Do you have enough dishes and silverware? Depending on the ages of your children, you might want to invest in stuffed animals or blankets to bring them comfort during their distressing transition. Or, at the very least, put money aside each payday to help cover these anticipated expenses when they arise.

You'll need to get ready for God to move for two reasons. (1) It displays trust in God. (2) You want to be prepared when you're suddenly alerted to a situation that opens the door for you to regain custody. Remember, you're praying for God to move; prepare for Him to move. This is what trust looks like. Trust is always accompanied by purposeful action, whether direct or indirect.

You must initiate the action. If you would like God's blessings on your life, you must live your life in obedience to His word by making the first voluntary move—an action that is absent of compulsion. This is why you cannot obey unlawful orders (e.g. child support orders) and trust God simultaneously. This is non-negotiable when it's time to pursue offensive actions and create obstacles for your enemy. You must pray earnestly, yield to God's will, and trust Him fully if you expect Him to move on your behalf.

Phase 3: Associate with Like-Minded Individuals

You need support. You need a friend—someone who listens to you, who asks questions to understand you, and believes in your innocence. Your greatest friend is the one who lifts you up when you fall or accompanies you to the courthouse or helps you build your case or speaks up in your defense when others are condemning you. The best friend you can have is someone that stands by you regardless of your circumstances—through the false allegations, financial struggles, emotional challenges, and court hearings. But it's vital that your friend shares your belief system.

He or she must advocate for both limited and decentralized government. Without this tenet, people generally believe that all government agencies, policies, laws, and programs are good while only the individual perverting them is bad. They fail to recognize that aggressive laws and orders, such as restraining orders and child support orders, are only weapons of destruction, *not* tools of righteousness. How can the law be good, but its enforcement bad?

He or she must reject conformity to Political Correctness. Well-meaning citizens who don't embrace this principle are inclined to pervert reality and falsely accuse, unaware. They accept the Communist slogans by believing them, and they may even repeat the mainstream narrative. Someone who believes that fathers are abusers or deadbeats won't truly believe in your innocence.

He or she must actively pursue Biblical, historical, and political truth. Everyone thinks they know the truth, but individuals who don't purposefully act have deceived themselves. Turning on the television, watching YouTube, or scanning Facebook posts is mindless behavior. These people are blinded to reality. Since God warns us in 2 Corinthians 11:14-15 that Satan transforms himself into an angel of light, and his ministers transform themselves into agents of righteousness, the blind generally favors the oppressor (government)—not the oppressed (you).

If even one of these convictions is absent, the individual lacks a foundation. Political Correctness, Communist slogans, and the shift in government operations have resulted in the Christian Army shooting their own wounded. Tragically, the government pits God's people against one another. Without standing on the foundation of Christ, even God's people wander aimlessly, lacking direction. They don't know how to love others, be a friend, and pray effectively. You need a friend with a solid foundation in place.

Get involved in a community ministry and find someone to work with, whether it's a homeless shelter or an animal shelter or a deaf school, or even a political campaign. Join a local church and share your time and talent with others. Freely share your political beliefs and educate people around you. Allow others who engage in the conversation to educate you. But avoid those who won't let you educate them, are unable to educate you due to their own ignorance, or doesn't appreciate the conversation.

Also, there are many organizations which you can join and work with such as The John Birch Society, The Constitution Party, and Eagle Forum. Find a local chapter or start one of your own. Search the Internet for pro-life groups in your area and get involved. You might be going through tough times yourself, but helping others and working with like-minded individuals is where you'll find friends.

And lastly, if you meet another person who is going through an ordeal similar to yours, help to educate him, provide resources for him, and work to defend him. The greatest friend is one who will help someone in need without expecting anything in return.

Phase 4: Study American History

Studying history is vital for several reasons. First off, history allows us to see God's work throughout time. History, which followed the conclusion of the New Testament Scriptures, is just as important as the Old Testament history. The appreciation of God's hand at work with man can only be acknowledged through history. Those who don't know history are clearly ignorant of the work of God.

Secondly, history alerts us to the dangers which lie ahead (Ecclesiastes 1:9). We must always look forward, but it's imperative to understand our history to avoid repeating mistakes of the past. The people in America and their elected representatives continue to pursue wrong courses of action, because they can't think critically about what has happened from the past. Those who don't know history are easily persuaded to advance their own destruction unaware.

Thirdly, history provides us with a standard of comparison. The direction in which we travel into the future will ultimately have an end. A standard of comparison allows us to identify the scenery on a route that's already been traveled and recorded, and then we can compare it to the route we're currently on. Now we can clearly see and understand what awaits us at the end of our journey. Those who don't know history have no standard of comparison, so they're ignorant of their direction of travel and destination. They are sheep being led to the slaughter.

Phase 5: Educate Yourself

If you intend to defeat your enemy, you must (1) understand proper strategic methods and plan accordingly, and (2) know the tactics of your enemy so you can counter them. This is what confuses most people, because they're not engaged in physical combat. The only warfare they can grasp is a conventional battle—army against army, with flying planes and bombs falling. The fight you're engaged in is a spiritual warfare—it may not be visible to the naked eye, but it's just as real. It cannot be fought with physical strength or human might. The real battle is waged against the Word of God. Words are powerful, and when war is declared against the very Word of God, then our everyday words are weaponized to kill and destroy.

To fight back and defend your liberty, your property, and even your life (or the lives placed under your authority), you must transform your worldview. This is because your worldview is formed by words—the very words which have become weapons. Here are a few pointers to assist you in restoring your vocabulary back to its original and healthy state.

Read and study the King James Bible. The King James Bible is politically incorrect. Don't be fooled, but newer translations conform to Political Correctness—changing words to increase vagueness, stealthily removing selective phrases, and slanting leftward to neutralize Christians in this warfare.

Read political and historical books for the sole purpose of seeking truth, not pleasure. I have provided a good reference list at the end of this book. History buffs generally read history for pleasure, not for truth. They can easily be persuaded to accept erroneous historical accounts, such as the false legacy that surrounds Abraham Lincoln or the myth that encompasses the Great Depression of the 1930's.

As you invest your time in reading political sources that are true and accurate, your education level will increase, your newfound knowledge and understanding will help you reason critically, your vocabulary will skyrocket, and your writing will improve. I didn't have to study a dictionary to break free from the shackles of Political Correctness and repair my vocabulary. All I had to do was read and saturate myself with truth.

Understand original intent. The purpose of language is to communicate a message. The proper interpretation of the message is what the transmitter (or author) intended to say, not what the receiver thinks it means. You need to be aware of the time period and the environment in which the author lived. Interpretation errors often result from applying an author's words within the context of our modern age, Western Civilization, or political ideology.

Stay informed about current events written from a source which is only biased towards the truth. You must refrain from newspapers, news sources on television, or Facebook. Keep in mind that many current events, whether written or spoken, are from people who have adopted Political Correctness. And they share their opinions as though they were facts. This results in skewing events and reporting to conform to America's new state ideology. And in the process, the truth gets suppressed. The best source of current events which reports objectively is "The New American" which can be found at www.thenewamerican.com.

Phase 6: Reject Political Correctness

Political Correctness can appear in several different forms, but the end is always the same: to force conformity to America's new state ideology through the suppression of unpopular or unrecognized speech. In today's culture, playing the role of the victim is politically correct. So by conforming to this ideology, you're abetting the victimhood mindset.

Political Correctness, which includes the Communist slogans, is intended to communicate unspoken words. An example might be helpful. Suppose a friend or pastor of yours asks you about your children. You regretfully respond that you're not allowed to see them because a restraining order was issued against you. Although that may be true, the unspoken message you're transmitting is that you've abused your children, and these are the consequences of your actions.

Let's change your conversation up a bit. Suppose you used words that reflected reality. So you regretfully respond that your children were kidnapped by your ex-wife who conspired with government officials to legalize her crime. And you suspect that ransom demands will soon follow. Nobody will understand what you mean. You're speaking a completely different language.

Political Correctness erodes free speech since the truth cannot be revealed. Political Correctness permeates our culture from the top down, not bottom up. The power to disseminate an entirely new language, which shifts thought patterns, originates from the higher echelons of government and the hidden powers of darkness.

Politically correct phrases and Communist slogans attach itself to the culture and begin to circulate through different avenues.

- Congressional or state laws—enforced by police, brought before the judiciary through criminal proceedings or a civil lawsuit.
- Executive or judicial orders—enforced by police.
- Administrative regulations or policies.
- Public speeches by political candidates from both parties.
- Colleges (government controls colleges who accept funding through their tuition assistance programs).
- School district curriculum (politically correct curriculum is promoted to the local school boards for adoption).
- Training or education that's required to obtain a government-mandated license to work in a specified field (e.g. teaching license).

Over time, our government gradually creates a separate language. This slow progress hides reality. However, the new language blurs the distinction between right and wrong. As the culture embraces redefined words and new phrases, a division emerges.

The desired outcome of Political Correctness is observable by the constant reference of respecting others and not saying things which might offend. Ultimately, it's not about respect; rather, it's about silencing dissent and suppressing the truth. However, God's Word tells us why people get offended. In Psalm 119:165, we read, *"Great peace have they which love thy law: and nothing shall offend them."* So those offended are actually the aggressors and despise God's law. But regardless, to maintain peace, those in higher positions (employers, landlords, etc.) accept the most popular language. And anyone with an inclination to resist is blamed for the division.

When your language conforms to this world, your actions inevitably follow. Political Correctness is more than just homicidal; it's suicidal. People can no longer defend themselves once they embrace this language.

For instance, suppose an elderly woman is shopping in her local grocery store. While in the check-out line, the cashier makes a political comment, which offends the customer. The cashier, however, is entitled to his own opinion, and the woman is free to disagree with him (or ignore his comment).

The cashier's comment, be it truth or error, she could not refute. Since she's unable to point out his error or defend her position adequately, she gets offended. So the customer doesn't want him free to share his opinion. Therefore, following her transaction at the cash register, she approaches management and complains, even threatening to take her business elsewhere. In response, the manager fires the cashier.

As an entire nation is consumed with Political Correctness, it becomes genocidal. One doesn't need to look very far to see the war against fathers. The Violence Against Women Act is a prime example of the Congressional war against men. The Standard Family Court Act illustrates the State's war against the family. This is genocidal, but wrapped up and packaged to disguise its appearance. This is the dangerous result of conforming to America's new state ideology.

Adopting Political Correctness may make life easier, but it's poisonous. It's like a cancer that spreads. When you are confronted with this dangerous ideology, counter their move by using words that accurately describe reality, not fantasy. If it's universally accepted and politically correct, it's satanic. Run the other direction.

Remember, your employer is not withholding child support; they are stealing—plain and simple. Too many people have swallowed this Communist poison. But you don't have to.

CHAPTER TWENTY

LAUNCH ATTACKS

Your situation and environment may be different than mine, but the State's strategy against you is all the same. Since they initiated the war, you are now justified to make offensive maneuvers. Your offensive actions should be directed at ending the war and stopping a tyrant's reign of terror.

Think of how you play the game of Chess. Will you win the game by moving your king out of check? No! You have to make an offensive move to checkmate the other player and end the game. You may have to make several offensive moves before you force your opponent into checkmate.

You can't win by defending; you must attack. However, there's a distinction between a vengeful attack and a defensive attack. The aggression of your spouse and the State is vengeful. They seek to inflict injury through deceit. Your attack against them should be a defensive maneuver. Your aggression should be directed at ending the hostilities. By spreading truth, your goal is to stop them from inflicting further injury. But you must attack if you want to end the fight.

Your spouse and the State may have launched this war, but you need to end it. You don't fight fire with fire (deceit and revenge); rather, you fight fire with water (truth and justice). It's time for you to engage in battle with an offensive mindset. There are several ways to go on the offensive, and each situation can determine a different offensive maneuver, but here's a sample to help get your creative juices flowing. This list is not all-inclusive, so brainstorm with others about various ways to go on the offensive.

Attack 1: Hire an Attorney

Imagine that you have an opportunity to have your own house built. This is your construction project, and you have the option of customizing it to your preferences. Others might offer suggestions, but ultimately, you have the final word. That's the privilege of funding the project. After weeks or months of planning, you hire a skilled architect and several carpenters to construct your home in accordance with your wishes. Their expertise allows them to customize the home's design into your vision of the end product. These skilled contractors usually ask questions, to bring clarity and understanding so they can complete your project according to your expectation. They might even offer suggestions or alternatives, if necessary. But one thing is certain, the architect doesn't design what he thinks is best.

This analogy is similar to the law profession. Your divorce case is your legal project, and you have the right to customize it according to your situational needs. After much thought and consideration, you hire a skilled attorney to litigate in your best interest, *not* the child's best interest. An attorney is an independent contractor whose expertise allows them to strategize in your favor. They should ask questions to bring clarity and understanding, so they can best represent you according to your wishes. They can offer suggestions or alternatives with possible outcomes. But one thing is certain, your attorney should never execute what he thinks is best for you.

Your lawyer should stick strictly with the facts and avoid imposing their beliefs. For instance, it's proper for your attorney to inform you of the unrestrained power wielded by the State and the consequences of defying a child support order. But it becomes improper for your attorney to pressure, intimidate, or threaten you to pay child support. The servant should never boss around his master.

With this in mind, attorneys have a moral obligation to comply with the law, follow judicial protocol, and always speak the truth in and out of court. You should never ask or pressure your attorney to violate his convictions. If a conflict arises, a good attorney would distance himself from the argument he makes in court. For example: your attorney could argue, "My client holds religious convictions that 10% of his income must go to his church. We pray the court to exclude that small amount from child support figures considering that my client never abandoned his parental responsibilities."

Research attorneys throughout the country and find one who will litigate in your best interest. He doesn't have to be from the local area, but he must be familiar with and recognize:

- False allegations of child sexual abuse.
- Parental alienation and the tactics deployed.
- The value of fatherhood and the willingness to aggressively attack your spouse in court for undermining this value.

An honest attorney understands that the child's best interest is always ruled by law, not deceit. In essence, child abuse arguments made in family court are invalid. Circumventing the judicial process, criminally playing the role of the victim, and conspiring with government employees automatically disqualifies the unfit and deceitful parent from child custody. An attorney with this mindset is more valuable than the one who believes that the courts are just trying to protect your children.

Attack 2: Contact the Media

There are various media outlets that you can turn to. The media is on television, in the newspaper, and on the Internet. It'll be in your best interest to prepare a solid case first. Gather evidence (tape recordings, court hearings, medical records, documentation, etc.) and write an argument in chronological order. Ensure to include vital questions, address inconsistencies, expose deception, etc. Once you have prepared your case, send the different media outlets a letter with the strongest excerpt of your argument. Urge them to report this incident because the people need to know what's going on behind the curtains for their own safety.

Feel free to turn over copies of the evidence to the media. Your spouse's crimes should be made public as well as the judge's ruling favoring criminal behavior. If your spouse doesn't want her actions made public, she shouldn't have committed the crime. If the judge doesn't want his ruling made public, then he should've upheld the law, not favor criminals.

Be mindful of the fact that since you're being denied due process, making your case public doesn't affect the integrity of the case since there was no integrity to begin with. You're being framed for a fictitious crime, and so the media can be used to sabotage the conspiracy against you. Maintaining the integrity of a case only applies when the law is being upheld, *not* when a crime is being committed.

Attack 3: Prove Your Spouse's Guilt

The biggest mistake anyone can make is to prove their innocence. This is similar to a cat chasing its tail or trying to catch the light from a laser pointer. Your innocence is elusive. You accomplish nothing by traveling a path which leads you in circles, but the end always remains just out of reach. You can see it alright, but you just can't prove it. This happens because you can't prove a negative. That's why the leverage of proof always resides with the accuser.

Falsely accusing others is waging war against them. Since you can't prove a negative, you're unable to prove that your spouse is *not* a victim. On the other hand, you can prove that she's the offender. By proving that she's committed perjury, abuses your children through brainwashing techniques, and tampered with testimonial evidence, you can discredit her claim as a victim. Through your petitions, responses to motions filed, and verbal testimonies in court, you should continually attempt to shift the court's focus from the accuser's false allegations to her psychological impairment, which is why she lied in the first place.

Your best defense is a strong offense. You can't checkmate the other party by playing defensive.

After I was indicted by the Grand Jury, my attorney requested a copy of the Grand Jury hearing. He compared the detective's testimony with the interviews conducted at the Children's Advocacy Center. Shockingly, this revealed that the Las Cruces police detective had perjured his statements.

My attorney didn't try to prove my innocence. He made an offensive maneuver and aggressively attacked the State by exposing the detective's crime. Naturally, this placed the prosecution on the defense. The State hates playing defense, so they'll forfeit first. This led to the dismissal of one of my cases.

The objective is to turn the tables on your spouse. Since she is the one who started the war, it would be up to you to end the war. If you give up and allow her to crush you, peace will not be ushered in. Your war-making spouse will only produce a reign of terror. To place an end to war and stop the reign of terror over you and your children, you must defeat her. This ultimately requires an attack on your part to place the other party on the defense.

Attack 4: Examine for Parental Alienation

This can be used as part of your investigation and gathering of evidence. The evaluation is indispensable in revealing psychological abuse. A medical diagnosis discredits your child, exposes the origins of their allegations, and damages the accuser's case.

More often than not, it's the custodial parent who opposes this medical evaluation. Child abusers frequently deprive children from medical attention to conceal their crimes. So even if your petition for an evaluation is denied by the courts, use their own ruling against them by exposing their crime to the media or other published material. Only cases with integrity would allow medical attention to be sought at the request of one parent.

If you're successful in seeking an evaluation for parental alienation, the specialist who agrees to examine and diagnose your children should have no previous knowledge of your circumstances. Any information provided to the doctor about allegations of abuse prior to the examination will lead to a biased and tainted diagnosis. The specialist you've chosen must reach his own conclusion following the examination. He shouldn't be swayed by anyone—not you, not through propaganda spread by the accuser, and not through the court system.

Attack 5: Demand a Custody Evaluation

Don't ever cease collecting evidence in your favor. A custody evaluation is intended to evaluate the mental and emotional capacity of both parents. But it should come as no surprise when the custodial parent is often the one who opposes this testing. Psychologically and emotionally sick people abhor this evaluation because it exposes their mental incapacity, and often demonic personalities. In a nutshell, if they intend to commit a crime against your children, they don't want their plans uncovered.

If you recall, I demanded a custody evaluation, but Judge Quintero empowered Amy to nullify my request. But there's still a lesson to be learned. If you request the evaluation, you need to be the one to hire the evaluator, not your spouse.

The evaluator you hire should be an expert with parental alienation. However, this evaluation should be conducted separately and from a different doctor who diagnosed your child with Parental Alienation Syndrome. You don't want to give the appearance of collusion.

Custody evaluations are usually requested because parental alienation is present. If you can locate a husband and wife couple to perform both evaluations, it might be more cost effective. But whomever you choose, the evaluator should have no previous knowledge of the divorce and child abuse allegations. They should reach their own conclusions based on merit.

Attack 6: Compel Your Spouse to Undergo a Psychological Evaluation

If you have previously identified numerous traits of a mental illness, petition the court to compel your spouse to seek an accurate psychological diagnosis. A formal motion or petition may require certain formatting guidelines, so ensure you check with the courthouse in which you plan to file. But don't forget, you'll want to specify the symptoms identified in her behavior and how this behavior is harmful to your children. You want to ensure she is seen by a psychiatrist so the court can make an informed decision in the "best interest of your child." (Feel free to use their own language against them.)

Attack 7: Request a Transfer of Custody Regularly

When a new judge is seated in your case, petition the court immediately to request a transfer of custody. You'll have to present your case each time you make this request. But focus on the guilt of your spouse and the abuse she's committing against your children.

Do *not* defend your innocence. Do *not* play the role of the victim. These are detrimental to your cause, and it can indicate that you care more about yourself than your children. Instead, levy a solid argument with several points showing how your spouse is deliberately committing acts of child abuse and neglect—and the transfer of custody is necessary for the protection of your children.

These acts can even include depriving your children of necessary medical care. For example: if your wife falsely accused you of rape or molestation, use this to your benefit. If she didn't take your child to the hospital to be examined for internal damage, that's medical neglect. Present your argument from a compassionate point of view. You are concerned about other men your wife may be inviting into her home, and she may be covering up this rape. (Hint: Just don't tell the judge that she accused you. Shift her accusation onto "other men.")

The trick here is not the quantity of bullet points, but the strength of your bullet points. Do not attempt to prove that you're a good, caring, or fit parent. This is not the place. Your focus must remain on the crimes of your spouse and the danger that your children are in. Be sure to reference outside sources or attach physical evidence that's relevant to your request.

If you reside in a jurisdiction where the same judge remains appointed over your case, you may still request a transfer of custody regularly. But your request would be triggered by an event or several events, not by the judge's reassignment. As your ex-wife creates drama that's harmful to your children, log those circumstances. If she violates the judge's order, file charges against her in court. This is, ultimately, building a case against her. Once you have reasonable claims or evidence, file your transfer request. If it is denied, you must wait for a new set of circumstances.

Attack 8: File Lawsuits

Has your spouse spread false accusations about you causing a burden for you in society? You can sue her for defamation of character.
This is not protected speech—she is injuring you. But there are two
conditions. First off, you must be able to prove that your spouse knew
the accusations were false, but was spreading them for revenge, black-
mail, or as a form of punishment.

Second, others would have to retaliate against you in response to
the lies she told them. For example, she runs to your employer, so he
fires you. She speaks to your landlord, so he evicts you. She spreads
the accusations throughout your church so the leadership removes you
from any positions you hold. She visits your neighbors, so they harass
you. She calls her family and friends who threaten you, stalk you, or
vandalize your property.

But consider, if your wife doesn't act unilaterally, but works with
various agencies (private, public, or governmental), file a lawsuit
against her and those agencies for conspiracy. But you have to prove
that you were injured in some way. Others potentially open themselves up for lawsuits when they assist the child support machinery.
Let's look at a few examples.

Has the Department of Motor Vehicles (DMV) suspended your
driver's license for non-payment of a court-ordered debt (e.g. child
support)? Consider filing a lawsuit against the DMV. Four states—
California, Kentucky, Georgia, and Wyoming—have no laws allowing
the suspension of your driver's license for unpaid court debt. Louisi-
ana, Minnesota, New Hampshire, and Oklahoma require a determination that you had the ability to pay and intentionally refused to do so.[50]
In the remaining states, your driver's license may be suspended without regard for or inquiry into your ability to pay at the time of suspen-

---

[50] Mario Salas and Angela Ciolfi, *Driven By Dollars: A State-By-State Analysis of Driver's License Suspension Laws for Failure to Pay Court Debt* (Fall
2017), Accessed April 27, 2021, https://www.justice4all.org/wp-content/ up-
loads/2017/09/Driven-by-Dollars.pdf.

sion. This is a violation of your procedural due process since this practice provides inadequate pre-deprivation procedural protections. At a minimum, you should receive a notice and have an opportunity to be heard.

In the case of Bell v. Burson, the Supreme Court recognized that,

> *"Once licenses are issued, as in petitioner's case, their continued possession may become essential in the pursuit of a livelihood. Suspension of issued licenses thus involves state action that adjudicates important interests of the licensees. In such cases, the licenses are not to be taken away without that procedural due process required by the Fourteenth Amendment."* (Bell v. Burson, 1971)[51]

So challenge your state's DMV in court for violating your constitutional protections (including your State Constitution's Bill of Rights), but also utilize Bell v. Burson as the precedent.

What about your child support order—has the amount been incorrectly calculated or imputed? Consider filing a lawsuit against the child support hearing officer (also called a support magistrate). According to NM Stat § 40-4B-4, *"Child support hearing officers shall be lawyers who are licensed to practice law in this state and who have a minimum of five years experience in the practice of law, with at least twenty percent of that practice having been in family law or domestic relations matters."* A hearing officer is an attorney licensed to practice law. These lawyers are not certified public accountants, not licensed tax preparers, not licensed bookkeepers, and not licensed financial advisors. Most states have similar statutes in place, so check the laws of your state.

The human error may have been an honest mistake (incorrect calculation) or a malicious intent (imputed calculation), but regardless, your state should be held liable for the damages. The hearing officer (or support magistrate) is appointed to make expert monetary recom-

---

[51] Bell v. Burson, 402 U.S. 535 (United States Supreme Court, 1971).

mendations without any financial expertise in that area. They are, in essence, performing an action with the same qualifications and experience as the judge presiding over the case. Thus, hearing officers are nothing more than figureheads—false experts.

Have you suffered the unfortunate circumstances of being arrested for failing to pay child support? Well, the arresting officers must ensure they're in possession of a valid warrant. To be valid, a warrant must contain all of the elements required under the Constitution.

> *"The right of the people to be secure in their persons, houses, papers, and effects, against unreasonable searches and seizures, shall not be violated, and no Warrants shall issue, but upon probable cause, supported by Oath or affirmation, and particularly describing the place to be searched, and the persons or things to be seized."* (Federal Constitution, Amendment 4, 1789)

Did you catch that? No warrants shall be issued but upon probable cause, supported by oath or affirmation. Was a support of oath or affirmation attached to the warrant? If not, the warrant was invalid and the arresting officers made a warrantless arrest. In these circumstances, file a lawsuit against the arresting officers. Ignorance of the law is no excuse.

In the case of Payton v. New York, the Supreme Court acknowledged the particulars of a valid warrant as opposed to the evils of a general warrant (also known as a bench warrant).

> *"It is familiar history that indiscriminate searches and seizures conducted under the authority of 'general warrants' were the immediate evils that motivated the framing and adoption of the Fourth Amendment...As it was ultimately adopted, the Amendment contained two separate clauses, the first protecting the basic right to be free from unreasonable searches and seizures, and the second requiring that warrants be particular and supported by probable cause...It is thus perfectly clear that the evil*

the Amendment was designed to prevent was broader than the abuse of a general warrant." (Payton v. New York, 1980)[52]

If your State Constitution's Bill of Rights has similar wording to that of the Federal Constitution's Fourth Amendment, more power can be inserted into your lawsuit against the arresting officers.

And finally, were you deprived of your civil rights under the color of law? If a state actor uses the legal system to deprive you of your constitutional protections, the state actor opens themselves up to a civil rights lawsuit. More specifically, you can file a civil action against the person or agency responsible under 42 U.S. Code, Section 1983.

A state actor is any person or entity who acts on behalf of the state. Social bureaucracies and private persons or agencies (usually offering medical, psychological, or therapeutic services) contracted with the government are state actors. In addition, joint activity between a private party and a government agent transforms the private party into a state actor.

In the case of Dennis v. Sparks (an action filed under 42 U.S.C. § 1983), the Supreme Court held, *"...Private persons, jointly engaged with state officials in a challenged action, are acting 'under color' of law for purposes of § 1983 actions."* The court ruled *"...against those private persons who participate in subverting the judicial process and, in so doing, inflict injury on other persons."*[53]

Of course, to file suit under a federal statute, there are requirements that must be fulfilled. The claimant must have had federal rights violated by someone acting under the color of state law. Although section 1983 has expanded dramatically since its passage in 1871, claims of this magnitude are complicated. There are a host of other elements that need to be established before a claim can be pursued and without careful preparation, your case could be sunk before it even starts.

---

[52] Payton v. New York, 445 U.S. 573 (United States Supreme Court, 1980).
[53] Dennis v. Sparks, 449 U.S. 24 (United States Supreme Court, 1980).

Contact an experienced attorney who can review your case and help you prepare an effective claim.

CHAPTER TWENTY-ONE

PLANT OBSTACLES

I would like to discuss some tactics you can employ to obstruct the State's movement. Obstacles don't stop the enemy's pursuit; it's only intended to slow them down. Planting a hidden obstacle in front of your enemy will take them some time to realize that a road-block has been placed in front of them. Once the State has realized what you've done, it won't be long until they find a bypass, and their pursuit continues. Setting obstacles will be a continuing effort until the battle ends.

The obstacles listed below are intended to complement the actions of another. So it would be beneficial to utilize several at one time. If you have a trusted friend or family member willing to help, you're sitting on a gold mine. This list doesn't encompass all possible options. Brainstorm some ideas with a friend, and find other ways to set obstacles for the State. But remember, its effectiveness is made only by the element of surprise.

Obstacle 1: Relocate to a Different State

For obvious reasons, residing within the same jurisdiction as the rulers who seek your destruction isn't wise. If someone is paid handsomely to assassinate you, it's irrational to stay in the local area. The rational person would flee; they wouldn't wait to have a job lined up first. By moving to a different state, the court loses jurisdiction over you (even though they claim otherwise). The government bullies become dependent on the federal government and other state jurisdictions to execute their unlawful edicts.

You don't want to transfer your citizenship to the new state, if you can avoid it. (Don't transfer your driver's license.) You just want to live there without a record of your existence. Avoid getting home services in your name, such as electric, water, cable, Internet, landline phone, etc. Rather, look to share a room or apartment with someone else where the services are already in someone else's name. Moving to a state and living with friends or relatives that are helpful is your best option. Additionally, you'll need to supply an address, which allows you to receive mail but protects your physical location and whereabouts. I'll discuss your options in the next section.

Drive as little as possible, especially your vehicle with out-of-state tags. Walk, ride a bike, take public transportation, or catch rides with friends and family. You may need to drive occasionally, but don't make it a habit. The less your vehicle is on the road, the better.

Your new state isn't motivated by greed, but by ideology. For your old state to get wealthy, your new state must pick up its pursuit after you—without reaping any of the monetary benefits. This is naturally de-motivating, which can potentially work in your favor.

You'll need this advantage later should you request that certain government officials or agents interpose on your behalf. Your petition will hold more weight when the officials aren't motivated by greed.

Obstacle 2: Conceal Your Physical Location

If possible, consider using an out-of-state address of a trusted friend. For example, let's say that your family court case is in California. You could live with a relative in Tennessee but utilize the address of trusted friend in Kentucky. However, your friend in Kentucky must have the means to contact you about your mail. They could scan and email your mail to you or they could mail it to the person you're living with. When your driver's license and vehicle tags are about to expire, this provides you the ability to get them renewed in a state you've never lived in.

Without the help of another person, you could look into obtaining a UPS mailbox. The UPS Store gives you a real street address, so feel free to use this as your mailing address, physical address, and billing address. It's best to manage a UPS mailbox from an adjoining state, but it may not be feasible. When filling out the paperwork at the UPS store, don't provide your physical location. You can use a friend's address, an old address, or a fictitious address.

But the utmost importance is to keep your physical location under tight confidentiality. The three credit reporting bureaus—Equifax, Experian, and TransUnion—receive your address through your financial institutions and any loans or mortgages you hold or apply for. Once these agencies get your address, it's accessible to anyone who wants it.

The United States Postal Service will gladly report your address change to anyone who mails you anything. And the auto insurance industry will be happy to provide your vehicle's physical location to any government agency demanding the information. They would prefer to protect themselves at your expense. Do yourself a favor and utilize a UPS mailbox or an alternate out-of-state address. You can still receive mail, but in the process, you can give the government a false location.

Caution: turning on home services in your name might negate all of your hard efforts. Such services include: electric, water, cable, Internet, landline phone, etc. However, the more services you can have in someone else's name, the better off you are.

Additionally, cell phone services are deceitful—they're tracking devices, even when they're shut off. This is not good if the service is in your name. If you must have your own phone, consider the Librem, a security and privacy-focused phone, made by Purism. The location tracking can be disabled. You can visit their store at https://puri.sm.

One final warning: avoid a Post Office Box since it cannot be used as a physical location.

Obstacle 3: Appeal for an Interposition

One strategic method used by the government is to pit citizens against one another. This happens when the courts demand one private citizen or government agency to commit a crime against another private citizen. It's masked by assigning a new name. In this case, the name "child support" conceals the crime of robbery.

The execution of this crime is conducted when the government secretly contacts an individual or group of individuals, which are positioned between them and their target (you). They make unlawful demands accompanied with propaganda, intimidation, and fear to force compliance of those demands.

Interposition is the act of interposing on behalf of another. You should appeal to those individuals to stand up on your behalf and refuse to execute the government's plot of malice. Although these people already stand between you and the government, don't expect them to interpose on your behalf if you don't request it. Some examples of those in a position to interpose would include:

- An employer can interpose on behalf of employees.
- The local police department can interpose on behalf of the community within its jurisdiction.
- The city mayor can interpose on behalf of city residents.
- The state governor can interpose on behalf of citizens.

When you request interposition, ensure you make the correct contact. For example, if an unlawful warrant was issued for your arrest, you might want to contact your local police chief. If he refuses to interpose, then contact your state's attorney general. If needed, you could work your way up to your state's governor, since he is the head of your state's executive branch—the branch of government intended to faithfully execute the laws. Always start with the lowest level possible and work your way up until you have received interposition. If you live in one jurisdiction, but you work in another, it might behoove you to request interposition from the law enforcement agencies in both jurisdictions.

Here are a few pointers to consider when writing a letter requesting interposition.

- Words are powerful and can impact your request. Utilizing the proper words and the right language has the potential to move the other person.
- Keep the letter short, brief, and to the point.
- Answer this question in your letter: "Why should they interpose on your behalf?"
- Sum up vital information. Don't get wrapped up in the details of your case.
- Avoid language that's vague, misleading, or deceptive. Instead, properly use words which accurately describe the action —stealing or theft as opposed to child support.
- Only use politically correct language when used as a proper noun—you want to address the name which has been assigned to the action, *not* the action itself.
- Address the unlawful order received by the government and bullet point what makes it unlawful. Don't point out the consequences or the criminal activity being committed if the recipient doesn't interpose.
- Don't play the role of the victim.

Should your request for interposition be denied, consider taking a different avenue. If your local sheriff denies it, how do you know that the attorney general won't approve it? If the payroll department with your employer denies it, how do you know that the president of your company (or owner) won't approve it?

If all levels of your employer deny your request, it might be best to terminate the relationship you have with your employer.

Obstacle 4: Transact in the Underground Economy

Open up a private PayPal (or PayPal alternative, such as Stripe) account. PayPal is primarily linked to your email address. So if the government (or your ex-wife) has your email address, you might want to open a new email account first. (I recommend ProtonMail since it is free, encrypted, and beyond the jurisdiction of the United States government.) People can transfer money to you through PayPal. You can buy and sell online by using your PayPal balance. The available products on the Internet have greatly expanded. You can purchase clothes, hygiene and bathroom supplies, and even groceries online.

If you need to shop at a retail business that doesn't accept PayPal payments, consider buying a gift card with your PayPal balance. You can check sites, such as www.egifter.com, www.giftcards.com, www.mygiftcardsupply.com, or www.paypal.com/us/gifts. You can also use your digital gift cards in brick and mortar stores. This method allows you to bypass your checking account—an account the government has access to. It would be a good idea to leave your bank account open. Just keep a very low balance.

In some circumstances, you wouldn't be able to pay with your PayPal balance, such as fuel or car repairs. Don't fall into the trap of opening a PayPal Cash Plus account with debit card. For the convenience of a PayPal debit card, you're sacrificing your account privacy. When you open a card account, PayPal records all of your private information. This is in accordance with federal law under the guise of fighting terrorism and money laundering activities. But regardless, your identity, linked with your account, is reported to the government —for your protection, of course.

In situations where you can't use your PayPal balance, a trusted friend or relative becomes a prized possession. They can physically make the payment, while you transfer money to them from your Pay-Pal account. Your friend or relative could even open up a new checking or prepaid account for you. (Your name, however, should *not* be on the account.) Some financial institutions may even issue a debit card in your name, but solely at the request of the account owner. This is a commonly seen with children's accounts. Whether it's a debit or prepaid card, use the account to deposit into and access the money through the card. (Re-loadable cards bought in the store is another great option.)

There's still yet another alternative for you to explore. If you'd rather throw off the shackles of government tyranny over your money, challenge yourself to live on cryptocurrency. Under America's centralized banking system, accounts are created, identifiable, and available to the government. This central authority issues fiat currency and controls the accounting ledger. This makes it possible for the court to order your bank to alter their ledger.

Cryptocurrency, however, is a decentralized system of exchange. The court's unchecked power over your money crumbles when the accounting ledger resides on every computer on the exchange. Therefore, the government doesn't have access to or control over your cryptocurrency. It cannot be taxed, inflated, or garnished.

There are several cryptocurrencies on the market, but the most widely recognized is Bitcoin. If you're interested in learning more about cryptocurrency, visit "https://99bitcoins.com/" and watch their videos. I also recommend watching a documentary titled "Life on Bitcoin," which is about a newly married couple and their challenges to survive when every living necessity can only be purchased with cryptocurrency. It's available to watch on Amazon Prime video.

Cryptocurrency can be mined or purchased. You can send and receive it. You can buy with it or sell it for traditional currency. But first, you must download a digital wallet to your desktop or smart phone. Tip: A hardware wallet is more secure if you intend to store cryptocurrency, while the wallet app on your smart phone is more effective if you intend to exchange it for goods or services. Visit "https://www.bitcoin.com/" to begin your journey.

But I must caution you about Bitcoin debit cards. These cards are issued by the centralized banking industry. They're subject to government finance laws, which require the financial institution to record all your personal information and report it to the government.

Bitcoin debit cards are usually prepaid. They're not linked directly to your Bitcoin wallet, so you're not actually spending Bitcoin at the grocery store. What happens when you transfer Bitcoin onto your prepaid debit card is that you're actually selling your Bitcoin (BTC) for United States Dollars (USD) at the current exchange rate.

The bank who issued your Bitcoin debit card creates an account that identifies you. Your debit card is linked to that account. The bank buys your BTC, and the money is held in your bank account until you spend it. But if the financial institution receives a court order to garnish all current and future wages, you'll never receive payment for the Bitcoin you've sold.

If you find it a bit overwhelming to switch to PayPal or cryptocurrencies and intend to continue using your bank account, consider transferring money to your PayPal balance or store some cryptocurrency as a form of savings. You can still be prepared if the government ever cleans out your bank accounts.

Obstacle 5: Employ with a Locally-Owned Business

Gaining employment with a small, locally-owned and operated business is a step in the right direction. This environment opens the door for your employer to see you as an individual, not a number. This is because the same person hires you, trains you, and provides you direction. This one person also observes your work ethics, punctuality, and attitude. The person who knows the most about you also controls your pay.

Which would be easier: to commit a crime against someone you know, trust, and appreciate or to commit a crime against a stranger? In our centralized economy, it's difficult to find work apart from big corporations. A local manager hires you, but someone else in another state pays you. You're just a name and a number, but there's no relationship.

Be mindful of the fact that out-of-state judges will place small business owners in the cross hairs. A business in one state (say Georgia) is not bound by laws from another state (say New Mexico). Similarly, New Mexico judges should only issue orders that comply with New Mexico laws, not Georgia laws.

State laws that violate the life, liberty, and property of others actually create a conflict. A judge might order your employer to withhold a certain amount of money from your paycheck, but that amount might be greater than the legal limit within your state. Naturally, your employer will likely comply with the judge's decree. That is, until you show him that he's violating the law. By writing a strong, solid, and compelling case, you might be able to place your boss' mind at ease and persuade him or her to interpose on your behalf. Let's face it, are you fearful of breaking another state's law? Of course not! Your fear is amplified when you're facing a situation that causes you to break the law of your own state.

But what happens if your employer doesn't interpose? You might request an interposition from your state's attorney general or the governor. If they are moved and intercede on your behalf, I'm certain that your employer would rather obey their own state officials than take orders from the judge in another state. This is a strategic tactic of using one government against another.

Obstacle 6: Explore Under-the-Table Employment

This option can be fairly difficult for most people. But hopefully you can be successful in this endeavor. I would highly recommend this option for a quick but very effective method, if you're able to meet one of the two criteria.

- You know somebody who can get you connected.
- You have the skill required to undertake the job without training.

Jobs in this field can include farming, carpentry, landscaping, or mechanics. You could also look into fields such as, electrical or plumbing. What about babysitting, being a nanny, or house cleaning? The common attribute with all of these fields is that they are either outdoors or are mobile. It's important to understand that under-the-table jobs are more common within these fields, but not all positions within these fields will be under-the-table.

Of course, if you possess high work ethics but lack the skills necessary for self-reliance, you might consider joining the WWOOF program.

Obstacle 7: Join the WWOOF Program

Worldwide Opportunities on Organic Farms, USA (WWOOF-USA) is part of a worldwide effort to link visitors with organic farmers. Through this program, you can volunteer to work on organic farms in exchange for lodging and three meals per day. You pay a yearly membership fee of about $40, but they will connect you with organic farmers looking for some help. The farmer will train you on your tasks, so no experience or skills are necessary.

There are over 1,500 organic farmers within the United States enrolled in this program. You can stay on one farm as long as the farmer wants to keep you, or you can move or travel around the U.S. visiting different farms. You work approximately 6 hours per day, 5 days per week, but verify this with the farmer before you accept the job. This still frees up some extra time for you to make a little money on the side.

If the State does to you what they're doing to me, this is a viable option since it allows you to bypass the monetary exchange for labor. You can be productive in exchange for direct food and lodging. Since our government is attempting to depopulate the U.S. without being noticed, you have to think about survival.

If you're interested in this program, visit https://wwoofusa.org.

Obstacle 8: Start Your Own Business

Starting your own business has become easier and more affordable with the invention of the Internet and the rise of e-commerce platforms. However, this option is a slow process and risky at the same time, but its success would be more permanent, and the long-term benefits would far outweigh other alternatives. In the meantime, other obstacles would still have to be employed.

If your expertise is administration or retail, under-the-table employment is hardly an option, but starting your own online business can become reality.

Take some time today to consider what type of work you enjoy doing. Do you possess the required knowledge? What resources would you need before you could begin? How would you acquire those resources? Could you borrow from family or friends? Could you rent them, or should you buy them?

Will you be selling a product or service as an individual or would you prefer operating a business to provide the product or service? Consider the difference. As an individual, business would be slower and profits would be lower, but operating an actual business will require you to register with your state's department of revenue and file monthly tax returns. Each method has its perks, but each also has its downfalls.

How would you market your product or service? Through email? Through social media? By word of mouth? Before investing any money, create a business plan. Then share your plan with someone you trust to get their input. If your supply of money runs short, consider ways to raise money.

Obstacle 9: Raise Money

There are numerous ways to raise money. You need money to fight the allegations, to pay for an attorney, to reestablish your living environment, or to start your own business. But I must warn you against the collection of government funds. It's nothing more than a scheme. If you remember, the government is the one who stole everything from you in the first place. So giving you a small portion of your property back and calling it food stamps (also known as SNAP) only produces poverty and reduces you to a slave of the State (your financial benefactor). Let's look at more honest and effective ways to raise money through persuasion, not government coercion.

Consider starting a fundraiser. With the effort of a couple of friends or relatives, you can be successful. Fundraising campaigns are vitally important because individuals who donate have limited resources. So you will need active fundraising efforts to reach out to the community, the state, and eventually the nation. Prepare fundraising materials, such as flyers, business cards, and a donation form. As your fundraiser grows, recruit others to help you raise funds. (Tip: sending emails, posting to social media, and starting a GoFundMe account has its place, but a successful campaign requires much more activity).

Also consider selling on Bonanza (an Ebay alternative). Acquiring products to sell can provide a continual flow of funds, but requires continual work. Find great deals at yard sales, the classifieds (e.g. Craigslist), liquidation or going out-of-business sales, estate sales, or after-holiday sales when stores discount their products up to 90% off. You might even find some things in the dumpster that you can clean, repair, and resell. Do you have friends or family that is spring cleaning and can give you things they don't want? The more products you offer...the more sales you get.

You can also write a book, short story, or novel and self-publish it. In this manner, you can get a commission from each book sold. E-books are very popular, easy to write and produce, and affordable to publish.

The key to successful obstacles is the element of surprise. Don't be fooled into thinking that you must give away your confidential, military strategy because you have nothing to hide. Rather, what do you have that's worth protecting? Your private information must be kept confidential from the State if you intend to triumph. This includes your new address once you move.

The State, on the other hand, has everything to hide. That's why they do things in secret, such as restraining orders and the CSD's ransom demands. The State's secrecy is to devise evil against the innocent, whereas confidentiality of your private information protects the innocent. There's a big difference between secrecy and confidentiality.

CHAPTER TWENTY-TWO

BYPASS LANDMINES

The State strategically plants minefields in and around your path, so your decisions and actions must be slow, deliberate, and carefully thought out. Decisions that are reactionary and made in haste are the most dangerous, since you risk stepping on a landmine. You cannot avoid the minefield, but you can bypass the mines without stepping on them.

A landmine is invisible to the naked eye. But once you step on it, the damage is often fatal. To bypass the mine, you must first recognize its existence. Many soldiers have died from stepping on landmines they didn't see, because the enemy had buried them.

You're at war! And the State is your enemy, so they will hide and bury landmines in hopes that you'll carelessly step on one. So how do you avoid a mine that you can't see?

Well, think about it. Each time a mine is planted, the natural area is disrupted. If you are observant to this disruption, you can step over or around the area. But one thing is certain; passing through a mine-field cannot be done in haste. It must be slow, and you must remain sober and vigilant. Let's examine some mines so that you're not fooled into stepping on them. This list is not all-inclusive. It's intended to give you a start. But keep in mind that the State will, in the future, invent new landmines that you must identify.

Landmine 1: Entertaining Negative Thoughts

A negative thought is a natural phenomenon, but entertaining those thoughts is a choice. You need to possess knowledge and understanding of a negative event without meditating on those negative aspects. You cannot defeat your war-hungry spouse if you're ignorant of her behavior and the hidden powers of darkness. But dwelling on your negative circumstances is self-destructive.

God provides us the only route to avoid this landmine. It's penned by Paul in Philippians 4:8, *"Finally, brethren, whatsoever things are true, whatsoever things are honest, whatsoever things are just, whatsoever things are pure, whatsoever things are lovely, whatsoever things are of good report; if there be any virtue, and if there be any praise, think on these things."*

Think...meditate...ponder on these things, and you'll bypass the first landmine planted. Here are a few pointers:

- Follow my advice from chapter 19: *Enduring Adversity*. Ensure you maintain a positive focus throughout your entire ordeal.
- Heed feasible recommendations from chapter 20: *Pursue Offensive Maneuvers* and chapter 21: *Plant Obstacles*. Don't be ignorant or naive about your circumstances.
- Stay productive. Work keeps you busy and focused on good things, which reduces the time you have to entertain negativity. Idleness, on the other hand, is always self-destructive.
- Read...Read...Read! Read and study the Bible. Subscribe to and read the print edition of The New American magazine at https://www.thenewamerican.com. Read wholesome books, fiction or non-fiction.

Reading engages your mind, a necessary component to remaining positive in a negative world.

But I must caution you about television. Watching videos is mindless behavior and seduces you to a hypnotic state. Television has nearly the same affect that alcohol has on the mind—it only conceals your problem. It doesn't help you endure it. So keep your television down to a minimum if you want to avoid this landmine.

Landmine 2: Losing Touch with Reality

Suppose a young female friend of yours, whom we'll call Sue, moved into a house located in a bad part of town. Crime was high, break-ins occurred daily, and illicit drug dealings and usage ran rampant. Regardless, she accepted the superficial notion that most people were good by nature. Sue never paid attention to her environment, so her ignorance led to some very strange behavior.

This young girl never locked her doors or windows. She didn't own a dog or a firearm, and she saw no need for an alarm or security system. In addition, it was odd that she had no window blinds or curtains. In fact, there were several nights during Spring when she opted to open her windows for a cool breeze. But through it all, Sue felt perfectly safe. She never felt in danger.

You recognized Sue's vulnerability as a result of those decisions, so you tried to warn her numerous times. But each time, she got very argumentative. Your friend brushed away "peeping toms" as a conspiracy theory, and often accused you of being a deceiver, uneducated, or mentally ill for always thinking the worst about people. To keep the tension down and avoid further arguments, you stopped talking about it. Sadly, this young girl's emotions had deceived her.

Then one night, you received a disturbing phone call. Sue's house had been broken into. You were informed that your good friend apparently stumbled onto the burglar in the middle of the night when she went to investigate a noise that woke her. Determined to leave no witnesses, the intruder brutally attacked her before fleeing the scene. Sue was hospitalized with internal bleeding, and it appeared she might also suffer from severe brain damage.

Every opportunity, you visited Sue in the hospital. Initially, she was unable to respond or talk to you. Several months later, Sue miraculously walked out of the hospital. But for the rest of her life, she will walk with a limp and live with a terrible scar on her face to remind her of that dreadful night. After you took her home, you were shocked to learn that she still thought you were being overly cautious with your ridiculous "conspiracy theories." She went right back to her old ways and her strange behavior. This happens when a person loses touch with reality.

Sue represents the average American. The innocent inmate who was in prison because they were railroaded are finally released, yet they go back to their old life. A father who loses access to his children continues living in his old ways. People often witness a tragedy befalling a relative, friend, or neighbor, but behaves as if that could never happen to them. The lack of political understanding and the hidden powers of darkness can easily cause us to make foolish decisions, which opens us for destruction.

We've all made mistakes. We've all been in a place where we didn't care what the government was doing or who they were hurting. But now it's time to put away our foolishness and educate ourselves. Avoid this landmine by visiting Appendix E: *Additional Resources* to begin your journey in seeking truth and understanding. Don't repeat past mistakes.

Landmine 3: Reading Government Correspondence Prior to Work

Have you ever heard the expression, "Garbage In...Garbage Out?" Well, what do you think will be the result if you open a threatening, intimidating, or provocative letter just prior to going to work? At work, your job may consist of stocking shelves, helping customers, running the cash register, etc. Your workplace doesn't allow you the opportunity to ponder your circumstances, reevaluate your strategy, and read between the lines. More often than not, proper scrutiny reveals that the government just created a little hiccup, but amplifies it in the letter to scare you into submission. You can't sort this out at work.

Therefore, you'll resort to entertaining this negativity. Then while you're at work, garbage will seep out through your attitude and behavior. You'll have difficulty focusing on your tasks and will tend to be more pessimistic during your shift. Your attitude and behavior will offend those around you, no matter how unintentional it may be.

People don't like being around someone who is constantly negative, has a poor self-image, or possesses a vengeful mindset. Your work ethics will deteriorate, which can place your employment in jeopardy.

The moral of the story is: your letter isn't going anywhere. You can hold off for another 8 hours before opening it. In the heat of the moment, things can look pretty grim. But after some time and careful reflection, the State's setback didn't change anything. It was just another challenge for you to conquer. Time, when used properly, can have a powerful advantage. Don't simply read the government's letter out of curiosity. Practice the virtue of patience.

Landmine 4: Requesting a Guardian Ad Litem

A Guardian Ad Litem is an attorney who claims to represent your children. This sounds very appealing so most people are easily duped. But it's a landmine that far too many people have stepped on. The assertions of a Guardian Ad Litem are in complete opposition to the truth found in Scripture.

- **Guardian Ad Litems are appointed by satanic forces.** Children are born with parents to represent their best interest, and God established the father as the head. The father is the sole representation of his family and children. This is God's order. God gives children a father to represent their best interest, but Satan gives them a Guardian Ad Litem.

- **Guardian Ad Litems are not representatives.** For a person to be represented, an individual must first possess authority, which can then be extended to their representative. Since children possess no authority over themselves, God assigns them a representative—their father—until they reach the age of maturity.

- **Guardian Ad Litems are unqualified to represent.** Extending one's authority to a representative must be free from deception, threats, intimidation, bribery, or compulsion. If any one of these is present, then the representative isn't representing. Guardian Ad Litems are always requested and appointed under these circumstances—without which their services wouldn't be necessary.

- **Guardian Ad Litems work for the State.** An attorney who is court-ordered has been hired by the State. This means that the State secures their salary, regardless where the money comes from. If the Guardian Ad Litem was hired by one of the parties without a court order, then the attorney is actually a representative of the party who hired them.

- **Guardian Ad Litems are not doctors or detectives.** Their expertise is litigation, not medicine or forensics. So if some form of child abuse is present, an attorney can easily be deceived.

Landmine 5: Compromising

Compromising is superficially accepted as an inherently good trait, but don't be deceived. Settling your differences by making a deal is deadly. The commandment for wives to submit to their own husbands

(Ephesians 5:22), intrinsically prohibits marital compromise. So teaching marriage partners to make concession is a false doctrine.

Compromising, however, is frequently brought to the forefront when an important issue is at stake. The question to ask is...On what are we compromising?

Suppose you request a custody evaluation. Your spouse and the judge will usually reach a mutual agreement that both parties must "compromise." Since you want the custody evaluation and are willing to pay for it, your ex-wife feels that she should get to choose the evaluator. It sounds a lot like this: "I'll give you what you want, if you give me what I want." But we must learn to read between the lines.

Your request for an evaluation is out of concern for your children. (Why else would you be willing to bear the cost?) Your wife's demand to choose the evaluator, however, is to control the outcome without bearing the cost. What good is an evaluation if your wife controls the outcome?

Many women, like Amy, attempt to turn that argument on its head by claiming that you would collude with the evaluator. The implication is that she'd never do such a thing—this is moral superiority (pride). However, collusion is possible for either party. So to be perfectly fair, the party who hires (chooses) the evaluator should also bear the cost. It's not really a compromise if one party hires (or colludes with) the evaluator, while the other party pays the fees.

What we're uncovering is that mothers ostentatiously claim to protect their children with restraining orders, but then demand to poison a medical or custody evaluation under the banner of "compromise." This rhetoric conceals their motives.

Furthermore, "compromise" is misleading terminology, because it implies that both parties need to reach a mutual agreement, and the refusal to compromise is equated with selfishness. However, mothers who deny the father access to their children usually have mental or emotional problems and are generally unfit parents. Impartial evaluations expose this reality. They are only a means to an end, *not* an end itself. No father *wants* an evaluation. They only want more access to their children. So this cannot be a compromise. Your ex-wife gets what she wants (to control the outcome of the evaluation), but you never get what you want (more access to your children).

And in my case, this was a negotiation between the judge and Amy. I had requested the evaluation, but the judge and Amy reached a mutual agreement on their own terms. I was exempt from the process. So they colluded together for fear that I might collude against Amy—all under the color of law.

Landmine 6: Disclosing Your Personal Information

The Child Support Division files a lawsuit against you, but never presents a case against you. They never even accuse you of fault. Their suit implies wrong-doing on your part without the need to directly accuse. But this is only accomplished if they perceive you as their adversary—an enemy. But if they make you their enemy, then by a parity of reason, they too would be your enemy.

Is it any wonder why the CSD always comes out on top? It's one thing for the legislatures to pass laws that prop up their agency and its operations. It's another thing for you to turn over your private and confidential information to the enemy. Doing so can have devastating consequences in your case.

Part of the CSD's procedure is to seize all of your private information without a warrant. If you fail to "voluntarily" relinquish it, have no fear, your ex-wife will sell it to them in return for future child support money. Therefore, you should expect that anything you say or write can and will be used against you.

Regardless of the CSD's method to steal your private information, you should take all precautions to secure new or future information. You'll have some limitations when altering personal information, such as your Social Security Number and birth certificate. However, setting obstacles is a great way to change other portions of your personal information, such as your address and email. But proceed with caution because the CSD continually breaks the law by cross-referencing your SSN to obtain the new information.

The most effective way to fool the government is to set a decoy. (e.g. Your address is in one state, but your physical location is in another.) Whatever tactics you utilize, just keep it confidential from your ex-wife and all government agencies.

If you intend to make a request of the CSD, they'll require you to fill out a Financial Affidavit or other documents, but don't fill anything out just because they want you to. When filling out any CSD form, I'd advise you to approach each line with caution, because anything you write or attach *will* be used against you. If it can't be used against you, they'll ignore it. Nevertheless, only attach information that's relevant to serve your purpose. Don't let them decide what's relevant—you decide.

For example: Suppose you were forced to move in with your parents, and so your father connects you with a high-paying job. But you know that this job is also only temporary. These are special circumstances, not the norm. Later on, the CSD wants you to attach your most recent tax return, which shows these high wages. Since your wages are not a reflection of your past—prior to the State's intervention—nor will it reflect future realities, the tax return will only be used against you, not in your favor. Remember, you're their enemy.

Another example could be if the CSD asks you how many hours or nights you spend with your children. By filling in "zero," you're leading them to believe that you refuse to see or spend any time with your children. Of course, they don't understand the circumstances behind the "zero," nor would they care. The CSD didn't take your children away; the courts did. Leave these types of questions blank.

Could they deny your application if you fail to answer all questions or attach all required documents? Yes! But the problem is that their questions are constructed for the purpose of self-incrimination, *not* justice. How would this situation be handled in the context of criminal court? Let's take a look.

You're currently on the witness stand, testifying in your defense. You glance to the left and see several members of the jury looking at you. You look off to the right, and the judge is staring down at you. You look out into the courtroom and it's full of people condemning you. The only person present who is on your side is your attorney.

A tragic thought crosses your mind. *Will the jury side with the State and mob?* You feel so small, so helpless, and so vulnerable. Suddenly, the realization sets in: you're on trial. You silently cry out in your thoughts, *Dear God, help me!*

Just then, the prosecuting attorney snaps you back to the present by shouting your name. Approaching the witness stand, he pops the question, "How many times have you seen your children in the past month?"

You respond, "None, but–"

"No further questions," shouts the prosecutor. He's determined to persuade the jury to convict you for abandoning your children.

Now, your attorney steps up and asks you, "Why haven't you seen your children?"

And you explain, "Because they were kidnapped and held for ransom."

Wow! The power of cross-examination. Proverbs 18:17 tells us the importance of cross examination. *"He that is first in his own cause seemeth just; but his neighbour cometh and searcheth him."* Remove this judicial procedure, and you lose your innocence. There's no jury to save you. The CSD has a free ticket to gun down whomever they please. They despise the goodness of God and embrace the wickedness of the devil. This is why cross-examination had to be eliminated. It exposes truth—and truth requires justice.

The CSD's attorney *does not* represent you. He's prosecuting you, but cannot be cross-examined or searched. Hence, your answers will be twisted, perverted, and taken out of context. They're propagandizing your statements to justify their existence and intervention. Your answers will *never* be used in your favor. You're their worst enemy.

Landmine 7: Leaving False Criminal Charges on Your Public Record

If criminal charges were filed against you but ended without a conviction, check the laws of your state for criminal expunction. You need those criminal charges and any arrest(s) associated with the false allegations to be erased from public records and sealed from public disclosure. Nobody has the right to know that you've been accused, arrested, or indicted of a crime, especially in the face of false accusations. Your privacy is paramount to the public interest. So clear your name and expunge your record today.

Landmine 8: Complying with Unlawful Orders

To avoid this landmine, you must possess knowledge and understanding of the law—Natural Law, Revealed Law (Biblical), and Constitutional Law. This is the higher law and is superior to case law, legislative law, and executive or judicial orders, as well as administrative regulations and policies. These inferior and sometimes fictitious laws will lead you astray.

This is a very oppressive landmine. Once stepped on, it becomes difficult, but not impossible, to regain consciousness. The casualty who remains in a comatose state is unaware that those inferior laws and orders are being used to perpetrate vile activities against them.

For instance, a black-robed tyrant orders you to:

- …pay the kidnapper of your children.
- …pay the salaries of CSD agents.
- …purchase unnecessary health insurance.
- …give away your privately-owned property, such as your house, car, or furniture.
- …abandon your children (restraining order).

However, if he doesn't enact a restraining order against you, he still has the power to order you to:

- …a specific pick-up or drop-off location to transfer your child.
- …turn your children over to your ex's friends (strangers).
- …remain in a certain locality.
- …send your children to a specific school.

Obeying one requires you to obey them all. This casualty is in a comatose state—an American slave. This is what ignorance of God's Word and the Rule of Law produces. Avoiding this landmine (or regaining consciousness if you've already stepped on it) requires you to seek the truth, recognize the truth, and put the truth into action.

The State doesn't care what you know. They care about what you do with what you know. Isn't it time to execute your knowledge by resisting unlawful orders? (This landmine is thoroughly addressed in chapters 12-14. Reread those three chapters if you need a refresher.)

Landmine 9: Appearing for Unproductive Hearings

Court appearances, either in person or by telephone, should be productive. Arguments should be heard, evidence should be submitted, the accuser and any witnesses should be cross-examined, and the truth should be sought. This is what a productive court hearing looks like. If you remove the productive process, only injustice can be dispensed. You cannot accidentally produce justice.

What would happen if you weren't productive in making supper? After working in the kitchen for an hour, you had made a mess with all the ingredients, but nothing was cooked, properly prepared, or even edible. Could you snap your fingers and have a full stomach? In a similar fashion, family court seems to think so when it comes to justice. But that begs the question: If injustice is the only thing that can and will prevail in court, what's the purpose of a court appearance? Couldn't everyone just stay home while judges sign whatever court order they intend to anyway? Why should anyone go to the courtroom if there's no procedure to produce justice?

Without production, family court attempts to rule you without your consent. They make you their slave and acquire your wealth in the process. When a court hearing is unproductive, your appearance means nothing to you but everything to them. You are "voluntarily" subjecting yourself to the powers of the State.

If you have reasonable belief that the court appearance could be productive and you are preparing to present your case, then do show up. On the flip side, there will also be some tattle tale signs that the court hearing will not be productive. A few of the signs include:

- **A hearing scheduled without a motion.** A motion is an application made to a court requesting an order or rule directing some act to be done in favor of the applicant. Without a motion, you don't know what's being requested or why. This prohibits you from preparing an argument or mounting a defense.
- **A hearing scheduled to appear in front of a hearing officer or support magistrate.** The hearing officer will only determine how much money to lay and collect from you. This isn't producing justice, it's only dispensing injustice. And if you try to advocate for paying less, it gives the appearance that you are trying to stiff your ex with your responsibility.
- **A hearing scheduled at a time which precludes you from arguing your case or mounting a defense.** Family court employs this method when they're looking for a smokescreen. For example: You're pending criminal charges for child molestation and a court hearing is set to determine custody.

- **A hearing scheduled, not at your request, which succeeds other unproductive court hearings.**

On a side note, refusing to appear for court doesn't apply to criminal court, because the criminal court system is set up differently than family court. In criminal court, you aren't being ruled without your consent because no one person is in charge. Instead, criminal court consists of a process with several checks and balances in place—a process abolished in family court. This procedure helps to maintain a productive court hearing.

Landmine 10: Responding Poorly to Bad Motions

Before any court hearing is scheduled, you should receive a copy of the motion that was filed with the court. When false allegations are in play, bad motions are always filed. Here are a few identification marks to look for:

A motion lacking explanation—A solid and fundamentally grounded argument is difficult to produce when the abuse has been fabricated. So attention to detail is imperative. Your spouse may use trigger words, such as abusive, dangerous, or violent. But these words are vague and lack explanation. What abuse have you committed? What makes you dangerous? How are you violent? Other trigger words include: fear, threaten, intimidate, anger, power, and control.

A motion deficient of support—All crimes produce some form of physical evidence. This makes it difficult for false accusers to reference what doesn't exist. Physical evidence could include a medical examination or psychological evaluation. But keep in mind, this evidence can only reveal the crime, not necessarily link you to the crime. Notes from therapy or counseling sessions as well as a Grand Jury indictment don't constitute proof. These methods are intended to manufacture evidence where none exists.

A motion shifting to inward motives—These are commonly re-ferred to as Red Flag accusations. They always begin with an outward action, such as "He would change her diaper…" Then shift to inward motives, "…so he could fondle her privates." The accuser may even exploit a photo of you kissing your toddler with a peck (outward ac-tion) to imply that you're sexually attracted to her (inward motive). False accusations must shift to the motive while innocent behavior is portrayed as a cover-up.

A motion using hearsay—Referencing valid evidence or quoting an expert from a published report or evaluation is not hearsay. On the contrary, quoting or paraphrasing any person without a published re-port is indeed hearsay. Published, in this instance, refers to a written or recorded statement being made available to both parties in the case.

A motion displaying representation—Telling the court what your child said about you is hearsay, but telling them what your child feels, thinks, believes, or desires (all internal characteristics) is representa-tion. "She was upset when he didn't show up or call…She's scared of her father…He frightens her…She doesn't want his last name any-more." These examples are false representations. Since you cannot validate them to ensure accuracy, the intent is to force you to believe them. That's a clear sign of oppression.

The motion for a restraining order that Amy filed against me con-sisted of all five attributes above. So if your spouse files a bad motion with the court, always respond with a rebuttal for each charge against you. Stay away from language that's obvious to everyone but the judge, such as, That doesn't prove anything…No child thinks like that…That's hearsay and isn't valid evidence. Remember, you cannot prove your innocence, so you need to prove your spouse's guilt in-stead. Here are a few examples of refuting those false allegations.

Place an accusation in context—Let's say that you're accused of building a tent for you to have sex with your daughter. The proper context may be that your daughter was actually having a sleepover with her best friend and they asked you for permission to build a tent over the bed. Hint: Accusers who attack the inward motive and utilize outward actions as a cover-up never explain how they came across that information.

Shift focus from the accusation to the medical neglect of your child—If your spouse accused you of molestation or rape, you might demand to know why your ex hasn't provided your child the proper medical examination and care necessary. What is she trying to hide from the judge? Could the crime have been committed by another man your ex invited into her home—and she's trying to cover it up?

Provide your own evidence to discredit your spouse's accusations—For instance, your spouse may say that your child is scared of you (a false representation), but just two days before the accusations started, your child wrote you a note telling you how much they loved you and thought you were the best dad in the world.

You cannot and will never be able to prove your innocence. These rebuttals are examples of discrediting your spouse and proving that she's the guilty party. All three of these examples do not deny the charge of sexual abuse. If you deny the charges, the judge will think you're lying, so why deny it? Instead, approach from a different angle. This is how defendants in criminal court sway the jury in their favor. This is the only way to prove that you're not guilty.

In addition to refuting the false allegations filed in the motion, it's also important to make a request from the court. Depending on your circumstances or the motions filed by your spouse, your request can be any number of things. You might ask the court to deny your spouse's motion, request a custody evaluation, or ask for a parental alienation evaluation. You may request that the court compel your spouse to undergo a psychological evaluation, or maybe a transfer of custody so you could seek medical attention for your child.

Maybe you need to file a new petition or motion with the court, or you may only be responding. But at any rate, make your request first, bullet point your supporting arguments, and attach copies of any evidence you have.

PART FIVE

RESTORING FREEDOM

CHAPTER TWENTY-THREE

VICTORY: THE LORD'S TIMING

Adversity is never fun to go through, but it's essential for maturity and growth. This doesn't mean that evil's necessary, but rather, God transcends our circumstances, so He can turn evil around for good. People often wonder why God allows bad things to happen to good people. The answer rests with His principle of freedom—the freedom to choose.

When you're faced with trials and tribulations, endurance is the secret ingredient to overcoming your circumstances and living a full life. This conforms to the law of sowing and reaping. But when a person sows a victim mentality, they'll reap the curses of a victim.

In retrospect, the toughest years of my life contributed to an expansion of knowledge, strength, and courage. With the proper perspective, you'll observe the handiwork of God. Battle for Control and Chilling Effects (chapters 3 and 4 respectively) both focused on the visible effect of propaganda. It probably left you in suspense. But I'd like to close this book on a positive note. God only blesses righteous people. So here's the rest of my story.

Pulling away from the curb, mom headed home. It was September 3, 2016, and she had just picked me up at the Cincinnati-Northern Kentucky International Airport. I must have stared out the window for the entire trip. I was glad to see her, but not under these circumstances.

I had been released from jail and was temporarily moving in with my parents. My father persuaded his employer, Multi-Color, to provide me a job. For the first time in my working history, I enjoyed the traditional routine of Monday through Friday from 7 am to 3 pm. But this employment wouldn't have been possible without Divine intervention.

My dad's boss sent me to their temp agency to fill out an application and the necessary paperwork for the position. I was hired without an interview and immediately scheduled to begin work. But the temp agency still performed their usual tasks of a drug screen and background check.

My background check was held up until after I started my first day of work. However, the results shocked everyone since it showed I was pending felony criminal charges. But due to the contract between Multi-Color and their temp agency, since I had already started work, they were required to keep me employed for a minimum of three weeks. But the manager in charge must have liked my work ethics, because Multi-Color chose to keep me on.

This job lightened my burden. It kept me productive, preoccupied, and allowed me the opportunity to pay my legal debt. My parents and I hired a private attorney familiar with these types of cases. He was expensive, but the price of a false conviction was far greater. My attorney's fee, bail, polygraph examinations, and other travel-related expenses easily surpassed $35,000. Then God took a portion of this debt upon Himself by turning another bad situation on its head.

Prior to my arrival in Cincinnati, my aunt had just collected a life insurance payout due to the tragic loss of her husband. So she gifted my parents $14,000 to help offset my legal expenditures.

I stayed with my parents for nearly 17 months, and during that time, I took it upon myself to learn about Borderline Personality Disorder, the rise of sexual politics, and the attacks against the family.

These resources, many of them online, never touched the invisible characteristics that this book addresses.

Then one day, I stumbled upon some online videos published by the John Birch Society (JBS). I was intrigued, partially because they spoke about limited government—a concept I had never heard of. But since my mind also lacked the nutrition of knowledge and understanding, I craved political truth.

The JBS website introduced me to The New American (TNA), a magazine with essential news for freedom-loving Americans. TNA appealed to me because of its reporting and educational style. Their integrity and knowledge of history are unsurpassed qualities. They are often the first (and sometimes the only) news source to sound the alarm on freedom-destroying tactics.

In fact, the JBS store was paramount to jump starting my library. For the first time, I had an appetite to read—and I just couldn't get enough. As I reflect upon my younger days, I wasn't much of a reader. In reality, I hated reading as a child, which carried into my adult life. But I thank the Lord for allowing these circumstances to change my attitude about reading. Indeed, Christ used the State's intervention to strengthen my mind and to bring the Scriptures to life.

A genuine understanding of history and current affairs in America is exciting. Studying the Scriptures, the principles of individual freedom, and Austrian economics (a laissez-faire school of thought), imparts critical knowledge necessary to discern truth from error. And by frequently surrounding myself with truth, I found it easier to spot counterfeits. Critical thinking, psychological nutrition, and purposeful action come by reading—reading truth.

A Planned Departure

Living with my parents was only temporary, and I was itching to get out of the Cincinnati metropolitan area. I lived in Valdosta, Georgia for part of my childhood years, so I elected to move back after the charges were dismissed or I was acquitted.

In the summer of 2017, I prepared myself for the cross county drive out to New Mexico. Purchasing a camper van, I converted it into a miniature home with the help of my nephew. I built some cupboards, a counter, and a table. There was plenty of storage for food, clothes, books, and other odds and ends. These preparations kept me active and focused on the positive. After the trial, I planned to move to Valdosta.

Trial was scheduled for the following February, so about a week before, I headed out to New Mexico. After arriving in Las Cruces, I found a nice spot in the desert to set up camp. (For all the curiosity seekers, I joined a nationwide gym membership, so I could use their showers.) Anyhow, two days before trial, I received a phone call from my attorney that all criminal charges had been dismissed. Only by God's grace and mercy, He prohibited the State from ramming me through criminal court.

Although I was ready to leave for Valdosta, I needed to wait until February 27. That was my scheduled hearing for a mock trial over the temporary restraining order. So I waited in the solitary desert for another two weeks. It wasn't all that bad—quiet and peaceful. That's a rare commodity.

Not surprisingly, on February 27, Judge Isabel renewed the restraining order. His decision may have been based solely on my daughter's statement that if he favored me, she'd be murdered. Maybe, he thought that just because the prosecution found no evidence and the abuse accusations had been discredited, that didn't mean I wasn't guilty. But whatever his reason, I clearly understood that the wicked protect their own.

I enjoyed my solitude in the desert, so I waited until the first day of March to leave New Mexico. Upon my arrival in Valdosta, I started searching for employment. Within one week, Publix Super Market called me in for my first job interview. A few days later, I was contacted for my second job interview. It was at this interview that I was offered a part-time position as a bagger, which I gladly accepted.

Meanwhile, I started attending Open Bible Baptist Church. One of the deacons owned a used 3-bedroom, single wide mobile home that he had considered selling. It had been sitting vacant for some time, and he hadn't listed it for sale yet. After prayerful consideration, he made me an outstanding offer. I purchased the mobile home with the cash I'd saved from my Cincinnati employment and moved it into a rural mobile home park a few miles outside the city limits.

Obtaining employment with Publix and reestablishing a living environment was accomplished in record time. (My employment with Multi-Color is the only exception.) This speed can only be explained in the context of God's blessings for His children. Those who have a personal relationship with Jesus and surrender their heart to Him aren't exempt from the sufferings of this life, but through perilous times, God still blesses those who submit to His authority.

I was employed with Publix for 15 months. But during that time, I failed to devise a plan to protect my earnings from governmental theft. At the time, I had no idea how powerful family court could be from clear across the country as they extended their tentacles into another state's jurisdiction. So to protect themselves, others surrendered me to the unlawful tyranny of New Mexico.

In July, 2019, I launched my own online business. However, the late startup resulted in a short-lived business. But fortunately, it sustained me briefly during a period of unemployment that I faced soon afterward.

Less than two weeks later, Hobby Lobby hired me in a seasonal position and worked me approximately 47 hours per week. The overtime hours provided enough funds to gradually build my business. But the excruciatingly slow process to increase my inventory and build my product line only lasted for six months.

By the end of February, 2020, I was out of work again. Shortly thereafter, the panic induced by the Coronavirus propaganda enticed state governors to unlawfully shut down their economy by edict. Consequently, their action threw millions of people out of work. Although disastrous to the economy, this spike in unemployment actually worked in my favor as my creditors were more lenient on my late payments.

However, the shutdown of the economy only masked the problem I faced. As businesses gradually reopened, it did nothing to improve my circumstances. The sales from my business alleviated some of the financial strain I was under. I didn't know what the Lord had in store for me, but I continued to trust Him.

I posted a free classified ad online to offer a helping hand around the neighborhood or city. I also informed my pastor and several members from two separate churches of my dire situation. But unfortunately, there was no response. I desperately wanted to regain employment, but any effort on my part was futile. The State was determined to confiscate the great majority of my wages, not leaving me anything to live on. And the part of my salary they couldn't justify stealing for themselves, they wanted to give away to their friends in the health insurance industry.

I was nearing the verge of financial collapse when the Lord opened a door and made a way of escape. His timing couldn't have been more perfect.

A Narrow Escape

At the beginning of May, 2020, I offered to sell my mobile home to the park landlord. Surprisingly, he joyfully purchased it. This immediately solved my financial troubles, but it left me homeless.

While searching the Internet, I stumbled upon the Worldwide Opportunities on Organic Farms, USA (WWOOF) website. This provided an opportunity to escape government oppression. By working on a farm in exchange for lodging and meals, I was effectively by-passing the monetary exchange. This is under-the-table work.

After joining the program, I was provided access to over 1,500 organic farms across America. I browsed several farms by location, contacted a few farmers, and requested to visit one. This appointment was scheduled for June 4, 2020.

As the month progressed, I was getting excited as numerous thoughts raced through my mind. I was moving to a farm...I would learn new skills...I would become more self-reliant...I would live in a secluded area...Nobody will know my whereabouts...The State doesn't have the power to extract money I don't have...In fact, the State won't even know where I am.

I stored some money in my PayPal account and kept some cash in my wallet for emergencies, but the great majority of my money from the sale of my mobile home was held by my parents.

I lived on the first farm for three months, and then moved to a second farm. I worked about six hours per day, five days per week, and I was compensated with lodging, three meals per day, and new skills in the process. I tended chickens and collected the eggs. I also helped repair fences along the farm's parameter and worked in the garden by planting, weeding, and harvesting. The farmer killed his meat chickens, and I even participated in eviscerating a few of them.

I learned to make bars of soap for the first farmer I lived with. He sold his soap to businesses and individuals at the farmer's market. Once I moved to my second farm, the first farmer invited me back on a weekly basis to make soap and get paid in the process. I now had my very first under-the-table job with a monetary compensation.

At my second farm, I learned to care for a horse named Willie and a cow named Rosie. Awake by 6:00 every morning, I fed and watered the animals. This farm also had goats, egg-laying hens, turkeys, dogs, and barn cats.

Only God could place me in a situation where the "omniscient" (all-knowing) State didn't know where I was or what I was doing.

And in the process, the "omnipotent" (all-powerful) government lost their power to garnish my wages.

Earlier this year, I petitioned the court, through my attorney, to expunge my criminal cases and arrest records from the public domain. A motion accompanied the petition to seal all proceedings and records from disclosure. On October 1, 2020, the court ruled in my favor. A total of seven government agencies were served with a court order to expunge my records from public databases and to seal my records from disclosure. It's as if the circumstances I endured in 2016 never occurred. I've come a long way to clear my name and erase those false records, but the most valuable—my children—have never been restored.

In December, I visited my sister and her fiancé for the Christmas holidays. But as of this writing, I never returned to a farm. My sister opened up her home and allowed me to stay for much longer.

At the time, my father was finishing his basement and offered to let me move so I could help with the work in exchange for food and lodging. The state of New Mexico periodically sends monthly statements or threatening letters, but that's the extent of their correspondence.

Overall, my trust remains in the Lord. Jesus was betrayed for money. And that's the whole scheme behind the child support mechanisms—betrayal. Yet, I feel honored to experience the same kind of betrayal that my Lord endured.

Remember Jesus' words: *"Blessed are they which are persecuted for righteousness' sake: for theirs is the Kingdom of Heaven. Blessed are ye when men shall revile you, and persecute you, and shall say all manner of evil against you falsely, for my sake."* Matthew 5:10-11

I now await the Lord's timing to reunite me with my children. When that day arrives, Amy's biggest fear will become a reality. The moment my children are removed by Divine intervention, Amy's parental rights will be severed. As for the State, the government will lose jurisdiction over my family. With men, this is impossible, but with God, all things are possible (Matthew 19:26).

However, if the Lord chooses not to intervene, I'll never bow to the Child Support Division.   But in the meantime, I move from one location to the next, without a place to call home.   And any wages must be earned on the black market. Communism at its finest—right here in America. Government is truly a dangerous servant and a fearful master.

To my beautiful children:
Addison, Kyndall, Tobie, Paige, and Lincoln

If you're reading this, I'm writing to tell you how much I love you. Circumstances from the past does not affect my love for you. I pray for each of you by name that you will come to have a personal relationship with my Lord and Saviour, Jesus Christ. He alone is our strength and refuge.

Safety is not found in government-induced fear, because fear is an enemy of freedom. It is written "There is no fear in love; but perfect love casteth out fear: because fear hath torment." When fear is present, love is not.

With all that I've been through, God has given me the strength to endure this hardship, rendering a hope that we will be together again on this side of Heaven. Even the family court system with all its array of forces is unable to separate us from the love of God that is in Christ Jesus.

The only thing I can offer you is the love of Christ, which flows through me. He alone can heal a broken heart. Maybe one day, we can see one another face-to-face. I have so much to tell each of you, but I also have so much to learn. But until that day, you will always be on my mind and in my heart.

Love always,
Dad

REFERENCE GUIDE

P art four: *Planning Your Strategy* is full of information, which can seem overwhelming. So I wanted to recap that part in an outline format. This allows you to bookmark this page, photocopy it, or print it to post in a location for your reference.

Protect Yourself — Secure Your Internal Faculties:

1. Enjoy a personal relationship with Jesus Christ.
2. Seek an equally-yoked partnership.
   A. Spiritual identity (your worldview).
   B. Spiritual legacy (your vision).
   C. Spiritual goals (your appetite).
3. Search for a politically-yoked companion.

Minimize the Damage — Purge Enemy Forces:

1. Identify high-risk situations or events.
   A. Filing for separation or divorce.
   B. Anticipating or currently involved in a custody battle.
   C. Petitioning for a transfer of custody.
   D. Altering visitation schedules.

2. Identify high-risk actions or behaviors.
   A. Exhibits symptoms of Borderline Personality Disorder.
   B. Adapts the new language of Political Correctness.
   C. Undermines your authority or endorses the child who challenges your authority.
   D. Negligently makes false accusations against you (blames you when things go wrong).
   E. Makes poor parenting decisions.
   F. Disciplines in anger or constantly yells at their children.
   G. Asserts being in charge, making decisions, or ruling the home (applicable only towards wives).
   H. Displays an "always right" attitude and makes use of hearsay or intuition as proof.
   I. Conveniently forgets recent events, but possesses a superb memory for past events.
   J. Acts in a manner that suggests she doesn't trust you or is suspicious of you.
3. Strike first.
   A. Document everything (a chronology timeline of events).
   B. Have an eyewitness account.
   C. Visit an expert Ph.D. or M.D.
   D. Hire an attorney.
   E. File for divorce and seek an ex parte order.
   F. Purchase a custody evaluation.
   G. Close all joint accounts.
   H. Remain in the house.

Endure Adversity — Escape the Enemy's Grip:

1. Encourage yourself in the Lord.
   A. Enjoy a personal relationship with Jesus Christ.
   B. Read the King James Bible.
   C. Memorize Scripture and pray.

2. Trust the Lord.
   A. Carry into action (direct).
   B. Resist forced action (indirect).
3. Associate with like-minded individuals.
4. Study American history.
5. Educate yourself.
6. Reject Political Correctness.

Launch Attacks — Attack the Enemy:

1. Hire an attorney.
2. Contact the media.
3. Prove your spouse's guilt, *not* your innocence.
4. Examine for parental alienation.
5. Demand a custody evaluation.
6. Compel your spouse to undergo a psychological evaluation.
7. Request a transfer of custody regularly.
8. File lawsuits.

Plant Obstacles — Slow the Enemy's Movement:

1. Relocate to a different state.
2. Conceal your physical location.
3. Appeal for an interposition.
4. Transact in the underground economy.
5. Employ with a small, locally-owned and operated business.
6. Explore under-the-table employment.
7. Join the WWOOF Program.
8. Start your own business.
9. Raise money.

Bypass Landmines — Avoid the Enemy's Traps:

1. Entertaining negative thoughts.
2. Losing touch with reality.
3. Reading government correspondence prior to work.
4. Requesting a Guardian Ad Litem.
5. Compromising.
6. Disclosing your personal information.
7. Leaving false criminal charges on your public record.
8. Complying with unlawful orders.
9. Appearing for unproductive court hearings.
10. Responding poorly to bad motions.

FICTITIOUS OR FACTUAL

Bona fide means honest, sincere. So a bona fide report is one that is made in good faith, with integrity. These mothers are child-focused. That is, they actually have a concern for the well-being of their children. On the other hand, fabricated reports are utilized primarily for attacking fathers. And by the very nature of government involvement, these attacks are usually violent. These mothers are self-centered. That is, they seek self-gratification at the expense of their children. (This is real child abuse.)

The following identification of child sexual abuse allegations includes an insight, which was summarized from Dean Tong's book, *"Elusive Innocence: Survival Guide for the Falsely Accused."*

Bona Fide Sexual Abuse (child-focused):

- Mothers will generally be upset, embarrassed, and keep everything private.
- She'll express remorse for not sufficiently protecting her child.
- Because she's looking for the truth, she's willing to consider other explanations for the child's statement or poor behavior.
- She's willing to allow her child to be interviewed without her present.

- The mother's first concern is always the child's well-being. How will testifying affect her child? Is there a suitable alternative to testifying in court?
- If the allegations can't be verified, the mother is willing to drop the investigative process as long as the child's well-being can be monitored.
- The child's descriptions or details of the abuse will be consistent, real, and serious.

Fabricated sexual abuse (self-centered):

- Mother has the need to tell the whole world. She acts like the victim, but displays no regret or concern for the child.
- She aggressively demands the decision-makers to act quickly.
- She's unwilling to consider other possible explanations for the child's statements or behaviors.
- She is eager for the child to testify at all costs.
- She seeks other professionals who will verify her suspicions.
- She involves the child in multiple examinations or therapeutic sessions.
- She'll demand the investigation continues, regardless of the previous outcome and irrespective of the impact on the child.
- When questioned for specific details, the mother can provide little information and may even turn hostile towards the questioner.
- She's reluctant to have her children interviewed alone.
- The child's descriptions or details of the abuse will be inconsistent and progressive.

Children from four to seven...

- Are easily persuaded to accuse by inappropriate discussions, encouragement, bribery, and promotions.

- Tend to over generalize.
- Fabricate in an effort to fill in the blanks.
- May remember two or more separate events and mistakenly merge them into one.
- Will begin to believe what they've said.
- Are very suggestible and prone to following the lead of the questioner.
- Often describe the abuse with preposterous scenarios.
- Also wants to tell the whole world.
- Are comfortable in the presence of the accused, and may even scream the accusations in the face of the accused parent.

Older children with a close relationship to the accused...

- Are forced to accuse, usually executed through propaganda, fear, intimidation, or threats.
- Fabricate in an effort to please the accuser and avoid future punishment.
- May remember what they're constantly told, but they won't have a recollection of the actual event.
- Over an extended period of time, they will start to believe what they've heard and have even repeated themselves. They'll often remember what's been drilled into their minds and trust this false memory to be an actual event. (This is a brainwashing technique that's very effective.)
- Often describe the abuse in vague terms and may even try to end the interview by saying, "There's nothing else" or "That's all that happened."
- Are uncomfortable in the presence of the accused as a result of fear instilled by the accuser through lies and deceit.
- The accusations are intended to hurt the child. By hurting the child, you can effectively hurt the father.

Accuser and abuser (one and the same):

- Impulsive and is driven to maintain control—control over others, events, and outcomes.
- Difficulty monitoring, directing, or controlling their own emotional reactions.
- Love has grown cold.
- Excessively selfish.
- Irresponsible, which requires dependency on others—usually in some form of government welfare.
- Continually executes poor judgment in behavior.
- Usually overzealous and dishonest.
- Histrionic or combative.

THE SCIENCE OF MARRIAGE

There are numerous books written about marriage, some from a Biblical perspective and others from a secular perspective. So why did I include this Appendix? Well, most books on marriage are written from a politically correct viewpoint, even the books with Biblical references. That is, they're usually directed towards the husband, but very little is actually geared towards his wife or their marital relationship as a whole. This approach to marriage implies that he's always at fault and must change, while she's always the victim and can never do any wrong. Yet, this victim mentality sows division and discord within the family by pitting a wife against her husband. This is why I don't trust any of those sources.

Popular opinion dresses up this approach to marriage by calling him the leader of his family. Thus, transferring all household responsibilities, relationship obligations, and gender roles onto his shoulders. And in the process, his wife loses her function within the family unit. She simply becomes a useless prop. To correct this deficiency, she finds and amplifies his faults. By pointing out his errors, she's no longer useless, but has taken on the decision-making role—a role without its corresponding responsibilities. She can now rule over her husband while escaping the consequences.

But the Bible never calls him, "the leader." Applying that terminology inappropriately is a perversion from man. Neither does God assign husbands all of the marital tasks, and leave his wife to float through life without a purpose in marriage. This is an invention of marriage counselors and self-help books—even those who quote Scripture.

I would like to correct some faulty ideas and beliefs about marriage that can revolutionize your home. This is not intended to cover the entire institution of marriage or family that God's Word addresses. This is just some of the most practical ways to increase the health of your marriage. My desire is to keep the State out of your home and the minds of your children guarded.

* * * * *

The husband and wife each have one role in marriage.
- The Husband is the Ruler *"...he shall rule over thee."* (Genesis 3:16)
- The Wife is his Helper *"...I will make him an help meet for him."* (Genesis 2:18)

In simple terms, the husband makes the decisions and his wife helps him execute them. The individual roles of both, the husband and his wife, are strictly action-based. Knowledge or emotions aren't prerequisites to the fulfillment of these roles. The number one cause of a deteriorating marriage is the breakdown of these roles.

- He makes a decision in which his wife disagrees, so she refuses to help him execute it, or
- She demands to be the decision-maker, so in an effort to please his wife, he allows her to make the decisions. However, she makes a bad decision, and he takes the fall.

A husband is greatly paralyzed in all he can accomplish for the sake of his family if his wife refuses to support him (be his helpmate).

He is not called a leader in the Bible and the reason is elementary. Leaders don't lead; they are followed. You are not born a leader.

You cannot learn to be a leader. You cannot be trained to be a leader. You cannot be voted to be a leader. You must be followed to be a leader. Jesus was the greatest leader of all time, but notice how He never tried to lead.

- "When He was come down from the mountain, great multitudes followed him." (Matthew 8:1)
- "...the Pharisees went out, and held a council against Him, how they might destroy Him. But when Jesus knew it, He withdrew Himself from thence: and great multitudes followed him, and He healed them all." (Matthew 12:14-15)
- "...as Jesus sat at meat in his house, many publicans and sinners sat also together with Jesus and His disciples: for there were many, and they followed him." (Mark 2:15)
- "...Jesus went over the sea of Galilee, which is the sea of Tiberias. And a great multitude followed him..." (John 6:1-2)

Contrary to popular belief, leaders are actually chosen by their followers. It's the followers who make the leaders, and it's the followers who can also unmake the leaders. When the husband makes a decision, his wife must follow his lead. If she doesn't, how can he lead someone who's not following? Ultimately, the wife must follow her husband first for him to have the ability to lead.

The follower is always commanded in the Bible first as to how that person is to behave toward the leader. Then God commands the leader as to how to behave toward the follower. God always requires the follower to initiate the action first. God tells the children they are to obey first (Ephesians 6:1). God tells the wife to submit first (Ephesians 5:22).

This principle is accepted and executed everywhere in society, except the home. God tells the employee that he is to obey first (Ephesians 6:5). And businesses couldn't function without this Biblical principle. An employee must perform his duties first before his employer pays him. He must meet certain conditions first before he's considered for a management position. And similar to this business model, the wife must follow her husband first before he can lead her. It's an impossibility to lead someone who isn't following.

Wives follow their husbands by simply submitting to them. Submission is yielding to the authority of another—the act of non-intervention. And the family cannot function correctly if the wife interferes with her husband's decision-making authority.

Today's marital crises results from a wife's interference with her husband's decisions. But unfortunately, professional counselors or pastors are unable to recognize the problem. They usually hear the wife accusing her husband of making bad or selfish decisions (a subtle tactic to shift focus). Because of this, the "professionals" seem to focus their counseling sessions on the motives of the decision, rather than the God-ordained roles. The "professional" couldn't care less if the husband executes his Biblical role and makes a decision. Instead, he looks to see if the decision made was unloving and selfish.

But what yardstick does the "professional" use to make his determination? How does he know when a decision is unloving or not? Marriage counselors never analyze the science behind the decision. They only look to see if the decision is unanimously accepted by both parties. Any marital conflicts act as "proof" that the husband's decision was unloving and selfish. These "professionals" are fueling the flame that's burning down the home by elevating the wife to a higher position of rule within the home. But to consider the wife as the ultimate arbiter of all decisions within the home is a very dangerous doctrine. Wives are as sinful as other men. To assume the power to check or strike down any decision is a usurpation of her husband's decision-making authority. But this power, in the hands of his wife, is more dangerous as she escapes the consequences of those decisions. If the decision is good, the wife takes the credit, but if the decision is bad, her husband takes the fall. Once again, we see the familiar tactic of ruling without responsibility.

The worldly perception is that all decisions between married couples must be unanimous. If his decision is loving and caring, wouldn't she unconditionally embrace it? Not necessarily! We have to remember that mankind has a fallen nature. Love and selflessness are conditions of the heart. And wives cannot see his heart. Nor can the husband see hers. His loving and thoughtful decision may be met with hostility because of her selfishness. Without the sin nature where selfishness abounds, God would never have to command the wife to submit. God knows that the husband will make decisions in which his wife disagrees. But challenging them is evident that she doesn't trust him to make any decisions. And marriage is built on trust. Where there is no trust, there can be no marriage.

Some of my readers might argue that I'm singling out women, but the reality is that I'm just presenting the other side of marriage that marital books and counselors leave out. When a child disobeys his parents, it's nearly impossible for them to see their parents' love in the midst of their discipline. The love is present, which is why their parents discipline in the first place, but the child is unable to see or feel that love while experiencing their parents' wrath. This same concept applies between a husband and his wife. When she refuses to submit, that doesn't mean he stops loving her. His love may still be present, but she's just unable to see or experience it in the midst of her rebellion.

But it's important to recognize that the State invades the home, divides the family, and destroys the children—and this is all accomplished through the wife. Therefore, to interfere with the State's abolition of the family, I must address the marriage through the wife, not the husband.

The following suggestions were taken from Dr. Jack Hyles' book, "The Science of the Christian Life." There are practical ways to set boundaries within marriage to help maintain the God-ordained roles in their proper perspective.

Never speak disagreement. If your mate says something in which you disagree, it's best not to respond. You don't have to express your opinion about everything. You are not the final authority on everything, so it is possible that you might be wrong.

Divide areas of choice. Each person within a marriage should have assigned areas, and that person should make all the decisions in that area. The husband is the head and so he should delegate areas to his wife where she makes the decision, such as grocery shopping, furniture arrangement, etc. He may occasionally have to veto a decision, but she should make decisions in her area most of the time without his interference.

Share interests, but not decisions. It's good when you share mutual interests with your mate. This is how you draw close to your spouse. However, it's unnecessary when you try to make mutual decisions. In trying to agree, you will begin to disagree. This is why the husband makes the decisions, and his wife helps execute them.

Have some time and activity apart from one another. Outside interests make spouses more engaging to each other. By participating in outside activities, you're experiencing delightful diversions in your routine that you can share with each other when you're together again. This expands your horizon and builds a mystique into your marriage.

Do not interfere with your mate's discipline of the children. Parents often disagree over the way they discipline their children. In these situations, it's best to say nothing. It is better for the child to be disciplined improperly than to see a heated argument between the parents about child discipline. In addition, the child quickly learns to play the parents against each other.

Put your mate before your children. When you were first married, you and your spouse had a close and romantic relationship. Then the children started coming, and suddenly you found your marriage and your relationship with your spouse put on hold. There's a baby to feed and diapers to change and baths to give and homework to do and laundry and scouts and little league and school activities and continuous childcare needs for the next 18 years or more. And during those turbulent, child-rearing years, if a couple isn't diligent about their lives together, they tend to drift apart. Your children will one day leave home and begin families of their own. Then it will be just the two of you again. But along the way, if you and your spouse aren't careful, something tragic happens. You allow your children to maneuver their way between mom and dad, causing your lives to revolve around them, instead of each other, and your marriage deteriorates. Never allow that to happen. Make certain that your mate keeps his or her rightful, prominent place in your life, rather than taking a backseat to the kids. Then once they're gone, you'll still have each other.

Put your mate before your parents. When you got married, that was the end of your old family and the beginning of your new. Your parents shouldn't be competing with your spouse for your love and affection. So don't run home to your parents when things don't go well. Even in-laws with good intentions don't realize that they are helping to divide your home.

Never criticize your in-laws. It's very hurtful to speak negatively about your spouse's parents—the very people who raised your spouse from childhood.

One should manage the finances, and the other should live on an allowance. The husband makes this decision. If he isn't good at managing finances, but his wife is, he should delegate this area of decision to his wife and live on an allowance himself. If both couples are employed, that doesn't change anything. The income of both spouses should go into the same account where only one spouse manages all household finances and the other lives on an allowance.

Do not have joint bank accounts.

These are very basic practices that have a very high success rate for the health of one's marriage. They are not just ideas, but they are formulas that have been developed over the years by Dr. Jack Hyles. Don't allow your marriage to fail because you didn't plan for success. Make a science out of it.

THE CONFLICT OF MARRIAGE: BIBLICAL V. SECULAR

Each year, Americans head to their county offices to apply for a marriage license. Yet, hardly anyone questions the marital procedure established by their government. *Everyone does it...the law requires it...you're not married without it.* These superficial statements lack depth.

If you're considering marriage or remarriage, educate yourself about marriage licenses. Don't run down to your county courthouse until you can make an informed decision on whether you should marry with or without a state-issued license.

Marriage licenses didn't always exist. Prior to the Scottish Reformation of 1560, religious marriage was very common in Scotland and regulated by the state-run church, but no statutory provision existed for non-religious civil marriage. The latter being known as an "irregular" marriage, prompted the Council of Trent in 1563 to issue its decree, *Tametsi*, which declared that marriage had to be contracted before a duly-authorized priest and two or three witnesses. [54]

---

[54] Council of Trent, "Decree Tametsi: Concerning the Reform of Matrimony (1563)," In *The Canons and Decrees of the Council of Trent*, trans. H. J. Schroeder (London: B. Herder Book Co, 1941).

This law, however, couldn't be carried out in the British colonies during the Colonial Era. As a result, the Albemarle County General Assembly in Carolina passed "An Act Concerning Marriages" in January 1670. This law authorized civil officers to perform marriage ceremonies, but only if the county had no minister. [55]

Then in 1741, North Carolina broke from tradition by increasing government control over marriages. The General Assembly, held at Edenton, enacted a law, which was also titled "An Act Concerning Marriages" (not to be confused with the Act of 1670).

> *"...That no Minister or Ministers, Justice or Justices of the Peace, within any of the Parishes of this Government, shall celebrate the Rites of Matrimony between any Persons, or join them together as Man and Wife, without License first had and obtained for that Purpose...That all Licenses for marriages shall be issued by the Clerk of the Court."* [56]

This gradual shift towards a statutory marriage replaces Biblical provisions with State control. These marriage license laws don't govern the institution of marriage, but rather, they govern its procedure. However, the procedure of marriage is inherently associated with its ideological origins. For instance, a minister performing weddings reflects religious or Biblical origins, whereas a Justice of the Peace is a reflection of secular or governmental origins. So when a couple gets married, they are either making a covenant before God (Biblical marriage) or the State (secular marriage).

---

[55] Assembly of Albemarle, "Acts of the Albemarle County General Assembly," In *The Colonial Records of North Carolina, Vol. 1: 1662 to 1712*, ed. William Saunders (Raleigh: P.M. Hale, State Printer, 1886): 183-187, Accessed May 3, 2021, https://docsouth.unc.edu/csr/index.php/document/csr01-0074.

[56] North Carolina Legislature, "An Act Concerning Marriages," In *The Colonial Records of North Carolina, Vol. 23: 1715 to 1776*, ed. William Saunders (Raleigh: P.M. Hale, State Printer, 1886): 158-161, Accessed May 3, 2021, https://docsouth.unc.edu/csr/index.php/document/csr23-0012.

There are three aspects to a marriage that we need to recognize: (1) permission to marry, (2) the joining of man and wife, and (3) proof of the marriage. A marriage license is only a secular provision to initiate the marital process. The marital covenant (or contract) follows, and the certificate of marriage concludes the process.

Traditionally, the marital procedure was decentralized. Permission to marry was granted by the father; hence the question, "Who gives this woman to be married to this man?" God, through the minister, would join the man and wife together (Matthew 19:6). Then the proof of marriage would be recorded with the church or local government.

A marriage license, however, centralized the marital procedure into the hands of government officials. According to Black's Law Dictionary, a marriage license is *"The document that is executed by the public authority that gives a couple the permission to marry."*[57] In many jurisdictions, once the marriage is complete, the license is exchanged for a certificate, and the marriage is recorded in the public domain. This is the statutory procedure for all marriages in America.

The marriage license is our only concern, because of its statutory requirement. Hence, the power over marriage is transferred to the civil government—an institution of force. But the authority to license implies the power to prohibit. And usurped power is always abused and weaponized. The statutory requirement sets the stage to control, limit, and restrict marriages as well as births (population control).

A case brought before the Supreme Court of Wisconsin exemplifies how marriage licenses are and will be used as weapons. In the case of State v. Mueller, the statute being challenged was § 245.10, a Wisconsin law requiring residents who are under child support obligations to get permission from the court to receive a marriage license.[58] And marriage licenses are withheld if the person is behind in child support payments.

---

[57] Henry C. Black, *Black's Law Dictionary 2nd Ed*, (St. Paul: West Publishing, 1910).
[58] State v. Meuller, 44 Wis. 2D 387 (Supreme Court of Wisconsin, 1969).

This statute required three obligations to marry: a marriage license, a court order, and proof that child support payments were not delinquent. If you married and just one condition was absent, you were charged with a felony.

The same Wisconsin statute was challenged again, but this time, in the Supreme Court of the United States. In the case of Zablocki v. Redhail, a Wisconsin resident was unable to enter into a lawful marriage in Wisconsin or elsewhere so long as he maintained his Wisconsin residency.[59] Redhail was a minor and a high school student when a paternity action was instituted against him for being the father of a baby girl born out of wedlock. Yet, the teenage mother's action and her role in bringing forth the child were completely ignored.

So under Wisconsin law, fornication isn't a crime, but marriage is. In the hands of the State, a marriage license is an avenue to attack the Biblical institution of marriage. Licenses can be denied for any reason or granted to any person at the sole discretion of the State. The spiritual warfare waged by the rulers of darkness (Ephesians 6:12), suggests that state-issued marriage licenses pose a great risk for the Christian and Biblical marriage.

The confusion about marriage licenses stems from a lack of understanding. Many websites and pastors tend to misrepresent the function of the license. Some claim that the license is your covenant before God. (Apparently, they don't know the definition of a license.) Others perceive an unlicensed marriage as unlawful and unrecognized. For some reason, many folks cannot visualize a marriage ceremony, covenant, witnesses, or certificate without a license. These superficial claims lead to one false conclusion: the marriage must be invalid.

It is true, however, that an unlicensed marriage is unrecognized by the State, but that doesn't invalidate Biblical marriage.

Ever since the Supreme Court ruled against the institution of Biblical marriage in the case of Obergefell v. Hodges, local jurisdictions routinely issue marriage licenses to homosexuals. This blatant ruling

---

[59] Zablocki v. Redhail, 434 U.S. 374 (United States Supreme Court, 1978).

should open the eyes to every Christian in America. Marriage licenses do not legitimize a marriage. The belief that people aren't really married without a marriage license simply reveals how statist their thinking patterns are. Tragically, our culture is unable to recognize valid marriages.

Fortunately, followers of Christ don't need the State for their marriage to be Biblical. The Bible's provision to initiate a marriage was the father's blessing regarding whom his daughter married, and she was to be given in marriage (Exodus 22:16-17; Deuteronomy 22:16; 1 Corinthians 7:38). Nevertheless, a marriage license and the Justice of the Peace provide the means for an end run around parental authority.

The early American colonists may have had pure intentions with the license requirement, but their statutory enactment was the wrong method. North Carolina wasn't the only colony. In 1632, Virginia passed an act that required marriage licenses to be issued by the Governor, except in banns marriages. And parental consent was required under the age of 21. [60]

Those who obtain a state marriage license, but are joined together by a minister are combining Biblical with secular marriage. However, this mixture is problematic because the flesh is at war with the Spirit (Galatians 5:17), and the carnal mind is enmity against God (Romans 8:7). For what communion does light have with darkness (2 Corinthians 6:14)?

So I would encourage anyone who seeks a full, Biblical marriage to marry without a state license. This would be a banns marriage (no eloping). Initiate the marital process by obtaining permission from the father of your future wife. (If your father isn't alive or cannot be located, seek counsel from your pastor or a Godly elder within your

---

[60] Virginia Grand Assembly, *The Statutes at Large; Being a Collection of all the Laws of Virginia From the First Session of the Legislature, in the Year 1619: Vol. 1*, ed. William Hening (New York: R. & W. & G. Bartow, 1823): 156-157, Accessed May 3, 2021, http://vagenweb.org/hening/vol01-07.htm.

church.) And above all, pray for God's guidance before proceeding with the marriage.

Locate a church or minister who will marry you without a state-issued license. (There are several churches out there. You just need to find one.) Purchase a Family Bible and obtain a certificate of marriage (the church may even provide this). The marriage will be recorded in your Family Bible, and the certificate is proof of marriage. Ensure you have at least two witnesses at your wedding. That's all there is to it. The entire institution of marriage and your covenant before God remains intact. *"What therefore God hath joined together, let not man put asunder."* (Mark 10:9)

Remember, when the State administers all three functions of a secular marriage (the license, the Justice of the Peace, and the certificate), your marriage becomes the product of the State. And the power to unite comes with it the power to dissolve.

ADDITIONAL RESOURCES

These particular resources are in no specific order of importance. When you constantly surround yourself with truth, spotting the counterfeit becomes easy. However, for those constantly surrounded by propaganda, when a nugget of truth shines through, these folks don't recognize it as truth. This is the importance of seeking the truth on your own.

Online Resources:

- **The New American** at https://www.thenewamerican.com Covers news on politics, economy, culture, and more based on the U.S. Constitution so that freedom shall not perish.
- **Hillsdale College Courses** at https://online.hillsdale.edu Pursuing truth, defending liberty since 1844. Their course catalog includes politics, history, economics, and more.
- **The John Birch Society** at https://www.jbs.org To bring about less government, more responsibility, and with God's help a better world. Visit the JBS store for additional resources.
- **Constitution Party** at http://www.constitutionparty.com The party of "Integrity, Liberty, and Prosperity." Join your state party and get involved now.

- **Mises Institute** at https://mises.org The world's leading supporter of the ideas of liberty and the Austrian School of Economics. Visit the Mises Institute bookstore for additional resources.
- **The Foundation for American Christian Education** at https://www.face.net Resolute in teaching Biblical Principles that sustain liberty. Visit the FACE store for training courses and home school curriculum.
- **Wallbuilders Store** at https://shop.wallbuilders.com Dedicated to presenting America's forgotten history and heroes with an emphasis on our moral, religious, and constitutional foundation. Shop from a selection of categories, which includes books, CD's, DVD's, Bibles, puzzles, and more.
- **Worldwide Opportunities on Organic Farms** at https://wwoofusa.org WWOOF is part of a worldwide effort to link visitors with organic farmers. Visitors or "WWOOFers" spend about half of each day helping out on a farm, learn about organic agriculture, and receive free lodging and meals during their visit.

Books on Politics, History, and Economics:

- *The Making of America: The Substance and Meaning of the Constitution* by W. Cleon Skousen.
- *Quest of a Hemisphere* by Donzella Boyle.
- *George Washington's Secret Six: The Spies Who Saved America* by Brian Kilmeade and Don Yaeger.
- *Thomas Jefferson and the Tripoli Pirates: The Forgotten War That Changed American History* by Brian Kilmeade and Don Yaeger.
- *Andrew Jackson and the Miracle of New Orleans: The Battle That Shaped America's Destiny* by Brian Kilmeade and Don Yaeger.

- *Sam Houston and the Alamo Avengers: The Texas Victory That Changed American History* by Brian Kilmeade and Don Yaeger.
- *Give Me Liberty: The Uncompromising Statesmanship of Patrick Henry* by David Vaughan.
- *The Real Lincoln: A New Look at Abraham Lincoln, His Agenda, and an Unnecessary War* by Thomas DiLorenzo.
- *Lincoln Unmasked: What You're Not Supposed to Know About Dishonest Abe* by Thomas DiLorenzo.
- *Hamilton's Curse: How Jefferson's Arch Enemy Betrayed the American Revolution – and What it Means for Americans Today* by Thomas DiLorenzo.
- *New Deal or Raw Deal: How FDR's Economic Legacy has Damaged America* by Burton Folsom Jr.
- *The Law* by Frédéric Bastiat.
- *The Doctrine of the Lesser Magistrates: A Proper Resistance to Tyranny and a Repudiation of Unlimited Obedience to Civil Government* by Matthew Trewhella.
- *Technocracy: The Hard Road to World Order* by Patrick Wood.
- *A Capitalist Manifesto: Understanding the Market Economy and Defending Liberty* by Gary Wolfram.
- *Economics in One Lesson: The Shortest and Surest Way to Understand Basic Economics* by Henry Hazlitt.
- *The Creature from Jekyll Island: A Second Look at the Federal Reserve* by G. Edward Griffin.
- *The Income Tax: Root of All Evil* by Frank Chodorov.
- *The Tragedy of American Compassion* by Marvin Olasky.
- *Taken Into Custody: The War Against Fathers, Marriage, and the Family* by Stephen Baskerville.
- *Crimes of the Educators: How Utopians Are Using Government Schools to Destroy America's Children* by Samuel Blumenfeld and Alex Newman.

- *Sustainable: The War on Free Enterprise, Private Property, and Individuals* by Tom Deweese.
- *Political Correctness: A Deceptive and Dangerous Worldview* edited by William Lind and Richard Hawkins.
- *A Republic If You Can Keep It: America's Authentic Liberty Confronts Contemporary Counterfeits* by Gia Ferdon.
- *COVID-19 and the Agendas to Come: Red-Pilled* by James Perloff.
- *The Shadows of Power: The Council on Foreign Relations and the American Decline* by James Perloff.
- *America's Secret Establishment: An Introduction to the Order of Skull and Bones* by Antony Sutton.
- *Crisis and Leviathan: Critical Episodes in the Growth of American Government* by Robert Higgs.
- *Liberty in Peril: Democracy and Power in American History* by Randall Holcombe.
- *Feardom: How Politicians Exploit Your Emotions and What You Can do to Stop* Them by Connor Boyack.
- *Prudent Jurisprudence: The Constitution's Framers and the Supreme Court* by William Graves.
- *Original Intent: The Courts, the Constitution, and Religion* by David Barton.

Other Essential Books:

- *Crowned With Glory: The Bible from Ancient Text to Authorized Version* by Thomas Holland.
- *Which Bible Would Jesus Use: The Bible Version Controversy Explained and Resolved* by Jack McElroy.
- *PsychoHeresy: The Psychological Seduction of Christianity* by Martin and Deidre Bobgan

ABOUT THE AUTHOR

Author Toby Strebe is the son of a retired United States Air Force Master Sergeant. He was born at RAF Lakenheath, England, but attended preschool in Georgia, started kindergarten in Greece, first grade in Oklahoma, and second grade in Ohio... Needless to say, school turned out to be an academic struggle.

But being a military kid also had its perks. As a six-year old, Toby got to climb on the pillars in ancient Corinth, Greece. A year later, his father took him to Disneyland in California. On a cross-country drive, he enjoyed a tour through Carlsbad Caverns in New Mexico. And Toby also explored Epcot Center and Busch Gardens in Florida with his cousin.

In 2001, Toby enlisted in the United States Army and served a three-year term. He re-enlisted in the summer of 2009. Between his first and second enlistment, he got married and had three children.

During his total time in the service, he earned his bachelor's degree from Manhattan Christian College. He spent two years in a war zone, and one in Korea. To celebrate special days with his wife and daughters and stay in touch, he communicated with them on a regular basis through Skype.

In 2014, his wife was hospitalized for three weeks in a behavioral health unit. The Army promptly authorized emergency leave for him to be with his family and care for his children. But unfortunately, he couldn't stay on leave indefinitely, and at this point his wife could barely care for herself, let alone the children. So towards the end of the year, he opted to separate from the military and was honorably discharged. He needed to be there for his family.

However, his wife's mental condition deteriorated. And in 2016, she divorced him and took his children. Since then, he's shifted his focus towards defending freedom and exercising individual responsibility.

If you'd like to share a personal story or contact Toby for any reason, he can be reached at strikingdownthehome@protonmail.com.

www.ingramcontent.com/pod-product-compliance
Lightning Source LLC
Chambersburg PA
CBHW060306030426
42336CB00011B/962